D0001845

Why Lawsuits Are Good
for America

CRITICAL AMERICA

General Editors: Richard Delgado and Jean Stefancic

White by Law:
The Legal Construction of Race
Ian F. Haney López

Cultivating Intelligence:
Power, Law, and the Politics of Teaching
Louise Harmon and Deborah W. Post

Privilege Revealed:
How Invisible Preference Undermines America
Stephanie M. Wildman
with Margalynne Armstrong, Adrienne D. Davis, and Trina Grillo

Does the Law Morally Bind the Poor?
or What Good's the Constitution When You Can't Afford a Loaf of Bread?
R. George Wright

Hybrid:
Bisexuals, Multiracials, and Other Misfits under American Law
Ruth Colker

Critical Race Feminism:
A Reader
Edited by Adrien Katherine Wing

Immigrants Out!
The New Nativism and the Anti-Immigrant Impulse in the United States
Edited by Juan F. Perea

Taxing America
Edited by Karen B. Brown and Mary Louise Fellows

Notes of a Racial Caste Baby:
Color Blindness and the End of Affirmative Action
Bryan K. Fair

Please Don't Wish Me a Merry Christmas:
A Critical History of the Separation of Church and State
Stephen M. Feldman

To Be an American:
Cultural Pluralism and the Rhetoric of Assimilation
Bill Ong Hing

Negrophobia and Reasonable Racism:
The Hidden Costs of Being Black in America
Jody David Armour

Black and Brown in America:
The Case for Cooperation
Bill Piatt

Black Rage Confronts the Law
Paul Harris

Selling Words:
Free Speech in a Commercial Culture
R. George Wright

The Color of Crime:
Racial Hoaxes, White Fear, Black Protectionism, Police
Harassment, and Other Macroaggressions
Katheryn K. Russell

The Smart Culture:
Society, Intelligence, and Law
Robert L. Hayman, Jr.

Was Blind, But Now I See:
White Race Consciousness and the Law
Barbara J. Flagg

American Law in the Age of Hypercapitalism:
The Worker, the Family, and the State
Ruth Colker

The Gender Line:
Men, Women, and the Law
Nancy Levit

Heretics in the Temple:
Americans Who Reject the Nation's Legal Faith
David Ray Papke

The Empire Strikes Back:
Outsiders and the Struggle over Legal Education
Arthur Austin

Interracial Justice:
Conflict and Reconciliation in Post-Civil Rights America
Eric K. Yamamoto

Black Men on Race, Gender, and Sexuality:
A Critical Reader
Edited by Devon Carbado

When Sorry Isn't Enough:
The Controversy over Apologies and Reparations for Human Injustice
Edited by Roy L. Brooks

Disoriented: Asian Americans, Law, and the Nation State
Robert S. Chang

Rape and the Culture of the Courtroom
Andrew E. Taslitz

The Passions of Law
Edited by Susan A. Bandes

Global Critical Race Feminism:
An International Reader
Edited by Adrien Katherine Wing

Law and Religion:
Critical Essays
Edited by Stephen M. Feldman

Changing Race:
Latinos, the Census, and the History of Ethnicity
Clara E. Rodríguez

From the Ground Up:
Environmental Racism and the Rise of the Environmental Justice Movement
Luke Cole and Sheila Foster

Nothing but the Truth:
Why Trial Lawyers Don't, Can't, and Shouldn't Have to Tell the Whole Truth
Steven Lubet

Critical Race Theory:
A Primer
Richard Delgado and Jean Stefancic

Playing It Safe:
How the Supreme Court Sidesteps Hard Cases
Lisa A. Kloppenberg

Why Lawsuits Are Good for America:
Disciplined Democracy, Big Business, and the Common Law
Carl T. Bogus

Why Lawsuits Are Good for America

Disciplined Democracy, Big Business, and the Common Law

Carl T. Bogus

NEW YORK UNIVERSITY PRESS

New York and London

NEW YORK UNIVERSITY PRESS
New York and London

Library of Congress Cataloging-in-Publication Data
Bogus, Carl T.
Why lawsuits are good for America : disciplined democracy,
big business, and the common law / Carl T. Bogus.
p.   cm. — (Critical America)
Includes index.
ISBN 0-8147-1319-X (cloth : acid-free paper)
1. Products liability—United States. 2. Torts—United States.
3. Law reform—United States.   I. Title. II. Series.
KF1296 .B64 2001
346.7303—dc21   2001001254

New York University Press books are printed on acid-free paper,
and their binding materials are chosen for strength and durability.

Manufactured in the United States of America

10 9 8 7 6 5 4 3 2 1

For Cindy

Contents

Acknowledgments | *xi*

Introduction | 1

1 Why Tell Tales? | 6
Danforth's Tale | 6
Proctor v. Davis: The Real Story | 11
Why Tell Tales? | 17

2 War on the Common Law | 22
Warriors | 22
War on the Common Law | 27
The Tort Reform Agenda | 34
The Common Law and America | 40

3 The Third Branch of Government | 42
Beginnings | 42
Separation of Powers and the American Judiciary | 45
The Common Law Tradition | 52
An American Bench and Bar | 60
An American Procedural System | 62

4 Disciplined Democracy and the American Jury | 66
Legends | 66
The Founders and the Civil Jury | 77
The Contemporary Civil Jury: England versus America | 79
Disciplined Democracy | 82
Is the Civil Jury Competent? | 88
The Civil Jury and Societal Values | 94

5 The American Common Law System | 102
Is *Proctor* an Example of System Failure? | 102
The Four Legs of American Common Law | 115
Why the Common Law Is Special | 123

6   Who Regulates Auto Safety?   138
     Administrative versus Common Law Regulation   138
     The Stunning Improvement in Auto Safety   141
     Administrative Regulation   145
     The Bronco II Story   159
     Who Regulates Auto Safety?   163
     Balancing Safety and Other Considerations   169

7   The Three Revolutions in Products Liability   173
     Cardozo's Paradigm   173
     The First Revolution: Strict Liability for
        Defective Products   184
     The Second Revolution: Strict Liability for
        Nondefective Products with Unreasonably
        Dangerous Features   190
     The Third Revolution: Strict Liability for
        Unreasonably Dangerous Products   193

8   The Common Law and the Future   197
     Tobacco and Guns   197
     Common Law in the Twenty-first Century   211

     Notes   221
     Index   259
     About the Author   265

Acknowledgments

I am fortunate that so many people helped me in so many ways. I am grateful to those who chatted with me about their work, cases they handled, or their areas of expertise, often at considerable length. These include John W. (Don) Barrett, Barry Goldberg, Sally Greenberg, Jonathan Grohsman, Edgar F. Heiskell III, David Novoselsky, David Pittle, Kristen Rand, and Harry Stoffer. I am indebted to three energetic research assistants—Christopher H. Lordan, Lorraine K. Newton, and Rebecca R. Yeager—all of whom are, or will soon be, alumni of the Roger Williams University School of Law. I benefited from the professional and cheerful assistance from the law library staff at Roger Williams; special thanks to Nan Balliot, Stephanie Edwards, and Lucinda Harrison-Cox. It was a pleasure working with the highly professional editors at New York University Press; thanks especially to Joanna L. Mullins for excellent copyediting work. And thanks to the *Chicago-Kent Law Review, Connecticut Law Review,* and *Missouri Law Review* in which portions of this work appeared in different form.

Last but far from least, many thanks to those who read and commented on drafts of this work: Christian C. Day, Richard Delgado, Jay M. Feinman, Cynthia J. Giles, Jonathan Gutoff, Niko Pfund, Jean Stefancic, and Eric Zinner.

Introduction

Imagine three hospital patients considering surgery. Their surgeons discuss with each of them the risks and benefits of the procedures. Every surgery entails risk. The patient may have an adverse reaction to the anesthesia; his or her system may fail under the trauma of the surgery; there may be uncontrollable bleeding, bacterial infection, a virus in the blood the patient receives by transfusion. And since the operation will be performed by human beings, there is always the risk of error. In their conversations with their patients, the surgeons describe the greatest risks but not all the risks. The list is too long, and besides, there is no point in scaring patients silly. Law and good medical practice, however, require physicians to inform patients about "material" risks, that is, the risks a reasonable patient would want to consider in deciding whether to have the procedure. The surgeons, therefore, tell their patients something about cumulative risk. Let us assume that these are young, strong patients who are undergoing low-risk procedures. The surgeons inform their patients that they have better than a 99 percent of surviving the procedures and a 90 percent chance of a successful outcome without major complications.

Since these are merely hypothetical cases and we can afford to be merciless, let us assume that all three patients die during surgery. To increase the pathos even more: each patient had young children and was the principal breadwinner in the family. The families want to know what went wrong. Unsatisfied with what the doctors and hospitals tell them, they hire lawyers. Investigations ensue. The lawyer in one case discovers, and can prove, that the anesthesiologist mistakenly used the wrong anesthesia. The lawyer in a second case learns that the anesthesia machine was defective and dispensed a dose ten times greater than what the doctor punched in on the keypad and the machine displayed. The lawyer in the third case, however, is not able to discover what went wrong. It is not for lack of trying; the third investigation is conducted

1

just as vigorously as the others. But either no one knows what went wrong or those who do know are not talking. "Joe's heart simply stopped beating during the surgery. We don't know why" is the best explanation anyone can offer.

If the lawyers in the first two cases have enough evidence to prove their cases, the first can prevail in a medical malpractice action and the second in a products liability action. The anesthesiologist who made the mistake and the manufacturer who made a defective machine each will have to pay a sum to compensate for the patient's loss of life and the family's loss of a spouse, parent, and breadwinner. The family in the third case will have to look elsewhere for financial help, however, to Social Security survivor's benefits or to private insurance, if they have it.

It is often said that the twin objectives of the tort system are compensation and deterrence. This book reflects a different view. Compensation is often a useful by-product of the tort system, to be sure, but it is a mistake to consider it a principal function of the system. If compensation were, in fact, one of its objectives, the system would make need a determining factor in whether it would give parties recoveries; but that is not the case. The family in the third case may need compensation every bit as much as the other two families. Indeed, their need may be greatest of all. Yet need is taken into account only when determining the amount that a defendant should pay a plaintiff, and even then rather obliquely.

All this, I believe, is quite appropriate. There are better mechanisms for compensation. The tort system is truly about something else—it is principally a regulatory system.

In the complex world in which we live, regulation has become increasingly important. The government regulates the practice of medicine by licensing doctors and other health care providers, for example, but that regulation is limited. The anesthesiologist who made the mistake that cost the first patient his life will not, and should not, have his license suspended or revoked because of his error. He may be a fine doctor. He may even be the most careful anesthesiologist in town, someone who has made fewer mistakes over a period of years than any of his colleagues. After all, everyone is sometimes negligent.

In some ways, it is unfortunate that a fine doctor should suffer the indignity of being sued for medical malpractice, have his error thrust into the public limelight, or have to pay considerable sums of money (either directly or for malpractice insurance) because he is, inevitably, sometimes negligent. The doctor may wish the investigation of his error were confined within the precincts of the hospital, not only to avoid widespread disclosure and embarrassment but because he believes his colleagues can better understand the facts. Indeed, the doctor who believes he did *not* make a mistake may wish even more fervently that he were judged exclusively by the hospital's peer-review committee.

We can both sympathize the doctor's predicament and nevertheless believe that, on balance, the tort system is a necessary adjunctive system of regulation. The state and the hospital peer-review committee may be the primary mechanisms of regulation, yet they have their limits. The state may lack the resources and the incentive to undertake effective investigations, relying instead on information provided by peer-review committees or volunteered by individuals. Meanwhile, peer-review committees may take their duties seriously but—being composed of human beings—are influenced by desires to protect friends and colleagues and to safeguard the institutional reputation. Peer-review committees may too readily accept statements that nothing untoward occurred.

Although the tort system cannot improve the performance of the most careful anesthesiologist in town, it can improve the performance of anesthesiologists generally. It does this by unearthing errors that would remain hidden, publicly exposing them ("Sunlight is said to be the best of disinfectants: electric light the most efficient policeman," said Justice Louis D. Brandeis),[1] and imposing monetary penalties. The combination gives business organizations powerful incentives to reduce errors as much as is feasible. While errors cannot be eliminated, unnecessarily high error rates are unnecessarily costly. The tort system, therefore, encourages effective self regulation, that is, regulation not by government agencies but by entities, including hospitals, that know their business best.

Although I have used a hospital example to illustrate my thesis that we should think of the tort system more as a regulatory than a compensation system, this book is not about medical malpractice. It is about the common law generally and products liability specifically, more about the action against the manufacturer of the defective anesthesia machine than about the lawsuit against the anesthesiologist.

Products liability is both the common law's greatest advancement of the twentieth century and a subject of great controversy. To big business, it is an affront. In the products liability system, courts—and that means jurors, laypeople—judge the reasonableness of product risk. A pharmaceutical company, employing armies of biochemists and physicians, designs a drug that saves lives but necessarily presents risks of side effects. The Food and Drug Administration (FDA) evaluates and approves the drug, instructing the manufacturer as to exactly what language it must use in the *Physician's Desk Reference* and on the package insert to inform prescribing physicians and users about the drug's risks. An automobile manufacturer designs a sports utility vehicle (SUV), juggling complex considerations of safety, utility, cost, aesthetics, and marketability. The vehicle complies with all regulations promulgated by the National Highway Traffic Safety Administration (NHTSA). People injured from taking the drug or driving the SUV sue the manufacturers. Manufacturers are appalled that, at this juncture, they will be second-guessed by judges and jurors who know nothing about pharmaceuticals or automotive engineering.

Prominent political figures—Ronald Reagan, Dan Quayle, George W. Bush, and Joseph I. Lieberman among them—have called for reform. They argue that bizarre cases (the McDonald's hot coffee action is the most infamous) demonstrate an irrational system, out of control. State legislatures have, in fact, enacted many so-called reforms. Congress has passed tort reform legislation as well, but as of this writing, presidential vetoes have stopped them from becoming law.

In this book I argue that the attack on the system—this war on the common law, as I call it—is misguided. The common law system is working well. Far from being a Mad Hatter world of avaricious lawyers, fluff-headed jurors, and permissive judges, the common law is a careful, conservative, and self-correcting system. Data reflect that jurors, in the main, are up to their jobs. They are neither overly sympathetic to the injured nor prejudiced against large corporations. They take their responsibilities seriously, are educated through a structured trial process, and generally make intelligent decisions. When juries make decisions that are not adequately supported by the evidence or hand up gargantuan verdicts, trial and appellate judges make the appropriate corrections. Indeed, I go so far as to argue that while the system can and occasionally does produce wrong results, it is almost incapable of flatly irrational results.

What about the crazy cases? What kind of system, for example, awards a woman millions for spilling a cup of hot coffee and penalizes a restaurant for giving her what she ordered? I argue that absurd cases are a myth—a myth deliberately and disingenuously created by a campaign to diminish the common law as a regulatory system.

I argue, further, that the common law not only is a sound ancillary system of regulation; it is essential. In the modern world, we expect health and safety to be regulated by administrative agencies possessing expertise in their specialized areas. We expect the FDA to regulate drugs, the Environmental Protection Agency (EPA) to regulate toxic substances, the NHTSA to regulate motor vehicles, the Federal Aviation Association (FAA) to regulate aircraft, the Occupational Safety and Health Administration (OSHA) to regulate industrial machinery, and the Consumer Product Safety Commission (CPSC) to regulate most, if not all, other products. While agencies must, admittedly, be the primary instruments of regulation, I argue that they cannot do the job alone. Focusing on NHTSA as an example, I show how big business compromises the regulators—and how weak the agencies have, in fact, become.

Finally, I argue that the common law's regulatory role is part and parcel of American democracy. Under products liability law, manufacturers are liable for injuries caused by "unreasonably dangerous" products. We consider a product unreasonably dangerous if it fails a risk-utility test, that is, if its risk exceeds its benefits. Ford's Pinto was unreasonably dangerous because the risks posed by a gasoline tank vulnerable to exploding in low-impact rear-end collisions exceeded the benefits of that particular design. Some have argued that only experts can competently evaluate whether a product's risks exceed its benefits. Only automotive engineers can evaluate the Pinto's design; only toxicologists can decide whether a pesticide's risks of cancer and environmental damage exceed its benefits of producing more abundant, less expensive grain. What this argument misses is that these decisions cannot merely be computed. They are value judgments, and we are a democracy. It may be a mistake to make such decisions directly at the ballot box. The issues are complicated, and the public is not informed about the intricacies of such issues. But the ballot box is not democracy's only instrument. The people, after listening to evidence and reasoned arguments, work their will in the jury box as well. The tort system is a system of disciplined democracy—and, I try to show in this book, it is good for America.

1

Why Tell Tales?

Danforth's Tale

On Monday, July 27, 1994, Senator John C. Danforth of Missouri rose on the floor of the Senate to explain to his colleagues, and via C-Span to the nation at large, why he believed it was critical to enact legislation known as the Products Liability Fairness Act, which was designed to displace all state products liability laws with a uniform but more restrictive federal law. To the casual observer, it may have seemed that the bill was destined to become law. It had been written by five senators—two Republicans, including Danforth, and three Democrats. It had garnered forty-four cosponsors who ranged the political spectrum, from liberal Democrats such as Christopher J. Dodd of Connecticut to the hardest of right-wing Republicans, including North Carolina's Jesse Helms. And it had been approved by the Senate Commerce Committee on a vote of sixteen to six. Danforth, however, knew better. This was one of the most fiercely contested pieces of legislation of the session. In fact, it was the continuation of a bitter war that had raged through a number of sessions of Congress. Danforth and his coauthors had expected to win before, only to taste cold defeat at end of the day. All that could be said with certainty was that each side was going to use every available tool of persuasion, politics, and parliamentary maneuvering—and whatever the outcome, it was going to be close.

Products liability may seem like a curious subject to be inspiring such a passionate struggle. It is neither a topic of wide public interest, such as health care or Social Security, nor a political wedge issue such as abortion, gun control, or affirmative action. Yet, for an arcane subject that has historically been the province of the courts, it has received a surprising amount of attention from politicians. A products liability plank was part of the Republican Party platform in 1988, 1992, 1996, and 2000. In 1994, one of the ten legislative proposals that made up Newt Gingrich's Contract With America was the so-called Common

Sense Legal Reforms Act, which the Contract promised would consist of "loser pays laws—reasonable limits on punitive damages and reform of products liability laws to stem the endless tide of litigation." And although the public was largely unaware of it, George W. Bush's commitment to "tort reform"—which seeks to constrict the ability of individuals to sue corporations—was a major factor in his raising unprecedented sums for his presidential candidacy.

Danforth spoke to the Senate just hours before the vote on the bill. It was an important speech. Danforth's voice might be expected to carry particular weight in this debate. He had earned degrees from both the law and divinity schools at Yale, had sharpened his legal skills practicing law with a New York law firm and serving as attorney general of Missouri, and as an ordained Episcopal priest had preached every Tuesday at St. Alban's Church at the National Cathedral. Danforth therefore was not only a lawyer who understood the technical aspects of products liability law but was considered "a figure of moral stature" within the Senate.[1] Years later, when U.S. Attorney General Janet Reno needed a special counsel to investigate whether the Federal Bureau of Investigation (FBI) had started the fire that killed eighty people at the Branch Dividian compound in Waco, Texas, and whether the government had suppressed information about the event, she turned to then-retired senator John C. Danforth. On the day of his appointment, the *New York Times* explained that Danforth would "bring immediate credibility" to the investigation among Republicans, and President Bill Clinton praised him as "an honorable man." And when George W. Bush was looking for a running mate who would add gravitas to his ticket, it appears that Danforth was one of the two finalists on his list.

On that day in the Senate, Danforth spoke slowly and earnestly. To illustrate why tort reform legislation was needed to curb a products liability system that was dangerously out of control, Danforth told his colleagues a story:

> There was a famous case a few years ago of a 70-year-old man who lost the eyesight in his left eye. Now, the loss of eyesight in one eye is not a minor matter. But what is the just result of a 70-year-old man losing eyesight in one eye? What is the reasonable compensation that such an individual should receive? Should it be in the thousands of dollars? In the tens of thousands? The hundreds of thousands? Should it be in the millions of dollars? This person filed a lawsuit, a products liability case, against Upjohn Co. and his recovery was $127 million.[2]

Danforth did not say more about this case. He did not have to. His short vignette delivered a powerful message of why the system desperately needed repair. Compassion and compensation of the injured are worthy goals, but how can pharmaceutical companies offer medicines at affordable prices if they must pay these kinds of gargantuan verdicts? How can American companies compete in the world market carrying these kinds of burdens? And how is justice served by turning a man who suffered an unfortunate outcome from a surgical procedure into a Vanderbilt? Danforth's story gave Congress a reason to act, despite the fact that the common law has traditionally been the province of the judicial rather than the legislative branch of government, and of the states rather than the federal government.

There was just one problem. Danforth told the Senate a cock-and-bull story. Though literally true in most respects, Danforth's version of the case was, as we shall see, flagrantly deceiving. Moreover, this was not the only canard served up by politicians promoting "tort reform" or "civil justice reform." It was one in a series of beguiling yarns. Indeed, so many of these fables have been told—and notwithstanding corrections brought to the attention of the storytellers, retold—that it is reasonable to conclude that deception is a deliberate tactic, if not on the part of politicians like Danforth who tell the tales then on the part of the people who put those stories in their mouths.

This book is about the common law—dynamic bodies of law that courts continually refashion while deciding private lawsuits. The gruel of the common law are cases brought by ordinary people who are focused not on making law but on their own affairs; yet the role the common law plays in American democracy is quite extraordinary. The common law is the one place in American society where a citizen without money, status, or political connections can battle the powerful on nearly equal terms. The contingent fee system—under which lawyers are paid from moneys they recover for their client—makes it possible for an ordinary individual to engage high-caliber legal talent and compel the largest corporation in America to account for its actions in a court of law.

Many believe the common law is an antiquated system that may have been well suited for postmedieval England but is out of place in contemporary America. One criticism is that the common law is too slow to respond to rapidly changing circumstances. Judge Guido Calabresi, who, before being appointed to the United States Court of Appeals for the Second Circuit, served as dean of Yale Law School, has written: "The slow, unsystematic, and organic quality of common law changes made it clearly unsuitable to many legal demands of the welfare state."[3] A second criticism is that courts lack the resources to deal intelligently with complicated issues. We live in an age of highly specialized expertise. Even Congress, with its large professional staff, can grapple only so far with complex issues, which is why modern society is now principally regulated by administrative agencies. A third criticism is that the common law is chaotic; courts hand down conflicting decisions—sometimes deliberately, since the courts of various states decide to adopt different legal rules—which makes it difficult for corporations and others to plan their affairs. A fourth criticism is that the courts are undemocratic. Most judges are not elected, and even those who are elected are not accountable to the people in the same way as legislators are. Probably the harshest criticism of all is that judges and juries are irresponsible, that all too often they make downright wacky decisions, which, of course, was the point Senator Danforth was making in his speech to the Senate.

The central theme of this book is that the common law is not a quaint antique—that law developed by court decisions plays just as important a role at the beginning of the twenty-first century as it has at any time in American history. I focus principally on products liability, the body of law under which people injured by unreasonably dangerous products may sue the sellers of those products. Less than forty years old, products liability is the youngest and most dynamic area in the common law. It is also the most politically contentious. Corporate America has created organizations devoted exclusively to lobbying state legislatures or Congress for so-called tort reform legislation, much of which is directly aimed at legislatively curtailing judicially created products liability law. Meanwhile, products liability law has been the subject of intense debate with law schools, think tanks, and professional organizations, including, most prominently, the American Law Institute, which promulgates influential "Restatements" of common law areas.

Products liability and tort law have played an important but little-understood role in presidential politics as well. In early 1999, the race for the Republican presidential nomination was considered wide open: eight candidates, a number of whom—including former cabinet secretary Elizabeth Dole, Senator John McCain of Arizona, and former

Tennessee governor Lamar Alexander—were considered formidable. None was a clear front-runner. Then, on June 30, 1999, the dynamics of the race changed overnight. George W. Bush announced he had received contributions totaling $37 million, a sum that was not only unprecedented but that so dwarfed his opponents' contributions (the Republican in second place, McCain, had raised $4.3 million) as to hobble the ability of their campaigns to be taken seriously.

This took many by surprise. Bush, although the son of a president and governor of the nation's second most populous state, had been in public life for only five years. How, at the very beginning of the race, did he catapult so far ahead?

What had happened was that, well before the race officially began, leaders of corporate America privately decided to do their best to make Bush president. Through a systematic series of discussions, beginning within various trade associations—such as the American Petroleum Institute, the American Chemical Council, the Food Marketing Institute, and the American Automobile Manufacturers Association—and moving upward into the councils of organizations such as the U.S. Chamber of Commerce, corporate leaders decided Bush was their man. Within the first ninety days of the announcement of Bush's candidacy, 1,542 chairmen and chief executive officers contributed to his campaign.[4] Why the decision to support Bush? When he first ran for governor of Texas in 1994, Bush declared: "Probably the most significant thing that I will do when I am governor of this state is to insist that Texas change the tort laws and insist we end frivolous and junk lawsuits that threaten our producers and crowd our courts."[5] As soon as he took office, Bush declared tort reform "an emergency issue," so that legislation could be passed without the usually required thirty-day waiting period, and pushed a tort reform package through the Texas legislature. When he ran for reelection four years later, Bush was rewarded with millions of dollars in contributions from businesses associated with Texas tort reform organizations. Indeed, officers and board members of two Texas tort reform groups, Texans for Lawsuit Reform and the Texas Civil Justice League, contributed a total of $4.5 million to Bush's two gubernatorial campaigns.[6] Tort reform was but one part of a collection of pro-business positions—Bush also supported free trade, tax cuts, and deregulation, especially in the environmental area—but it was an important part. When he traveled from city to city for $1,000-a-plate fund-raisers early in his presidential campaign, Bush was careful to mention that he would fight for tort reform in Washington, even including the issue in comments to the mainstream media. It wasn't for the electorate at large that Bush gave tort reform so prominent a position. By publicly committing himself to make tort reform a high priority for his administration, Bush was essentially signing a tacit agreement with American industry.

Eventually, McCain was able to give Bush a run for his money. After McCain stunned Bush in the New Hampshire primary, corporate America quickly covered its bets by making contributions to McCain's campaign too. McCain also had long been a backer of tort reform.[7] Still, big business much preferred Bush. Bush was a reliable ally; McCain was unpredictable. Throughout his political career, McCain had raised large sums from corporate America, and using his powerful position as chair of the Senate Commerce Committee, McCain had paid his debts to his benefactors. But now McCain was running for the presidency by pronouncing the arrangement unholy and making campaign finance reform his battle cry.

After New Hampshire, Bush began to give tort reform an even more prominent place in his campaign rhetoric.[8] In part this was to simply to exploit the phrase. Bush was trying to position himself as a reformer; but seeking both to replenish his own campaign treasury and to suppress bet-covering contributions to McCain, Bush also wanted to remind big business of the stakes. Ultimately he prevailed. Part of the equation were the vast sums of money contributed to the Bush campaign—$68.7 million as of the end of 1999. McCain raised an impressive $15.7 million of his own. Still, with over four times as much money, Bush was able to out-organize and out-advertise McCain. It is difficult to beat corporate America.

To paraphrase Finley P. Dunne's Mr. Dooley, the battle over products liability has not been a game of beanbag—which brings me back to Senator Danforth's Senate speech.

Proctor v. Davis: *The Real Story*

Although Danforth did not identify it, the case he described to the Senate was brought by a retired public relations worker in Illinois named Meyer Proctor.[9] In 1983, Proctor experienced blurred vision and went to see Michael J. Davis, a board-certified ophthalmologist. Dr. Davis diagnosed

Proctor's condition as uveitis, a potentially serious inflammation of the middle layer of the eye, and began treating Davis with steroid eyedrops. This treatment did not significantly help, however, and as often occurs with uveitis, Proctor developed complications. Indeed, the vision in Proctor's left eye deteriorated so badly that he could be considered legally blind in that eye. After having Proctor examined by a retinal specialist, Davis decided to institute a new regime of treatment: he would inject a drug known as Depo-Medrol near Proctor's eyes.

Depo-Medrol is a steroid manufactured by Upjohn, a pharmaceutical company headquartered in Kalamazoo, Michigan, that produces Motrin, Rogaine, and the tranquilizer Xanax, as well as many other products. (Upjohn has since merged with a Swedish pharmaceutical company and changed its name to Pharmacia & Upjohn.) Depo-Medrol was by no means a new drug; the Food and Drug Administration (FDA) approved it more than twenty years earlier for use in treating a variety of inflammations throughout the human body, by injecting it directly into inflamed muscles and joints. The FDA, however, had never approved the drug for injection near the eyes—and for good reason. One of the benefits of Depo-Medrol is that it is an especially long-acting steroid. It is insoluble, and when it is injected into tissue with adequate blood supply, it is released gradually in the body over a period of six to eight weeks. But the eyes have lower blood flow than muscles and joints, and if Depo-Medrol is deposited into an eye, it will remain there—in a toxic, crystalline form—for a relatively long period of time.

Shortly after Upjohn introduced Depo-Medrol, two ophthalmologists independently contacted Upjohn and inquired about using the drug to treat inflammations of the eye. They wanted to know if Depo-Medrol could appropriately be administered by periocular injection, that is, by injecting it near the eyeball. Other steroids were used this way, but the doctors thought Depo-Medrol might offer advantages because it was long-acting.

Upjohn did not direct the doctors' attention to the fact that the very feature they found attractive—Depo-Medrol's long-acting effect—presented potential risks. And, although medical researchers normally consider animal tests a prerequisite to testing drugs on humans, Upjohn neglected to advise the doctors it had conducted no animal tests related to administering Depo-Medrol near the eyes. Instead, Upjohn sent the doctors vials of Depo-Medrol and a letter stating, "We do not have any reports concerning this use for preparation and we would very much like for you to evaluate it in this way."

Once a drug has been approved by FDA, nothing prevents physicians from using it for any purpose they consider medically appropriate, even if that use has not been approved by FDA. A pharmaceutical manufacturer encouraging physicians to use its products for unapproved purposes is another matter, however. Upjohn not only sent vials of Depo-Medrol and letters urging ophthalmologists to try administering it by periocular injection; it encouraged them with money as well. It sent at least one ophthalmologist $3,000 to support his testing of the drug. This doctor later told Upjohn he had given two talks in Chicago praising Depo-Medrol's use by periocular injection, even though, according to the doctor's own report to Upjohn, his experiment with the drug "fell flat" and did not justify his public remarks. This same doctor later published an article endorsing the use of Depo-Medrol for eye disease while, again, privately reporting to Upjohn that he did not include animal tests he conducted in the article because the results were "very unsatisfactory." Upjohn distributed twenty-five hundred copies of that article to physicians and hospitals.

Upjohn continued to promote Depo-Medrol aggressively for periocular use. It urged other ophthalmologists to experiment with the drug and told them that if they sought to publish their results, Upjohn would compensate the doctors for both their own and their secretaries' time and would even make the "Upjohn Writing Staff" available to help write the articles. These anecdotal reports by practicing physicians inexperienced in devising clinical trials had little or no value in determining the safety or effectiveness of Depo-Medrol in treating eye disease. Internally, Upjohn characterized some of these reports as "lousy data" and "almost worthless." One doctor's case reports were so amateurish that they failed to include such basic data as the patient's diagnosis, the strength of Depo-Medrol administered, and frequency of injections. Upjohn offered to pay this doctor's secretary to "re-work" the reports. Meanwhile, it continued furnishing even this self-appointed investigator with free vials of Depo-Medrol—that is, for as long as Upjohn could continue to consider him "a good friend of ours," as he was described in an internal company memorandum.

Upjohn could have conducted methodologically sound testing, including double-blind animal and human studies, either in house or by engaging professional outside consultants. If Upjohn were to file a supplemental request with the FDA asking that Depo-Medrol be approved for periocular administration, it would be required to furnish such data. But Upjohn chose never to seek such approval. It never had to. Upjohn was able to have its cake and eat it too: the company was able to develop a profitable ophthalmologic market for its product without incurring the expense of conducting serious studies—and, perhaps even more important, without running the risk that studies might show Depo-Medrol was *not* appropriate for periocular injection. By the time Meyer Proctor consulted Dr. Davis, twenty-four years after Depo-Medrol was originally introduced, ophthalmologists were routinely using the drug. In fact, at the trial in Meyer Proctor's case, Dr. Davis testified that he had himself injected Depo-Medrol near patients' eyes sixteen hundred times, and he believed ophthalmologists were using the drug about 1 million times a year.

Because the use was unapproved, Upjohn did not provide physicians with a recommended dose for periocular administration. An unknown number of ophthalmologists were apparently using one cubic centimeter (cc) of the drug, which may have been a common dosage for intramuscular injection but presented different risks when used near the eyes, where, with reduced blood flow, the crystalline material would remain for longer periods of time. Upjohn knew that when Depo-Medrol was administered subcutaneously in other areas of the body, as it is near the eye, it sometimes caused tissues to atrophy, and it expected that Depo-Medrol might cause eye pressure to increase as well. Moreover, periocular injections are made extremely close to the eye, where a physician might inadvertently deposit the drug into the globe of the eye itself. This possibility exists whenever any drug is injected near the eye, but the crystalline nature of Depo-Medrol means that when this happens, a toxic solid has been deposited into the eye. One published medical article reported that in four cases of accidental intraocular injection of Depo-Medrol, two patients suffered a complete loss of vision.

About twenty years after Depo-Medrol was introduced, and three years before Meyer Proctor went to see Dr. Davis, Upjohn made one attempt to warn the profession about some of the dangers of periocular use. Under a heading "Adverse Reactions Reported with Nonrecommended Routes of Administration," Upjohn proposed to the FDA issuing a warning that periocular administrations were associated with "[r]edness and itching, obtuse, slough at injection site, increased intraocular pressure, decreased vision" and listing "blindness" as having been associated with "retrobulbar" administrations, that is, with injecting Depo-Medrol beneath the eyeball itself. The FDA denied Upjohn's request to make this change, a fact that Upjohn, quite understandably, wanted to introduce into evidence in Meyer Proctor's case. The court found, however, that the FDA denial was less than it appeared. Upjohn made its proposal while responding to a request for a proposed labeling change relating to an entire class of drugs—not only Depo-Medrol, and not only Upjohn products. The FDA advised Upjohn that it had not decided to approve the global changes, and its communication could not reasonably be read as a decision about the merits of the proposed change relating specifically to Depo-Medrol. Indeed, the FDA's letter to Upjohn specifically stated that if important new information became available, Upjohn should revise its labeling under a different procedure. Upjohn never did so. The trial judge held that, under these circumstances, Upjohn's request to include a warning relating to periocular use was not admissible, and the Illinois appellate court agreed.

Dr. Davis testified that had Upjohn informed him of the dangers of the drug, he would not have administered Depo-Medrol to Meyer Proctor—a claim that perhaps should have been taken with a grain of salt, since it was to Davis's benefit to shift the blame to codefendant Upjohn. We do know, however, that the second time Davis administered Depo-Medrol to Proctor, he accidentally inserted the needle into Proctor's eye.

Although Davis was aware of the risk that this type of accident might occur, Proctor's lawyer questioned whether Davis followed the standard of care to ensure against injecting the drug into the eye. Some ophthalmologists claim that one can tell by pressure when the needle is encountering the eyeball, and a skilled physician making a subconjunctival injection should never puncture the eyeball. Davis testified that on this occasion he felt no sensation of pushing through tissue.[10] One expert testified at trial that, after inserting the needle but before injecting the medicine, a prudent physician should use two techniques to ensure that the needle has not penetrated the eye. First, the physician should withdraw the plunger slightly to see whether fluid is drawn into the syringe; if so, the tip of the needle is in the eye. Next, the physician should rock the needle back and forth to see whether the eyeball moves. Again, if it does, the needle is in the eye and the physician should not push the plunger on the syringe. Another expert disagreed about the propriety of using these techniques and testified that as of 1983, when the incident occurred, no technique had been devised that eliminated all risk of ocular penetration.

In any event, Davis, who had planned to inject one cc of Depo-Medrol, did not realize the accident had occurred until he had injected one-quarter cc directly into Meyer Proctor's left eye. Within a few weeks, Proctor's retina detached. Three times Proctor underwent surgery to reattach his retina, but after each procedure the retina detached once again. Proctor's left eye—now permanently blind and painful—was removed five months later.

When he offered this case as the prime example of an out-of-control tort system in need of reform, Senator Danforth asked what "reasonable compensation" was for a seventy-year-old man's loss of sight in one eye; then he told the Senate this individual's "recovery" was $127 million. The jury that heard the case did, in fact, render a verdict against Upjohn of more than $127 million, but not because it deemed that to be reasonable compensation for Meyer Proctor. Only $3,047,819.76 of the award for was compensatory damages, which were designed to compensate Proctor for his injury and included not only "loss of sight in one eye," as Danforth suggested, but the pain, discomfort, and anguish of three unsuccessful surgeries and the ultimate loss of the eye itself. The lion's share of the verdict, $124,573,750, was for punitive damages. Punitive damages are not awarded to compensate the plaintiff but to punish a defendant for outrageous conduct and to deter both the defendant and others from similar conduct in the future. Under Illinois law, which is typical of American common law generally, "outrageous conduct" includes both conduct inspired by an evil motive and conduct undertaken with a reckless indifference to the rights of others. The *Proctor* jury awarded punitive damages to punish Upjohn for deliberately promoting the use of its drug in a manner not approved by the FDA, without warning physicians about the risks of such use, and to deter both Upjohn and other pharmaceutical companies from engaging in similar conduct in the future.

Senator Danforth also neglected to mention that the trial judge had reduced the punitive award to $35 million and that an appeal seeking a further reduction was pending. After two separate reviews by the appellate court of Illinois, the punitive award was finally reduced to $6,095,639.52, a sum equal to twice the compensatory award. The case was settled by the parties at this stage, before this award was appealed to the Illinois Supreme Court. When I telephoned him, plaintiff's lawyer declined to tell me whether Meyer Proctor agreed to accept a lower sum to avoid the risk that the state supreme court would further reduce or eliminate the award (presumably because the settlement forbids him from disclosing the terms of the settlement), but it is a likely guess that this is exactly what happened.[11]

Why Tell Tales?

Why did Senator Danforth, a man who cultivated an image of "moral authority," misrepresent the facts of *Proctor* on the floor of the Senate? I argue that Danforth's misrepresentations—in service of political patrons in big business—were deliberate, if not intended by Danforth himself then by those who wrote his speech or who furnished the speechwriter with the distorted story. I shall show that this sort of deception is common. When those who argue that the tort system is broken and needs to be fixed serve up examples of the system run amok and, repeatedly, those examples turn out to be falsified, we can draw some conclusions about how abundant patently absurd court decisions actually are.

Prior to Danforth's Senate speech, there had been a history of prominent politicians, particularly Republicans, telling stories about outlandish court decisions, only to discover that the stories were inaccurate. Vice President Dan Quayle told a story about a psychic who won a jury award of $986,000 because a CAT scan allegedly robbed her of her psychic powers. The story was a hit on the lecture circuit and became something of a poster child for a system out of control. When the real case was identified, however, it was apparent there were a few things Quayle failed to mention. The plaintiff was a forty-two-year-old woman named Judith Richardson Haimes, who entered Temple University Hospital to discover the cause of tumors on her ear.[12] Haines suffered an allergic reaction to contrast dye administered in connection with a CAT scan and went into anaphylactic shock. Haimes testified that before the test she told the neuroradiologist who was preparing the dye that she knew from prior experience she was allergic to the dye but was told she was being "ridiculous" and was embarrassed into consenting to the procedure. After fewer than a dozen drops of the dye were injected into her, Haimes experienced a severe reaction. She said she felt "as if my head was going to explode." Her blood pressure dropped; she vomited and had trouble breathing. Hives and welts covered her body. Another doctor who was present took immediate action and saved Haimes's life. These facts state a sound cause of action and, if proved, warrant a monetary verdict.

Judith Haimes also testified that she made her living as a psychic and that after this event she experienced extreme headaches whenever she tried to use her psychic powers. Three police officers testified that Haimes had used her powers to help them solve cases. There is a question of whether the judge who presided over the trial in state court in Philadelphia, Leon Katz, should have allowed these officers to testify or allowed any evidence about Haimes's psychic powers to be introduced. Nevertheless, Judge Katz was not the Mad Hatter Quayle would have his audiences believe. After hearing the evidence, Judge Katz held there was not adequate evidence for a loss of psychic powers theory and instructed the jury to disregard that portion of the claim. The jury returned a verdict of $600,000, which was increased to $986,465 as a matter of law to provide for prejudgment interest that accrued. In a forty-two-page opinion, Judge Katz held the jury's award was grossly excessive and ordered a new trial. Haimes was unsuccessful in the second trial.[13]

Quayle's story about the clairvoyant and the CAT scan was sufficiently captivating to bamboozle even people who portray themselves as products liability experts. W. Kip Viscusi, a professor at the Harvard Law School, puts this case on the very first page of his book *Reforming Products Liability,* to help explain why, as he puts it, "[s]eemingly outrageous cases have come to epitomize the malfunctioning of the tort liability system."[14]

In one of his standard stump speeches, Ronald Reagan told of a cat burglar who fell through the skylight of a home he was burglarizing and sued the homeowner for his injuries.[15] When the real case was identified, it turned out that the plaintiff was not a cat burglar at all. He was high school student who had been sent to retrieve athletic equipment stored on the roof of the school and had fallen through a skylight that had been painted black.

Reagan also told the story of a man in a telephone booth who was injured when the booth was struck by a car operated by a drunk driver. According to Reagan's version, the man sued and recovered from the telephone company rather than from the drunk driver.[16] The real case involved a man named Charles Bigbee, who was seriously injured when an allegedly intoxicated woman lost control of her car and slammed into the booth.[17] Bigbee sued the driver and the club where the driver had allegedly become drunk. Those claims were settled before trial.

Bigbee did also sue the telephone company. He said he saw the car veering toward him and tried to escape, but the door jammed and, trapped, he watched helplessly while the car careened into him. Another witness supported Bigbee's version. The man said he was standing next to the phone booth, saw the oncoming car, and, although frozen for several seconds before starting to run, still had enough time to get out of the car's path. Plaintiff argued that the phone booth, in a liquor-store parking lot, was too close to a busy boulevard on which cars sped by. He also presented evidence showing that a booth in the very same location had been demolished by a hit-and-run driver twenty months earlier.

Reasonable minds can—and indeed did—differ as to whether the telephone company should be liable under these circumstances. The trial judge dismissed the claim against the phone company, and in a two-to-one decision, the appellate court upheld that decision. By a vote of six to two, however, the California Supreme Court reversed. The court noted that a number of other state courts held that telephone companies are responsible for the location and maintenance of their phone booths, and it wrote: "Here, defendants placed a telephone booth, which was difficult to exit, in a parking lot 15 feet from the side of a major thoroughfare and near a driveway. . . . In light of the circumstances of modern life, it seems evident that a jury could reasonably find that defendants should have foreseen the possibility of the very accident which occurred here."[18]

The most infamous tort case involves the woman who won a $2.9 million jury verdict against McDonald's after burning herself with a cup of hot coffee.[19] As nearly everyone knows, the woman purchased coffee at the restaurant's drive-through window, put the cup between her legs to remove the cover, and spilled it. Some other facts are not as well known. The trial evidence was that McDonald's served its coffee between 180 and 190 degrees Fahrenheit, while coffee made at home is between 130 and 140 degrees Fahrenheit, and that over the past ten years McDonald's had received seven hundred reports of patrons burning themselves with its superheated coffee. The woman, who was seventy-nine at the time of the incident, suffered third-degree burns. She spent eight days in the hospital undergoing a series of painful skin grafts on her thighs, groin, and buttocks. It took her two years to recover, and even then 16 percent of her body was left with permanent scars.

Before trial, plaintiff had offered to settle for $10,000, to cover her medical expenses and some compensation for her pain and suffering. The trial judge urged McDonald's to settle at that figure, but McDonald's refused. So plaintiff proceeded to trial asking for compensatory damages—based on the difference between the injuries she would have suffered if she had spilled 140-degree coffee and injuries caused by superheated coffee—and punitive damages. The jury awarded $200,000 in compensatory damages and $2.7 million in punitive damages (to which the court added interest in accordance with an established formula). The trial judge denied McDonald's motion to eliminate the punitive damage award, stating that the evidence showed McDonald's was guilty of "willful, wanton, reckless and what the court finds was callous" behavior. Nevertheless, the judge reduced the jury's $2.7 million punitive award to $480,000. The jury found plaintiff was 20 percent responsible for her injuries, and accordingly, her compensatory award was reduced by 20 percent to $160,000. McDonald's appealed, but we shall never know if these sums would have been reduced further or reversed altogether, for McDonald's elected to settle privately with the plaintiff for an undisclosed sum.

An article in the trade publication *Tea & Coffee Journal* stated, "Regardless of your views on the legal system, tort reform or matters of personal responsibility, the incidents of people spilling hot coffee on themselves raises [sic] issues that the coffee industry needs to be aware of and take very seriously."[20] Wendy's reevaluated its hot chocolate—which was sold mostly to children and heated to a scalding 180 degrees—and decided to voluntarily suspend selling that product until it could lower the temperature. For this book, I wrote to several of the national fast-food restaurant chains to find whether they had reformulated their hot beverages as a result of the McDonald's case. Most ignored my letters. Burger King sent a vaguely threatening reply declining to furnish any information but stating I had be sure whatever I said about Burger King was accurate. I then dispatched my research assistant to eight local McDonald's, Burger King, Dunkin' Donuts, and Wendy's restaurants, armed with a candy thermometer and instructions to purchase cups of coffee and hot chocolate and measure their temperature immediately on receipt. He found that no beverage was hotter than 157 degrees Fahrenheit. Moreover, the hot chocolate at Burger

King and Dunkin' Donuts was seven to nine degrees cooler than their coffee.[21] The McDonald's case may still provide ammunition for tort reformers and late-night talk-show hosts, but it may well have saved many people—children especially—from serious injury.

2

War on the Common Law

Warriors

By the time Danforth told his version of the Depo-Medrol case to the Senate on that Monday in July 1994, the stories about the clairvoyant, the cat burglar, and the man in the phone booth had became popular legends of an Alice in Wonderland world of rapacious lawyers, dippy jurors, and Mad Hatter judges.[1] Yet everyone working in the tort reform area knew the stories had been debunked.

Reagan had gotten away with his stories because he was Ronald Reagan. The American people accepted Reagan as sincere and well intentioned. Quayle's escaping unscathed had proved something else, however. It is an understatement to say that Quayle lacked Reagan's Teflon quality, yet he told tort reform stories with equal impunity. Political operatives learned that this is an area where truth does not catch up. Probably only a small fraction of the people who heard the distorted tort stories ever encountered corrected versions, and even those who had probably did not blame the politician for the fabrication. They assumed the politician was an innocent victim of a speechwriter. But while on many matters politicians may be held accountable for mistakes by their staff, experience showed that tort reform is too low on the national radar for this kind of vicarious responsibility. Danforth's speechwriter—and whoever furnished the anecdote to the speechwriter—probably understood all this. A newspaper might publish a correction after the Senate voted, but it would not matter. A correction would get little visibility; and besides, a colorful story is more enduring than truth. By the time Danforth gave his speech on the Senate floor in 1994, crafting horror stories about the judicial system had become an art form.

Proctor's $127.7 million award was the largest jury verdict in the nation in 1991[2] and received publicity. Danforth himself called it "a famous case," although that probably overstates it. Why not assume that

Danforth or his staff took the facts from an incomplete or inaccurate newspaper clipping, and that the distortions in Danforth's tale were innocent? The modus operandi of members of Congress and their staff makes it more likely that Danforth or his staff got their information from an advocacy organization than from a newspaper clipping they had filed.[3] Moreover, as Danforth and his staff were almost certainly aware, there had been a series of distorted tort stories coming from the mouths of politicians, and they knew they had to be careful if they wanted to avoid doing the same thing.

One of Danforth's aides was a lawyer named Sherman Joyce. After beginning his career as one of Danforth's legislative assistants, Joyce became counsel to the Republican members of the Senate Commerce Committee's Subcommittee on the Consumer, where he helped draft the Products Liability Fairness Act, the legislation Danforth was urging his colleagues to vote for when he made his remarks about *Proctor*. Two months after Danforth's speech, Joyce left the Senate to become president of the American Tort Reform Association (ATRA), an organization of large manufacturing companies and trade associations—including the Pharmaceutical Manufacturers Association—that lobbies for legislation cutting back on tort law and, especially, products liability law. ATRA was the moving force behind the Products Liability Fairness Act, about which Danforth was speaking when he made his remarks about *Proctor v. Davis*.

Danforth retired from the Senate at the end 1994 and today is general chairman of the American Tort Reform Foundation, an arm of ATRA. Sherman Joyce is still president of ATRA as well as its foundation. And ATRA continues to lobby vigorously—and, as we shall see, successfully—for tort and products liability reform. ATRA maintains a Web site that features a page called "Horror Stories!" with the latest supposed outrages of the judicial system. Most of ATRA's horror stories are not about judicial decisions but merely about bizarre claims, that is, lawsuits filed but not yet adjudicated. Undecided claims, no matter how outlandish, are hardly evidence of a flawed judicial system. In our society, the courts are open to all; and in much the same way that claptrap and blather are part of the price a society pays for permitting free speech, outlandish lawsuits are part of the price of an open judicial system. The test is not whether outrageous claims are filed but how they are handled.

From time to time, however, ATRA posts an alleged horror story about a decided case. A recent description of a case, titled "Pickled Justice," reads in full as follows:

> A West Virginia convenience store worker Cheryl Vandender [*sic*] was awarded an astonishing $2,699,000 in punitive damages after she injured her back when she opened a pickle jar, according to the Charleston Daily Mail. She also received $130,066 in compensation and $170,000 for emotional distress. State Supreme Court Justice Spike Maynard called this award an "outrageous sum," stating in his dissenting opinion: "I know an excessive punitive award when I see one, and I see one here." The court, however, upheld most of the punitive damages: $2.2 million.[4]

The case surely sounds like a product of a loopy judicial system. The reader wonders: How does one get injured opening a pickle jar? How could this possibly lead to a serious enough injury, including emotional distress, to justify punitive damages and an award of more than $2 million? And is it not daffy to hold the pickle company responsible? "Pickled Justice," however, is very much like Danforth's description of *Proctor v. Davis* in that, although nothing said is literally untrue, the capsule description has been carefully crafted to create a false impression.

Here are the facts of the actual case.[5] Cheryl Vandevender was an assistant manager of a convenience store owned by Sheetz, Inc., where she had worked for about a year and a half before hurting her back while trying to open a large pickle jar. This was probably the aggravation of a preexisting condition; Vandevender had injured her back and had surgery before taking the job at Sheetz.

Apparently hoping her back would get better on its own, Vandevender waited more than two weeks before seeing a doctor. She continued working during this time; indeed, she worked for a number of months after the injury. But her back did not improve. About seven months after the injury she began receiving disability payments, and two months later she underwent back surgery again. People with imagined or concocted injuries may have diathermy treatments and physical therapy, but they seldom have surgery.

Somewhere between ten and twelve months after the surgery, Vandevender told Sheetz's store manager, Karen Foltz, that with the permanent limitation that she could do no heavy lifting, she was ready to return to work. Foltz told Vandevender that she could not come back unless she were "100 percent," and the company later sent Vandevender a letter informing her that she was being discharged in accordance with the company's policy that a twelve-month absence from work was to be treated as a resignation. A West Virginia rehabilitation counselor called Foltz on Vandevender's behalf, only to be told that it would be futile for Vandevender to apply for rehire.

Vandevender never sued the pickle company. She filed an action against Sheetz for violating the state workers' compensation law by firing her because she had a work-related injury, and for violating the state anti-discrimination law by refusing to consider reemploying her because she had a disability. Foltz testified that the company's requirement that an employee holding Vandevender's job be able to lift up to fifty pounds and stand for eight hours a day was not actually essential. Five weeks after giving this testimony, Foltz was herself fired. Sheetz resisted attempts by Vandevender's lawyers to discover whether Foltz was fired because she had given testimony unfavorable to the company.

In any event, based on Foltz's testimony, Vandevender asked to return to work. Sheetz agreed to take her back on the condition that, one month before reporting for work, Vandevender undergo an independent medical examination. Vandevender had the exam. The results stated that—with the limitations that she should not lift more than fifteen pounds at a time and should periodically use a stool for standing breaks—Vandevender was able to work.

Sheetz, however, apparently had no intention of letting Vandevender work. When she reported for work one month later, Vandevender was greeted by the company's district manager, Ms. Imler. Although Imler knew the results of Vandevender's medical examination, she feigned ignorance. Imler told Vandevender she did not "see" physical problems and would not recognize any restrictions unless Vandevender got another medical exam by the end of the week. Moreover, Vandevender was to accomplish this notwithstanding being scheduled to work every day that week. Imler told Vandevender that until she produced the results of a new exam, "you're just like one of the others." Vandevender was afraid to tell anyone when she suffered back spasms twenty minutes later. On her attorney's advice, she did not return to work the next day.

Vandevender's complaint was amended to include the claim that Sheetz's actions on the day she returned to work were in reprisal for her filing an action against the company. After a trial lasting three days, a jury awarded Vandevender $130,066 for lost wages and uncompensated medical expenses, $170,000 for emotional distress, and $2,699,000 in punitive damages.

Sheetz asked the trial judge to vacate or reduce the award. The judge, however, found that Sheetz had a "policy and practice" of violating the state's workers' compensation law by firing and refusing to rehire injured workers. Sheetz's practices, wrote the court, "have the effect of increasing [its] profits at the expense of honest competitors, other honest employers and their employees, and to the detriment of the citizens of this State." Sheetz conceded its conduct had been illegal but argued this was due to "mistakes" rather than deliberate violations of law. The court found that this claim was "simply not credible." "Indeed," the judge continued, Sheetz "paid bonuses to managers based on their ability to reduce Workers' Compensation premiums, thus encouraging conduct that violates State public policy."

The judge reduced the compensatory award by $6,200 for medical expenses he found unsupported by evidence but upheld the rest of the verdict. In evaluating whether the punitive award of more than $2.3 million was excessive, the trial judge took into consideration that Sheetz's revenues were approximately $1.5 million per day. Punitive damages are designed to punish and deter, and they must be substantial enough to sting. The judge also considered that Sheetz's conduct—its initial refusal to resolve the matter amicably, even though it had clearly violated West Virginia law, followed by a scheme to pretend to allow Vandevender back to work while apparently intending to harass her into quitting—forced Vandevender's attorneys to advance more than $53,000 in fees and costs to see the matter through trial.

This is all relevant for two reasons. First, it relates to the egregiousness of Sheetz's conduct and therefore to the appropriate level of punishment. Second, the judge may have believed that Vandevender deserved to not have her compensation damages reduced by litigation expenses and that her lawyers deserved to be compensated for taking a considerable risk. If their arrangement was typical, Vandevender's lawyers represented her on a contingent fee arrangement. They advanced their time and paid the out-of-pocket costs of litigation. If they obtained money for their client, they would receive a fee equal to an agreed-upon portion (often about one-third) of the net recovery. If unsuccessful, however, they would receive nothing. Litigation is always uncertain, and thus Vandevender's lawyers ran a financial risk to vindicate her rights. In a case such as this, courts may conclude the attorneys should receive a premium or bonus to compensate them for taking that risk and to encourage them to take risky but worthy cases in the future. Although punitive damages are not theoretically designed for this purpose, they can provide a large enough pool to adequately compensate plaintiff's lawyers for their efforts and, after the attorney's fees are subtracted from the award, to fully compensate the plaintiff for her injuries.

Sheetz appealed. The Supreme Court of Appeals of West Virginia held that Sheetz's conduct in firing and refusing to rehire Vandevender fell more "into a category of reckless disregard" of her rights than of malice or an intent to cause her harm. It held that while punitive damages were justified, the ratio of punitive damages to compensatory damages for this portion of the case should not exceed a ratio of five to one. The appellate court, however, found that Sheetz's patterns of conduct on the day Vandevender actually returned to work—Imler's pretended ignorance of Vandevender's recent medical exam, her insistence that Vandevender have another exam by the end of the week, her refusal to recognize Vandevender's medical restrictions, and her directing Vandevender to engage in strenuous work—"suggest a mean-spirited intent to punish" Vandevender for filing a worker's compensation claim against Sheetz, and the court refused to reduce any of the punitive damages assessed for this part of the case. The final result was that the appellate court reduced the punitive award from $2,699,000 to $2,327,400 and made no reduction in the compensatory award of $293,866.

As noted in ATRA's description of the case, one of the five members of the court dissented. "I know an excessive punitive damages award when I see one, and I see one here," he wrote. But even that dissenting justice declared that Vandevender "was treated badly by" Sheetz and that Sheetz "should have to pay her a fair amount of damages." Reasonable minds can disagree about what represents fair or excessive remuneration for damages, but either way this case is hardly an example of an unhinged judicial system.

War on the Common Law

ATRA's capsulized description of *Vandevender v. Sheetz* is something of a work of art—literally true yet carefully crafted to create a false impression. The reader is told that Vandevender was awarded punitive damages "after she injured her back when she opened a pickle jar." Because this is the entire description of the dispute, the reader assumes that plaintiff was not only awarded punitive damages *after* but *because* she opened a pickle jar. Otherwise, why describe the case this way and call it "Pickled Justice"?

In fact, the pickle jar is wholly irrelevant. The jar is mentioned only once in the court's opinion, in a minor footnote. This was not a products liability action against the pickle jar manufacturer; the matter arose from Vandevender filing a workers' compensation claim. For workers' compensation purposes, it did not matter whether Vandevender hurt her back opening a pickle jar or walking across her work area. Workers' compensation covers employees for injuries occurring at work irrespective of fault.[6] Punitive damages were awarded in the case because Sheetz engaged in a deliberate and malicious scheme to evade its responsibilities under state law.

ATRA's vignette also invites the reader to imagine the plaintiff as a goldbrick, a malingerer, or both. The question that leaps to mind on hearing the story is: How could one be seriously hurt and suffer emotional distress from opening a pickle jar? It is impossible not to suspect that the plaintiff concocted the injury to stay home from work and get rich through litigation—and that a silly judiciary helped her get away with it. Ironically, the case is really about the fact that Vandevender wanted to work and Sheetz did not want her to. And the bona fides of her injury seem validated by her back surgery.

Of course, we cannot know some things with certainty. Did Vandevender genuinely hurt her back at work rather than at home? If the latter, was she attempting to get Sheetz's workers' compensation insurance to pay for a previous condition? West Virginia's workers' compensation system has been in operation since 1913 and has worked out methods of evaluating all kinds of claims, including, specifically, claims by workers with preexisting back conditions who claim to have suffered new injuries on the job.[7] But Sheetz, who had the most to lose, did not dispute the underlying facts relating to Vandevender's workers' compensation claim.

Perhaps most telling of all, ATRA's vignette identifies the plaintiff as Cheryl Vanender rather than Cheryl Vandevender. Did ATRA misspell her last name to make the court opinion more difficult to find? Most legal research today is conducted through computerized legal research systems. These systems are strictly literal, and if instructed to locate cases with the name Vanender, they will not produce cases with Vandevender. The misspelling may have been a typographical error, but one wonders, given the rest of ATRA's behavior.

It is impossible to mistake the strong similarities between ATRA's "Pickled Justice" and Danforth's description of *Proctor v. Davis*. The vignettes are alike in length, form, organization, and style and create false impressions from a selective use of facts that can be defended as literally true. Each vignette is designed to make listeners shake their heads at the stupidity of the courts. They are examples of the same art form.

But it is not only Danforth and ATRA who are using the distorted vignette. Two years after organizing ATRA to lobby state legislatures, the business community formed a second entity, the Product Liability Coordinating Committee (PLCC), to lobby for federal tort reform legislation. PLCC claims to represent more than seven hundred thousand companies and organizations, but its main sponsors are the U.S. Chamber of Commerce, the Business Roundtable, and the National Association of Manufacturers, in whose reports PLCC's financial and lobbying information are included.[8] On July 31, 1998, the *Des Moines Register* took the unusual step of running a short article signed personally by one of its editorial writers. It read in part as follows:

> The Product Liability Coordinating Committee . . . cites several "legal abuses," including these two, which were repeated in a July 16 essay I wrote:
>
> A man fell from a ladder atop a wobbly scaffold, "sued and won twice," from the ladder's manufacturer and a retailer.
>
> A brewery was sued because the plaintiff said its beer did not improve his love life, as its advertising implied. "The man was awarded $10,000," according to the PLCC.
>
> In fact, in the ladder case, the plaintiff dropped his suit; in the brewery case, the suit was dismissed with no award.
>
> . . . I regret having used the anecdotes. I regret trusting the veracity of PLCC, assuming that a lobbying group for the U.S. Chamber of Commerce and the National Association of Manufacturers . . . would not weaken its position by submitting the anecdotes as fact.

There can be little doubt, in light of the pattern, that the misrepresentations are knowing and deliberate—at least by those who are furnishing the horror stories, if not by the politicians, journalists, and stand-up comedians who are repeating them. This suggests that those who charge the tort system is in disrepair are themselves having difficulty finding genuine examples of a malfunctioning system. And that is significant.

Lawyers file something in the neighborhood of 1 million tort cases annually in state and federal courts throughout the country. About 95 percent of all cases are resolved before trial. Because the courts cannot be fairly blamed for the results in cases that the parties themselves have settled (even though, according to the *Des Moines Register* article, that is exactly what the PLCC is doing), and because the facts of such cases are not spread across a public record, settled cases are not a good place to look for horror stories. About 75 percent of all tort cases are automobile or premises liability cases, and most of these may be too mundane to provide colorful material for horror stories. But that still leaves about 12,500 other kinds of tort cases tried to conclusion each year. Moreover, about three thousand of these are products liability and medical malpractice cases, many of them defended by manufacturers and insurance companies who would be only too glad to report genuine horror stories to ATRA and PLCC. No system is perfect, and any system that processes thousands of complex matters makes many mistakes. But if the courts were routinely making ridiculous decisions, tort reformers should have little difficulty finding genuine horror stories. The conclusion that emerges from the horror-story campaign is exactly the reverse of the intended message.

The horror stories are designed to diminish the courts in the eyes of the public and, perhaps even more important, in the eyes of legislators. Tort reformers find it necessary to weaken confidence in the courts for two reasons. First, tort reformers are trying to persuade legislatures to intrude into common law areas that have traditionally been the province of the courts. Nearly everyone who has been to law school—and that includes up to a third of all state legislators and more than half of all members of Congress—has a special reverence for the common law.[9]

Second, in asking Congress to enact tort reform legislation, tort reformers are requesting federal intervention into an area that has traditionally belonged to state government. This places Republicans particularly in a difficult position. Big business is the bedrock of the Republican Party—so much so that during the nadir in the party's popularity after the Clinton impeachment effort, Governor John G. Rowland of Connecticut told a Republican caucus, "[T]he good news is that the rich people and business people still like us"[10]—and Republicans are therefore the natural allies of the tort reform movement. Since Reagan, however, the Republican Party has advocated a devolution of power back to the states. To avoid a charge of hypocrisy, Republicans need a compelling reason to violate their principle of bringing government "closer to the people." By portraying the courts as incompetent, the tort reformers offer legislators justification for taking matters in their own hands.

On another level, however, tort reform's assault on the courts fits well with a separate strategy of the Republican Party's right wing. Since the Warren Court era, Republicans have found it politically expedient to attack both Democrats and the courts as "soft on crime."[11] But Republicans lost this issue in the 1990s. Not only have Democrats generally supported what are perceived to be tough, punishment-oriented anti-crime measures, but Democrats have also advocated preventive measures such as gun control and federal funds for neighborhood police officers, which Republicans wound up opposing.

The political tables turned. By the late 1990s, more Americans had greater faith in Democrats than in Republicans when it came to crime policy, and Republicans have been scratching for a way to reclaim the issue. No longer able credibly to scapegoat the federal judiciary as a whole for being soft on crime—two-thirds of the justices of the United States Supreme Court and about 60 percent all currently sitting federal judges were appointed by Republican presidents—Republicans tried attacking individual judges.[12] In 1997, a group of right-wing Republicans, led by House Republican Whip Tom DeLay of Texas, announced a campaign to try to impeach three federal district judges for making allegedly soft-on-crime decisions in particular cases. Later in the year, three Republican senators tried to rack up political mileage by introducing legislation to overrule a decision in a particular criminal case by another federal district judge (who happened to have been appointed to the bench by President Bush).[13] And Republican presidential nominee Robert Dole joined in denouncing one of the judges.

These attacks sent tremors through the federal judiciary. "The bar must support the judiciary . . . when it is under attack," remarked Justice Anthony M. Kennedy, and the American Bar Association started a project to do just that.[14] The two sets of attacks on the courts—those by tort reformers and those by the soft-on-crime accusers—are mutually reinforcing. Both portray judges as witless enemies of public order and stability. The more the public hears this message, the more it is likely to perceive the courts not as temples of justice but as strange and dangerous places.

Of the two sets of attacks, that by tort reformers is the more pernicious. The soft-on-crime attacks tend to come in short, loud bursts, whereas the tort reform attacks are a steady and corrosive drip, year after year. The soft-on-crime attacks are generally made directly by politicians with obvious political motives. Politicians make tort reform speeches too, but tort reform horror stories are more likely to reach the public through news articles, editorials, or, most effective of all, in David Letterman and Jay Leno monologues.

The courts are not sacred. As one of the three branches of government, the judiciary is a proper subject of public scrutiny and criticism. The public has every right to know when and why courts make mistakes, regardless of how embarrassing or atypical those mistakes may be. And as Justice Brandeis famously observed, "Sunlight is the best of disinfectants."[15] The courts, however, should be criticized honestly for what they actually do. A program that makes courts a laughingstock for deeds they have not done is an effort in judicial slander.

Public confidence in government has seriously eroded over the past thirty-five years. In 1964, three-quarters of the American public had a great deal of confidence in the federal government and thought the government could be trusted to do the right thing.[16] When asked today how much of the time they trust the federal government to do what is right, three-quarters of the public say "only some of the time" or "none of the time," while only a quarter say "most of the time" or "just about always." Theories vie to explain the change. Some observers blame the Vietnam War and Watergate, during which public confidence in government took its biggest tumble; others suggest the slow growth (only 0.1 percent per annum) of real hourly wages from 1979 to 1995 may be responsible.

Thomas E. Patterson has demonstrated that since 1960 there has been an increase in negative news coverage of presidential candidates, fueled by increasing media focus on campaign strategy rather than policy and by attack journalism replacing investigative journalism. Patterson also shows that peaks in negative news coverage correlate almost exactly with the public's dissatisfaction with candidates.[17] Some believe that negative campaigning fuels public cynicism. They suggest that if, instead of running advertising campaigns promoting themselves, McDonald's, Burger King, and Wendy's devoted their advertising to trashing each other, they would have succeeded in persuading the public to avoid all fast-food hamburger restaurants. In the same way, they argue, negative advertising by candidates at all levels of government has succeeded in persuading the public that politicians, as a group, cannot be trusted.

But whatever the reasons may be, the unhappy fact is that the public today holds all branches of government in low regard. No more than 20 percent of the public has "a great deal of confidence" in the White House or the executive branch, and no more than 12 percent has such confidence in Congress. These are not post-Lewinsky Clinton impeachment figures; the numbers have remained at these levels throughout the 1990s. While the Supreme Court enjoys the highest level of respect among the three branches of government, the percentage of Americans expressing a great deal of confidence in the Court seldom exceeds 32 percent.[18] That is dangerously low. The judicial branch is the most vulnerable to public opinion. As Alexander Hamilton put it, the judiciary "has neither force nor will but merely judgment."[19] It is the judiciary that is charged with protecting the nation against the tyranny of the majority. The public need not—and should not—think of the courts as infallible. Yet, since from time to time the courts must stand against popular opinion, it is essential that even when the public passionately dislikes a particular decision, it nevertheless have confidence in the courts' integrity, devotion to the law, and essential wisdom.

As Jack Greenberg observed, prior to 1960 "nearly all advances in racial justice came through the courts."[20] Beginning with important but not widely remembered decisions by the Supreme Court under the leadership of Chief Justice Charles Evans Hughes, the courts led the way when the political branches could not. The Warren Court continued the legacy. When it handed down *Brown v. Board of Education* in 1954, more than one hundred members of Congress signed a document denouncing *Brown* as substituting "naked power for established law"; Senator Strom Thurmond of South Carolina called the Supreme Court "a great menace to this country"; seven states threatened to abolish public education in its entirety rather than integrate their schools; hundreds of thousands of citizens, including at least one governor and three United States senators, joined white supremacist organizations. Crosses burned throughout the South. Riots and bombings broke out. Angered by Supreme Court decisions in this and other areas, the John Birch Society launched an "Impeach Earl Warren" campaign, and pickets attempted to club Earl Warren as he entered a bar association meeting in New York City.

It was not clear at the time whether the effort to defeat federal judicial authority would succeed. In this precarious environment, it became the duty of the fifty-eight judges in the federal district and circuit courts in the South to ensure that schools were, in fact, desegregated with all deliberate speed. We know today how things turned out. The Supreme Court continued to hand down decisions promoting racial justice, and the lower courts enforced those decisions, if not perfectly, then further and with less strife than might have been expected.

Historian Lawrence M. Friedman observes that the civil rights revolution "would be unthinkable without the federal courts."[21] The courts were able to lead the nation through this dangerous terrain because, despite fierce hostility, the judiciary still retained a deep reservoir of respect. We cannot know whether, if that reservoir had been drained prior to *Brown* by a concerted campaign to make judges a national laughingstock, the Supreme Court would have possessed the moral authority to declare segregation to be unconstitutional, or if it had, how matters would have turned out. In theory, it might be possible to attack the state courts without diminishing the United States Supreme Court or vice versa, but a media-targeted campaign of judicial slander cannot be waged without weakening respect for courts at all levels. A nation cannot at the same time honor the rule of law and hold its courts in low regard.

The Tort Reform Agenda

The assault on the common law is being launched by a coalition of big business, which resents and hopes to weaken common law regulation of business activity, and an increasingly influential group of political libertarians, who favor weakening all forms of governmental regulation. The assault began in earnest in 1986, when hundreds of the nation's largest manufacturers, trade associations, and insurance companies joined forces to form ATRA.

ATRA's *raison d'être* is to enact legislation that would make it more difficult for citizens to sue business enterprises. The label "tort reform" is a savvy choice. *Reform* has a progressive connotation; by labeling their campaign a reform effort, ATRA and its supporters help camouflage their regressive agenda.

ATRA's membership has included petrochemical companies such as Dow, Exxon, Mobil, Monsanto, and Union Carbide; pharmaceutical giants American Home Products, Merck, Johnson & Johnson, and Pfizer; the Sporting Arms & Ammunition Manufacturers Association and handgun manufacturer Sturm, Ruger & Company; Philip Morris, the tobacco company that owns Miller Brewing (among a host of other enterprises); the National Pest Control Association; Anheuser-Busch and the Beer Institute. Most of ATRA's members are probably most concerned about products liability, but a significant group—the American Medical Association, the American Hospital Association, the American Osteopathic Association, the for-profit hospital chain Humana, and dozens of physician professional associations, among others—are concerned with medical malpractice litigation.

Because the coalition is comprised of major corporations located in every state, if not in every congressional district, it is no surprise that, despite being condemned from many quarters—the *New York Times,* for example, described one major effort as "an attempt to replace traditional American civil jurisprudence with Britain's class-based system of fixing the courts in favor of businesses and wealthy individuals"[22]— tort reformers have succeeded in winning support from majorities in both houses of Congress. Nevertheless, and perhaps amazingly, tort reform efforts have, so far at least, not succeeded at the federal level.

Since Republicans took control of the House of Representatives in 1994, tort reformers have generally been confident of moving legislation through that chamber.[23] It is the Senate, where sixty votes are required to end a filibuster and bring legislation to the floor for a vote, that has been difficult. During the first effort in 1992, supporters believed they had the sixty votes needed to invoke cloture and pass legislation known as the Products Liability Fairness Act—until Senate Majority Leader George Mitchell took the extraordinary step of suspending voting midstream and persuading two senators to switch sides.[24] Although, more often than not, tort reformers continued to command a simple majority, they again failed to overcome filibusters in 1994, 1995, and 1998. When, in 1996, they succeeded in moving legislation through both houses of Congress, President Clinton vetoed it and challenged Robert Dole to make the bill an issue in the presidential campaign that fall.

In 1998, an effort to enact a more modest measure seemed certain to succeed. The bill had two main provisions. First, it protected wholesalers and retailers from products liability actions, as long as they had not altered the product and the plaintiff had recourse against the manufacturer. Second, it capped punitive damages for small businesses—defined as those with fewer than twenty-five employees or annual revenues of less than $5 million dollars—at either $250,000 or twice the amount of the compensatory damage award, whichever was lower. The bill's appeal lay in protecting small businesses but not large manufacturers. President Clinton said he found the bill acceptable and would sign it, and at least a dozen Democrats were expected to join all fifty-five Senate Republicans to create a comfortable filibuster-proof margin of support.[25]

Then, just as it was coming to the Senate floor, the bill's prospects were blown apart by a sudden political maelstrom. The *New York Times* reported that Republican Senate Majority Leader Trent Lott had handwritten a provision in the margins of the bill specifically to protect Baxter Healthcare Corporation. Baxter, a biomaterial firm with $6.1 billion in annual revenues, was one largest companies in Lott's home state of Mississippi. Moreover, Baxter had products liability problems. Just months earlier an $18 million judgment had been entered against it in a case in which a woman allegedly suffered brain damage as a result of using a Baxter product. Even Republicans were furious; Lott had been urging them not to endanger the bill's prospects by adding amendments. Senator Jay Rockefeller, a Democrat and one of the two main sponsors of the bill, said under the circumstances he would vote against it himself. The White House also withdrew support. Lott insisted that both the White House and Rockefeller had known about his handwritten provision and suggested they were guilty of "duplicity" by feigning shock. *CongressDaily* reported that Rockefeller had told it about the provision a month earlier.[26] The next day the bill failed by fifty-one to forty-seven, nine votes short of the number required to invoke cloture.[27]

In forms filed with the House of Representatives, PLCC reported it had paid lawyers in three large Washington firms a total of $840,000 for lobbying services during a period that roughly coincided with the effort to pass the 1998 bill.[28]

It has been a different story in the state capitals. Since ATRA's formation in 1986, at least forty-five states and the District of Columbia have enacted some portion of its agenda. ATRA and its members have lobbied for a wide range of proposals, depending on what was politically achievable, and in various states have successfully obtained legislation that limits joint liability by multiple defendants, shortens time periods for filing lawsuits, reduces recoveries by compensation available from other sources, exposes parties to sanctions if the court considers their claim or defense to be frivolous, and creates a host of other pro-defendant rules.

Probably ATRA's strongest efforts have targeted punitive damages. Since 1986, at least thirty-one states have enacted tort reform legislation involving punitive damages. Some states made it procedurally more difficult to get punitive damages. In 1997, for example, Montana enacted legislation that requires unanimous jury verdicts in punitive damages cases, rather than majority verdicts as had previously been the case. But the biggest battles have been over arbitrary ceilings on punitive damage awards.

Generally, ATRA has proposed capping punitive damages at twice the amount of economic damages. (In *Vandevender*, for example, where lost wages and medical expenses totaled $123,866, this rule would have capped punitive damages at $247,632. In *Proctor*, the Illinois Supreme Court reduced the punitive award to twice the amount of compensatory, rather than economic, damages. Although the distinction did not matter under Illinois law and the *Proctor* jury was not asked to break it down, the lion's share of Proctor's compensatory award was almost certainly assessed for Proctor's loss of an eye and not for lost wages or other "economic" losses.) Tort reformers have lobbied for, and won, a variety of punitive damage caps. In 1987, for example, the Alabama legislature enacted a package of bills known collectively as the Alabama Tort Reform Act that included a $250,000 cap on punitive damages.[29] Six states have enacted a monetary ceiling on punitive damages; in all but one the ceiling is between $200,000 and $350,000.[30] Another five states have capped punitive damages as a multiple of compensatory damages, often two or three times the compensatory award.

In some states, legislative enactments led to pitched battles in the courts. A number of state courts held certain tort reform measures to be unconstitutional. In 1993, the Alabama Supreme Court held that a statutorily imposed cap on punitive damages violated the provision of the state constitution that provided "the right of trial by jury shall remain inviolate."[31] "Just as a trial court cannot insist that a given jury 'should' award punitive damages, the legislature cannot prohibit juries from awarding an amount commensurate to the wrongdoing shown by the evidence in a particular case," the court reasoned.[32] "In performing this function, the jury is an institution of the body politic," it said. "It acts in particular cases, whereas the legislature makes rules for general classes of situations. Legislation cannot take into account the particular circumstances of a particular wrong."[33] It was not a unique view. Statutory damage caps have been held unconstitutional in at least half a dozen states, including Illinois, Ohio, and Texas.[34]

To ward off courts declaring tort reform legislation unconstitutional, tort reformers have worked to change the composition of the courts. Although the American Bar Association and the American Judicature Society strongly advocate that judges be selected through a merit selection appointment process, forty-one states still elect judges to their highest court.[35] Both ATRA and the United States Chamber of Commerce are working with corporations and state tort reform groups to elect pro-business justices to state supreme courts. In 1998, the chamber targeted elections to state supreme courts in eight states, encouraging its members and allies to contribute to pro-business candidates.[36]

This may prove to be a potent strategy. Judicial campaigns used to be, at least ostensibly, conducted on a thoughtful and dignified level. Candidates would speak to civic and professional groups about jurisprudential philosophy or the administration of justice but would avoid sound-bite-style media campaigning. That has changed. When two seats to the Alabama Supreme Court came up for election in 1996, the candidates collectively spent about $5 million on the race. In Ohio, where the state supreme court held various tort reform measures unconstitutional, candidates in the 2000 election spent unprecedented sums, perhaps as much as $12 million, fighting over a single seat on the state supreme court. The money is disturbing enough. To whom are these candidates beholden? But the nature of the campaigns themselves is also distressing. Judicial candidates now pledge to support or overturn particular precedents, and they run attack ads on opposing candidates. Alarmed at how bad these have become, during the fall of 2000 the chief justices of fifteen states decided to hold a "summit meeting" to discuss the debasement of judicial elections.

Television ads by the opponent of Republican Harold F. See Jr., who was running for one of the two supreme court seats in Alabama, depicted See as a skunk and "a slick Chicago lawyer" who never passed the Alabama bar exam.[37] The implication was that See was a carpetbagger who had failed the state bar exam. In fact, See practiced in a

Chicago law firm before joining the faculty of the University of Alabama law school, where he taught for twenty years, and had been admitted to practice in Alabama without having to take the bar exam. But the TV commercial was nothing compared to the radio campaign. A group calling itself the Committee for Family Values ran a radio ad stating, "See abandoned his wife and two children, had an office love affair, got divorced, and fled Illinois for Alabama"—allegations taken from papers in a twenty-year-old child custody dispute. The Committee for Family Values was formed just before and dissolved soon after the election, and more than 99 percent of its funds came from a political action committee administered by an official of the Alabama Trial Lawyers Association.

Trial lawyers are hardly an impoverished group, but if judicial elections are decided on the basis of who can raise more money, big business is likely to win. And so it was in Alabama. With large contributions from the Alabama Business Council and the energy, insurance, banking, and forestry industries, Harold See raised $2.59 million, winning both the fund-raising contest and the election. The other pro-business candidate won the election for the other open seat, and business was able to boast that a conservative, Republican, and presumably pro-business majority now controlled the Alabama Supreme Court.[38]

Business got what it paid for. In 1999, in a footnote to an opinion in a case in which the parties had not raised the issue, Justice See wrote, "[W]e question whether [the decision that a cap on punitive damages is unconstitutional] remains good law."[39] Two justices wrote separate opinions disavowing this gratuitous comment, but four justices concurred without reservation—including one Republican member of the court who, when campaigning for a seat on the court in 1994, promised "to end excessive punitive damages that drive business from Alabama."[40] See's invitation to bring the issue back to the court will undoubtedly be accepted, and it appears the court will reverse itself and reinstate the cap.

The tort reform wars have reduced the Alabama Supreme Court to a popular assembly, where members raise money for media campaigns, make promises to interest groups and voters, and, instead of judging, vote in accordance with their campaign promises. The high courts of other states are also becoming casualties of war.

One is reminded of the observation by Alexis de Tocqueville, when he commented on American democracy in 1840: "[Under some state] constitutions the members of the tribunals are elected, and they are even subjected to frequent re-elections. I venture to predict that these innovations will sooner or later be attended with fatal consequences; and that it will be found out in some future period, that the attack which has been made upon the judicial power has affected the democratic republic itself."[41]

The Common Law and America

Most Americans understand how issues of public importance are contested and at least temporarily resolved in constitutional litigation. Court cases such as *Brown v. Board of Education* and *Roe v. Wade* are as well known as any act of Congress. What is not as well understood is the role common law litigation plays in American democracy. Here, too, issues of societal importance are debated and decided.

The common law and constitutional litigation systems are very different. It is often elites with policy agendas—strategists and lawyers at organizations such as the American Civil Liberties Union (ACLU), the National Association for the Advancement of Colored People (NAACP), the National Organization for Women (NOW), Common Cause, the National Rifle Association (NRA), the National Right to Work Legal Defense Foundation, the National Right to Life Committee—who select what constitutional issues will be litigated. The litigation is often financed by members of and contributors to these advocacy organizations. Constitutional cases are generally decided by judges sitting without juries and may ultimately be resolved by just five individuals—a majority of the United States Supreme Court—whose decisions may endure for decades or longer.

Judges have much to say about how common law cases are resolved, but contrary to constitutional litigation, they do not act alone. Citizens in the jury box play an equally important role. Few common law cases become household names, for juries do not make sweeping pronouncements. A jury decides only the individual case before it, and juries in similar cases may reach different conclusions. Yet consensuses emerge and exert powerful influences. It was, for example, common law litigation that drove asbestos from the market, something that—given the wealth and power of the asbestos industry—neither Congress nor regulatory agencies were able to do, even in the face of medical knowledge that asbestos was causing eight thousand to ten thousand cancer deaths every year.[42]

The American system is unique. No other society has, or ever had, anything quite like it. Many people think of the common law as an English legacy—an Anglo-Saxon system with Roman and Norman roots that was more or less handed to America by William Blackstone. We think of the common law world as a unity. The English and American systems are very different, however. American common law is both more democratic and more dynamic than its British counterpart. The people play a larger role in American than in British common law, and the common law plays a larger role in the American than in the British system of governance.

The American system did not evolve by happenstance. It was molded by distinctively American ideas and by deliberate choices of American founders. One cannot fully appreciate why or even how the system functions without understanding something of the past. The next two chapters therefore deal with history.

3

The Third Branch of Government

Beginnings

When, in the early seventeenth century, small bands of Europeans set out on dangerous voyages across the Atlantic to establish tiny settlements on the shores of North America, they could not know that the forces propelling them across the ocean would combine with the circumstances awaiting them in such a way as to produce concepts of law and government radically different from any the world had ever known. A new idea was to be born: the separation of religious and secular spheres of authority. This concept of differentiated spheres of authority would lead to a parallel idea of dividing powers within the government itself, that is, to the principle of separation of powers among governmental departments. And this idea, in turn, would give rise to an independent judiciary existing as a coequal branch of government, with profound implications for both law and governance.

For our purposes, it may be best to begin with the observation that many of the early settlers were dissidents fleeing compulsion to conform to orthodoxy. The Puritans who settled the Massachusetts Bay Colony wanted to worship as they pleased. They had not, however, generalized the idea of freedom in religion or speech. Within five years of establishing the Massachusetts Bay Colony, the Puritans decided they could no longer tolerate Roger Williams, the pastor of the congregation in Salem, Massachusetts, who refused to conform to the Puritans' own orthodoxy.[1] Williams had come to the New World to bring Christianity to the Indians and was displeased that the Puritans were more intent on taking Indian land than on giving Indians religion. Worse, Williams preached religious heresy. He believed that God made His covenant not with congregations, through ordained ministers, but directly, with each individual. This was dangerous. It meant a layperson's claim to know truth was as authoritative as that of church officials.

A friend tipped off Williams that he was about to be arrested and deported back to England. With his family, Williams slipped away, made his way through the wilderness, and founded what is now Rhode Island.[2] Williams, however, grasped the concept of freedom for all, and Rhode Island opened its doors to Antinomians, Quakers, Jews, and Catholics. What made Williams's tolerance of these groups so remarkable was that he no more accepted their views than the Puritans in Massachusetts had accepted his. Historian William G. McLoughlin writes:

> Williams remained throughout his life an orthodox Calvinist in theology and at the age of seventy-two rowed eighteen miles down the Narragansett Bay in his boat to debate the obnoxious views of a new sect called the Society of Friends (or Quakers) who entered Rhode Island as a refuge from Puritan intolerance. Of course Williams did not say that Quaker opinions were so dangerous to civil order as to justify civil persecution. He merely thought them theologically wrong-headed and tried to argue them out of their errors. Punishment for what he called their "ignorance and boisterousness" he left to God.[3]

Moreover, Williams did not merely tolerate these sects as neighbors; he accepted them as citizens. While no one was to be "molested for his conscience," everyone was subject to "orders or agreements made for the public good of the body in an orderly way by the major consent," but "only in civil things."[4] Williams believed a commonwealth was like a ship at sea, and the community's well-being depended on its members meeting their obligations to the group. Everyone was required to pay taxes, but Quakers were not forced to violate their faith by bearing arms.[5]

It is impossible to overstate how important it was to the development of American government and law that the colonies were established by dissidents attempting to escape pressures to conform to religious, political, and social orthodoxy. This gave them an ambivalence toward authority, including majoritarian authority. On the one hand, many colonists were members of sects that had been disdained or mistreated by the dominant culture and its government and therefore had reason to find ways to limit government's role. But at the same time survival in an often hostile, new world required colonists to create an effective social order. Weak government was not an option. They needed effective governments that worked the majority's will while respecting—indeed, even protecting—minority rights.

The tradition from which Roger Williams came knew no clear boundaries between civil and religious spheres, or between civil and religious authority. The court system in England included the Ecclesiastical Courts, which had jurisdiction over matters involving marriage and sex, including criminal jurisdiction over fornication, adultery, and sodomy. Until the reign of Henry VIII in the middle of the sixteenth century, these courts were under the control of the Catholic Church; later, even though controlled by the Crown, judges were appointed by bishops of the Church of England. It is futile to argue about whether they followed civil or religious law; any division between the two was blurred. Roger Williams's clear wall of separation between the two spheres was radical and profound.

Williams was a theologian, not a political scientist. His argument was based more on what was good for religion—and for promoting freedom of conscience, which Williams considered important to spiritual development—than on good government. That is exactly why it was so powerful in its day. For, as his audience understood it, a government that was not good for religion could not be a good government.

Williams's argument was strong enough to persuade the devout about the religious benefits of a secular judicial system. "It is," Williams wrote, "indeed the ignorance and blind zeal of the second beast, the false prophet . . . to persuade the civil powers of the earth to prosecute the saints, that is, to bring fiery judgments upon men in a judicial way, and to pronounce that such judgments of imprisonment, banishment, death, proceed from God's righteous vengeance upon such heretics." It was "vain, improper, and unsuitable" to use weapons employed throughout the ages by persecutors against saints. "[C]ivil weapons are improper in this business," he declared. Moreover, they were unnecessary since the spiritual weapons of the church were "able and mighty, sufficient and ready for Lord's work, either to save the soul, or to kill the soul."

Williams went an important step further. Not only should civil authority not be invoked to punish people for religious disobedience, but civil authority could not permit others to do so through use of violence. Because the civil magistrate "is bound to preserve the civil peace and quiet of the place and people under him, he is bound to suffer no man to break the civil peace, by laying hands of violence upon any," even if such violence were done in the name of religion and brought against one "as vile as the Samaritans, for not receiving of the Lord Jesus Christ."[6] It was this step that gave full force to the idea of separate jurisdictions. Inherent in Williams's argument was the idea not only of a

neutral civil authority that would interpret and enforce the law to promote public, without regard to religious policy but that it would be
supreme within its jurisdiction.

Although Roger Williams never achieved great fame in the colonies
beyond Rhode Island, he became a celebrated figure in intellectual circles in England, where, as Daniel Boorstin puts it, he was regarded
as something of "a by-word of heterodoxy and rebellion."[7] His idea
of separation of church and state was reimported through European
political thinkers, particularly Locke and Montesquieu, back to the
colonies, where it eventually became a bedrock principle of the American political structure. Moreover, it seems impossible that this idea of
separate spheres of authority was not a major inspiration for another
fundamental feature of American government, namely, separation of
powers.[8]

Separation of Powers and the American Judiciary

The division of powers among three branches of government is perhaps
the most fundamental feature of American government. It is also the
feature most distinctly American.

There was no separation of powers in the early colonies, at least not
by contemporary standards. At the time the Massachusetts Bay Colony
banished Roger Williams, Massachusetts already had a three-level court
system, but it was not the kind of independent judiciary we are accustomed to today.[9] The county courts at the base of the system were not
only courts of general jurisdiction, hearing criminal cases and private
lawsuits, but "general instruments of government," mapping out where
highways were to run, determining how bridge repairs and the ministry
were to be financed, administering probate, and performing other roles
that today would be classified as administrative functions.[10] One level up
was a court of assistants with original jurisdiction to hear certain cases,
including divorce actions and criminal matters that could result in capital punishment, amputation of limbs, and banishment. Members of the
court included magistrates and the governor and deputy governor of the
colony. The Massachusetts General Court, at the pinnacle of the system,
was both the final court of appeals and the legislature of the colony. Indeed, until the end of the eighteenth century, the American state assemblies continued not only to enact public legislation but to decide private

matters as well, with little recognition of a distinction between the two functions.[11] "As in England," writes legal historian Lawrence M. Friedman, "separation of powers was notably absent."[12]

While England has never fully adopted the concept in its own government, two seismic events in England helped give birth to the idea of dividing power among separate governmental departments. The first was civil war, which in 1649 resulted in the trial and execution of Charles I and the abolition of both the monarchy and the House of Lords. Eleven years of rule by the House of Commons alone was enough to convince England that consolidating all power in one set of hands, even a body of the people's elected representatives, was a recipe for disaster; and both the monarch and the House of Lords were resurrected.[13] The second was Glorious Revolution of 1689. James II failed to recognize parliamentary prerogatives, and in a bloodless revolution, Parliament replaced him with a new monarch, William of Orange. As a condition of being granted the crown, William recognized the principle that Parliament was the sole source of law.[14]

These two events produced some notion of separate spheres of governmental authority. This was, however, muddled by theory, which insisted that there were not separate governmental departments but three estates—the monarch, the aristocracy, and the people—within one governmental department, namely, Parliament.[15] Only the monarch could convene or dissolve Parliament; only Parliament could make law; and the bicameral nature of Parliament meant that no law could be enacted without the consent of both the aristocracy in the House of Lords and the elected representatives of the people in the House of Commons. Thus, in 1765, Blackstone wrote that Parliament was "coequal with the kingdom itself" and that its power was "transcendent and absolute."[16] Or, as another commentator put it, since England's civil war "the only ultimate source of law is the King in Parliament."[17] Nevertheless, after the Glorious Revolution there was a practical division between executive authority residing in the king and legislative authority residing in Parliament, and John Locke and other liberal political theorists began talking about separation of powers.

In the main, however, the notion was limited to dividing power into two branches of government. Administration of the courts was considered part of the executive function and the province of the king. One of the triggers of the Glorious Revolution was James II packing the Court of the King's Bench with judges who would do his bidding, with that court then holding that the "the laws of England are the king's laws" and thus that the king could dispense with parliamentary laws as he saw fit.[18] After the Glorious Revolution, Parliament enacted a statute providing that judges' commissions entitled them to serve *quamdiu se bene gesserint* (as long as they conducted themselves properly). The king could remove judges only for serious misconduct. Parliament, however, reserved the right to remove judges for whatever reasons it deemed sufficient.[19]

It is Montesquieu who is generally credited with devising the concept of separation of powers ultimately adopted by the United States.[20] In his *The Spirit of Laws*, published in 1748, Montesquieu argued that three sorts of power exist in every state: legislative power, executive power, and "the power of judging," by which a magistrate "punishes crimes or judges disputes between individuals."[21] He continued:

> Nor is there liberty if the power of judging is not separate from legislative power and from executive power. If it were joined to legislative power, the power over life and liberty of the citizens would be arbitrary, for the judge would be the legislator. If it were joined to executive power, the judge could have the force of an oppressor.[22]

This struck a chord among the American colonists. The principle that judges would serve during their good behavior and could not be removed by a king displeased with their rulings was now considered sacred in England. In 1761, King George III described it as "one of the best securities of the rights and liberties of his subjects."[23] Yet that very same year the king issued an order providing that colonial judges were to serve at "the pleasure of the Crown" and thereafter made judges dependent on the Crown for their salaries—an act that infuriated the Americans and was later listed in the Declaration of Independence as one of the grievances justifying separation from England.

In their original constitutions, adopted at the onset of the Revolutionary War, four states followed Montesquieu's prescription and established governments with expressly separate legislative, executive, and judicial departments.[24] The Articles of Confederation, adopted in 1777, did not create a judicial department. It can be argued that there was no reason for the drafters to even contemplate doing so, since the Articles created not so much a government as a confederation among thirteen sovereign state governments. Nevertheless, the Articles contained provisions for adjudicating certain disputes (disputes between states and questions about the structure of the confederation itself), and it entrusted this authority to Congress.

Drafters of the Articles were most afraid of executive tyranny. They considered King George III to be the villain. But why had the Americans demonized the king and not Parliament? The revolutionaries argued that much as he corrupted colonial judges by making them dependent on him for the amount and payment of their salaries, the king corrupted Parliament through patronage and other nefarious techniques.[25] Parliament might be supreme in theory, but the monarchy had reestablished practical control over the kingdom by employing and finding other techniques to manipulate members of Parliament.

There is irony here. To move his programs through an often resistant Parliament, King George III employed a member of the House of Lords, Lord North, as his "prime minister." North was one of England's first prime ministers, and the original vision of the job may be thought of in modern terms as the king's lobbyist. English Whigs and the Americans found this to be part of the corruption of Parliament. History has shown they were right in being concerned that the king's employment of a member of Parliament might undermine the balance of power; but they were right for the wrong reason. Beginning with the appointment of William Pitt the Younger—who accepted the post of prime minister in 1783 on the condition that he, rather than the king, select the other ministers—power flowed not from Parliament to king but from king to Parliament. From the Glorious Revolution to the appointment of William Pitt, the idea of separation of powers flickered in England, then sputtered out.[26]

Although it was impossible for Americans to foresee the future, they may have misread the present because they wanted to demonize King George rather than the English people or their elected representatives (or even the British aristocracy, whom many American leaders emulated). But regardless of whether the revolutionaries were persuaded by their own rhetoric or by reality, at least prior to the Revolution Americans feared monarchical power above all else.

The experience under the Articles of Confederation changed that view. The state legislatures were exercising unchecked power, and the results were terrifying. There was little regard for the rule of law. Assemblies enacted *ex post facto* legislation when it pleased the electorate. Many small farmers, merchants, and tradespeople, whose incomes and enterprises had suffered when they went off to war, had amassed large debts. State legislatures issued paper money and enacted legislation permitting debts to be paid off in devalued currency. This form of debtor relief was popular but perilous for a new nation with a fragile financial system. As Thornton Anderson put it, "The threat to republican government thus shifted from the man on horseback to legislative tyranny."[27]

When, in the summer of 1787, delegates convened at the Constitutional Convention in Philadelphia under the guise of revising the Articles of Confederation, there was general agreement that they needed to go beyond their mandate and create a new government. Moreover, from the beginning of their deliberations there was consensus that governmental power should be separated and balanced among the three branches of government recommended by Montesquieu.[28] So many subjects were passionately debated that it is, in one sense, surprising that this fundamental and radical premise should have been taken almost for granted. But what alternative did the founders have? They feared placing too much power in the hands of either an executive or a popularly elected assembly, and they believed the English system showed that dividing power between executive and legislative departments did not work either.[29] Thus, they created a judiciary that was to be a coequal branch of government.

In creating this independent new department of government, the founders borrowed some features of the English judicial system and added innovations. One of the most important features borrowed from the mother country was life tenure of federal judges (i.e., that judges "shall hold their Offices during good Behavior") and that Congress be precluded from diminishing a judge's salary as long as he or she continued to serve. A "power over a man's subsistence amounts to a power over his will," explained Alexander Hamilton in *The Federalist* No. 79. James Madison and Hamilton would lament that in this matter, so critical to the independence of the judiciary, the states in the main failed to follow the federal example.

The founders not only made the judiciary an independent branch of government; they consciously laid the foundation for federal courts to assume the power of judicial review—that is, to declare invalid laws enacted by Congress or state legislatures when, in the courts' judgment, these violated the Constitution.[30] This was an American innovation; it had no English precedent. Some of the founders entered the unchartered waters reluctantly. John Dickinson of Delaware said he believed "no such power ought to exist" but at the same time was convinced it was necessary to curtail misuse of legislative power and was "at a loss what expedient to substitute."[31] While, particularly during the ratification struggle, some anti-Federalists expressed concern over judicial review, their focus was not so much on whether courts should have the power to declare statutes unconstitutional as on whether making the United States Supreme Court the final authority on whether state (as well as federal) law violated the United States Constitution would unduly weaken the states vis-à-vis the federal government.[32]

The idea of judicial review did not spring full blown into Madison's mind. It had been broached but rejected in England. Moreover, some state courts had already begun to insist they had the prerogative to declare acts of their legislatures unconstitutional, but with mixed results—the legislatures in New York and Rhode Island, at least, were resisting.[33] Here again, the framers hoped that the federal example would be followed in the states; and in this instance their hopes were realized.

Some of the framers wanted the courts to have even greater authority. James Wilson of Pennsylvania told the Constitutional Convention that the power to declare laws unconstitutional did not go far enough. "Laws may be unjust, may be unwise, may be dangerous, may be destructive; and yet not be so unconstitutional as to justify the Judges in refusing to give them effect," he argued. Wilson proposed that a revisionary council consisting of federal judges and representatives of the executive branch be empowered to invalidate acts of Congress on policy grounds. Madison declared the motion "of great importance" and seconded it. "Experience in all the States has evinced a powerful tendency in the Legislature to absorb all power into its vortex. This was the real source of danger to the American Constitution," he said. Antifederalist George Mason of Virginia agreed. Nathaniel Gorham of Massachusetts questioned whether judges possessed particular knowledge of policy matters. Others worried the council would breach the principle of separation of powers and that judges would be reluctant to find laws unconstitutional after having previously approved them. To modern ears, a revisionary council has a discordant ring; yet it was defeated by the slimmest of margins—four states to three, with two states divided.[34]

The founders themselves realized they could not fully envision how such a judiciary would develop. Only one thing was certain: a constitutionally created, independent branch of government would be different from a court system operated as a governmental service, providing citizens with adjudicatory services in much the same way as a government post office provides mail service. Though the courts in England achieved important aspects of independence in 1700, when Parliament provided that henceforth judges were to have life tenure and irreducible salaries, the English system grew largely out of a tradition of government- (and church-) furnished adjudicatory services. As Shannon C. Stimson has noted, English courts "were 'independent' only in the sense that they were a source of rules—'judge-made law'—for the settlement of private disputes."[35] (And that remains the case today. As one commentator has put it, even in modern England the concept of an independent judiciary "remains primarily a term of constitutional rhetoric."[36]) Thus, a powerful difference developed between the two systems, not only in structure and jurisdiction but—even more important—in attitude and psychology.

Separation of powers and judicial review would profoundly affect how the courts handled disputes among the three branches of federal government or between the federal and state governments. It would also obviously influence the adjudication of disputes between the government and private citizens. Although less obvious, these features of the American system would also affect how courts decided disputes between private citizens—contract, tort, and property actions that comprise the common law and lie at the heart of the legal system.

By elevating the judiciary to a coequal branch of government, the founders created a system that would become more self-confident, robust, and dynamic than its colonial or English counterparts. The psychological difference between a judicial system operated by government and one that is a coequal branch of government is profound. As it gained plenary power in England, Parliament became the instrument ultimately responsible for the national welfare. Constrained only by its own view of the constitutional limits on its authority, Parliament made law that it deemed in the national interest. The duty of the courts was to help effectuate Parliament's public policy objectives. With respect to adjudicating disputes between private parties, the duty of the courts was to provide fairness and predictability.

A different attitude develops when a judicial system is a coequal department of government. American judges see themselves not as civil servants but as government officials. Their role is not limited to effectuating policies developed by others; they are participants in the governmental process. Although they recite the mantra that "the legislature makes the law and courts enforce it," American judges know their role is more complex and greater than a high school civics lesson suggests. The attitude is visible in many ways, large and small. American judges have, for example, been known to summon high-ranking government officials into their courtrooms to explain what the judge considers to be incoherent government policy or action—an event unthinkable in England.[37] It is not that American judges actually possess such authority; in most instances they do not. The point is that, right or wrong, they presume to take such action.

Such judges approach the common law with a different sense of confidence and responsibility. They see their duty as not only to provide parties with fairness and predictability but to fashion a body of law serving other public policy objectives as well. That is why, as the next sections demonstrate, American tort law developed not merely into a compensatory system, designed to provide justice to the injured, but, more important, into a regulatory system designed to protect public health and safety.

The Common Law Tradition

The term *common law* is often used to refer broadly to the English legal tradition, as opposed to the *civil law* tradition that was developed on the European continent. In the English system, the fabric of the law was woven largely by courts. There was no written constitution (although a variety of writings, including the Magna Carta and the Declaration of Rights of 1689, were considered part and parcel of an unwritten constitution). While Parliament enacted statutes, it did so on an ad hoc basis, addressing individual matters as deemed necessary. Statutory law was, however, relatively thin compared to the far fuller and richer body of law produced by courts.

Common law courts decided cases based on custom and precedent. Judges were respectful not only of the lawful authority of past rulings but also of what they believed must have been their essential wisdom. Nevertheless, the law was considered a dynamic, evolving system. Courts modified legal rules that appeared not to be working and adapted rules to new factual situations or changing societal circumstances. Change was cautious and incremental. Change came only as demanded by the cases before the court, and the court seldom moved farther than necessary for the cases then before it. Moreover, each modification was, in a sense, an experiment. Courts knew they would see the results of their handiwork in future cases and would be prepared to modify their work again if necessary. As Oliver Wendell Holmes famously put it: "The life of the law has not been logic: it has been experience. . . . The law embodies the story of a nation's development through many centuries, and it cannot be dealt with as if it contained only the axioms and corollaries of a book of mathematics."[38]

By contrast, the civil law tradition was closer to Holmes's book of mathematics. The pillar of the civil law tradition is codification. Some codes have tried to be detailed and comprehensive compendiums, providing answers to every foreseeable legal question. Others are intended as broader and more flexible collections of principles. But in either case, the underlying theory has been to have a commission of experts, who understand the science of law best, produce a written code that judges are to follow, not modify. Although the origins of the civil law tradition are thought to come from ancient Roman law, the first modern civil law codes were produced in Prussia in 1794, in France in 1804, and in Germany in 1896—all after the founding of the American Republic. Alexis de Tocqueville captured something of the difference between the common law and civil law systems when he wrote: "The English and American lawyers investigate what has been done; the French advocate inquires what should have been done: the former produce precedents; the latter reasons."[39]

The civil law tradition probably considered itself the more scientific system. It was rooted in a belief that there are objectively correct legal principles that legal experts are best able to divine and state in an orderly fashion, just as (to use Holmes's analogy) there are correct mathematical principles that mathematicians are best able to divine and state. The civil law system values central planning, order, and *a priori* reasoning. Paradoxically, the common law process more closely resembles the scientific method, where principles are constantly subject to experimentation and accepted only as long as they continue to work.

Dean Anthony T. Kronman of Yale Law School has argued that two competing traditions run within American law.[40] One tradition, descended from Aristotle, places its faith in practical wisdom gained from experience. Aristotle believed that human affairs were far too messy to be reduced to mathematical-type axioms, and thus theories and principles could never be sufficient for matters of governance. Kronman calls this school of thought "prudential realism." Competing with this, Kronman argues, is a tradition of scientific realism descended from Thomas Hobbes. Hobbes saw mathematics and political science in much the same light; each could be reduced to an ordered set of axioms through the use of logic. In an essay titled *A Dialogue between a Philosopher and a Student of the Common Laws of England*, published in 1681, Hobbes argued that principles of justice could be discovered through pure reason. "Reason is the Soul of the Law," wrote Hobbes. "*Nihil quod est Retioni contrarium est licitum*; that is to say, nothing is Law that is against Reason: and that Reason is the life of the Law, nay the Common Law itself is nothing but Reason."[41]

Kronman argues that disciples of scientific realism include Christopher Columbus Langdell, who founded Harvard Law School in 1817, and Richard A. Posner, the founder of the modern law-and-economics movement. Kronman maintains that while Langdell and Posner both claim to be its friend, they are, in fact, apostates to the common law. Kronman's argument, however, is stronger with respect to Posner than to Langdell.

Langdell sought to make the study of law something of a scientific enterprise. He believed that just as botanists attempt to discover the natural order of plant life by studying individual specimens, classifying individuals into species, and organizing species into genuses and subgenuses, legal scholars should attempt to discover the underlying order of the law by studying and categorizing case decisions.

In fact, Langdell's taxonomic approach to the law was not new. As the historian Gordon Wood notes, Blackstone's *Commentaries* was hugely popular in eighteenth-century America "not so much from its particular exposition of English law . . . but from its great effort to extract general principles from the English common law and make of it, as James Iredell [a North Carolina Supreme Court justice and champion for ratification of the Constitution], said, 'a science.'"[42]

Kronman recognizes that Hobbes and Langdell differed in an important way. Hobbes wanted to bring order to the law by replacing the jumble of the common law with comprehensive legislation. By contrast, Langdell was seeking not to impose order on the law but to discover order that he believed already existed. Yet, Kronman argues, though they took different routes, Hobbes and Langdell reached the same place. Both sought to make the law into an organized structure of objectively true principles, and thus both were scientific realists and enemies of the common law tradition.

Although there is something to what Kronman says, his argument about Langdell ultimately misses the mark. The common law tradition is not essentially nihilistic. It does not require a belief that the law lacks all form or structure, that it is merely a random jumble of ad hoc rules. It is not inconsistent with the common law tradition to believe that deep within the law are normative principles or experiential lessons that have exerted common influences on the development of seemingly unrelated rules, and that therefore there is structure below the surface.

At the same time, common law lawyers are taught to be skeptical about attempts to place cases into too tidy an order. One of the hallmarks of American legal education is to have students read judicial opinions and to require that the students themselves discern the legal principles and doctrinal architecture that arise from those opinions. The instructor's job is not to provide *ex cathedra* answers but to challenge whatever answer the student claims to have found. By contrast, legal education in civil law systems typically starts not with raw judicial decisions but with lectures about the principles and the architecture of the law.[43] But that common law lawyers are taught to be skeptical about universal truths and overarching principles proclaimed by others does not mean the law is wholly lacking in form and structure.

Nor, as Kronman seems to believe, is the common law anti scientific. Scientists employ reason to develop hypotheses and mathematicians use reason to develop axioms, but in each case the proposition is tested through experimentation. Common law courts approach rules in much the same way. Rules may have originally been devised because they seem to make sense, but they are subject to continuous real-world testing—that is, courts are continually observing the consequences of rules previously propounded—and are modified or rejected when they fail to work. Common law judges are acutely aware of the law of unintended consequences.

Where Kronman goes off the track is in his suggestion that the common law relies on experience but science does not. In fact, both science and the common law place their greatest faith in empirical knowledge. The acid test in both systems is how well the rule works. A rule—no matter how elegant or logical, no matter how well it fits within grand theory—will be rejected or modified when it fails to work. In both science and the common law, *a posteriori* reasoning trumps *a priori* reasoning.

The operative word, however, is *trumps*. Neither science nor the common law rejects reason and logic. Both employ reason as an important tool. In fact, American legal education can be seen as having some rough similarities to the scientific method. Students begin by studying raw data (i.e., judicial decisions) and work from there toward general truths and structure, remaining skeptical of whatever answers they find.

The relevant distinction with respect to the common law is, therefore, not between scientific realism and prudential realism; it is between pragmatism and rationalism. There are always those in the common law tradition who succumb to rationalism, believing that the law can be divined by reason alone. In 1842, for example, in a famous case known as *Swift v. Tyson*, the United States Supreme Court was faced with the question of whether a federal court should resolve a commercial dispute by applying New York case law or principles of the general common law. The applications led to different results. The Court held that general common law should apply. The essence of its reasoning was that the common law existed in an objective, permanent way, which the courts were striving to discover through the exercise of reason. Court decisions "are, at most, only evidence of what the laws are; and are not of themselves laws," Justice Joseph Story wrote for the Court. He continued: "The law respecting negotiable instruments may be truly declared in the language of Cicero, adopted by Lord Mansfield [an eighteenth-century English judge] to be in a great measure, not the law of a single country only, but of the commercial world. Non erit alia lex Romae, alia Athenis, alia nune, alia posthac, sed et apud omnes gentes, et omni tempore, una eademque lex obtenebit."[44]

But this philosophy has seldom been more than a backwater in the common law tradition. James Madison (who, incidentally, appointed Justice Story to the Supreme Court) certainly did not believe that judges in every jurisdiction were all searching for the very same, purely rational common law. When, in 1799, Madison was confronted with the suggestion that the same common law existed in England and all of the United States, his reaction was one of "astonishment and apprehension." Madison wrote:

> In the state, prior to the Revolution, it is certain that the common law, under different limitations, made a part of the colonial codes. But whether it be understood that the original colonists brought the law with them, or made it their law by adoption; it is equally certain, that it was the separate law of each colony within its respective limits, and was un-

known to them, as a law pervading and operating through the whole, as one society.

It could not possibly be otherwise. The common law was not the same in any two of the colonies; in some, the modifications were materially and extensively different. There was no common legislature, by which a common will could be expressed in the form of a law; not any common magistracy, by which such a law could be carried into practice. The will of each colony, alone and separately, had its organs for these purposes.[45]

Story's view of a universal common law dictated by pure reason may have enjoyed temporary popularity within certain circles. It was increasingly rejected by legal commentators, however, and by 1893 had fallen under sharp attack in other Supreme Court opinions.[46] Justice Oliver Wendell Holmes, in particular, lambasted the notion of a "transcendental body of law" as nothing but "fallacy and illusion."[47] "The common law so far as it is enforced in a State," Holmes wrote, "whether called common law or not, is not the common law generally but the law of that State existing by the authority of that State without regard to what it may have been in England or anywhere else." Any remaining doubt that the Supreme Court endorsed a natural law conception of the common law was laid to rest in the landmark 1938 case of *Erie Railroad v. Tomkins*.[48] In an opinion by Louis D. Brandeis, the Court reversed *Swift v. Tyson*. There is no federal common law, the Court declared, and when a matter is governed by common law, a federal court must apply the common law of the state in which it sits.

The ideology of the common law is, therefore, not rationalism but pragmatism. The common law judge is a pragmatist. He or she is interested in how rules work in the real world. A rule might have been devised because reason suggested it would yield positive results, but if it turns out that the anticipated benefits do not flow, or if they are more than counterbalanced by adverse consequences, the rule will be scrapped.

Pragmatism, said William James, asks the question: "Grant an idea or belief to be true . . . what concrete difference will its being true make in any one's actual life? How will the truth be realized? What experiences will be different from those which would obtain if the belief were false? What, in short, is the truth's cash-value in experiential terms?"[49] The very same may be said of the common law tradition.

Ironically, though Richard A. Posner holds himself out as a pragmatist, Anthony Kronman is on firmer ground when he argues that Posner is, in fact, an enemy of the common law tradition. Posner believes he and his colleagues in the law-and-economics school have found the logic of the law—and the logic of the law is economics. He argues that "the common law is best (not perfectly) explained as a system for maximizing the wealth of society," and legal doctrines are "best understood and explained as efforts to promote the efficient allocation of resources." He maintains that these and other universal principles discovered by the law-and-economics school have "been generalized, empirically tested, and integrated" with the law "to create an economic theory of law with growing explanative power and empirical support."[50]

The common law tradition can make room for those who claim to have found theories and patterns that help explain the law. The tradition can hardly encourage the search but condemn all who claim to have found underlying explanations. Yet it may well be that the common law tradition insists that the explanations be plural. Arguably, one places himself outside the common law tradition when he claims to have found a single, unified theory of the law. At the very least, one who claims to have found a synoptic explanation carries a heavy burden of persuasion.

When Posner states the theories of law-and-economics have been empirically tested, he is making a claim for legitimacy in the very terms the common law demands. So what is the problem? The answer to that question has three strands. The first strand concerns credibility. Posner concedes that law-and-economics "has normative as well as positive aspects," by which he must mean that law-and-economics not only reveals what the underlying goals of the law *are* but also what they *ought* to be. It is not clear, however, when the normative features end and the positive aspects begin. The law-and-economics school may claim that having discovered the underlying objectives of the law, it is using economic analysis to show how best to achieve those existing objectives. The goals that law-and-economics claims merely to have discovered, however, have a distinctly ideological flavor. This weakens law-and-economics' credibility about its objective, "empirically tested" discovery, making it difficult to carry the heavy burden of persuasion the common law places on those claiming to discovered a grand theory.

The second strand concerns consequence. Regardless of whether the claims of law-and-economics are true, there are profound normative consequences to accepting those claims. Once we accept that the principal aim of the law is about maximizing societal wealth and turn our attention to honing legal rules in order to advance that goal more efficiently, then that is what the law will be about. Law-and-economics may argue that since this is already what the law is about, there is no normative consequence at all. The only change is that, because we now understand the law's ultimate objective, we can work consciously to make doctrine more effective in achieving it. But it can just as easily be argued that now that the underlying agenda of the law has been revealed, we should consciously reconsider the merit of that agenda. After all, a theory that explains the law is not the same as a theory that explains why apples fall to the center of the earth. Gravity exists whether humankind likes it or not, while the law is a human construct. The disciples of law-and-economics, however, seem to skip past this stage. They are disturbingly quiescent about accepting—and becoming agents in perpetuating—what they claim is the law's preexisting agenda.

The third strand concerns methodology. Because it is pragmatic, the common law tradition is eclectic. Judges bring all sorts of knowledge to their decision making. They may seek to illuminate issues by using any of the social or natural sciences. What they use depends on the area of law in which they are working and the particular case before them. Most of all, they use the law itself and their own and their colleagues' experiences in observing the law in action. Law-and-economics, however, does not merely seek to offer judges economic insights in the same way, for example, that child psychology might offer a family court judge knowledge that will help inform child custody decisions. It invites judges to resort to law-and-economics theory in all kinds of cases, and in so doing, it seeks to radically alter the way in which courts decide cases.

When the three strands are pulled together, law-and-economics emerges not merely as a field of knowledge but as a system of belief. It has its own values, and like all creeds it seeks to have its values prevail over competing values. Suffice it to say that (1) the tradition of the common law, and especially American common law, is pragmatism; (2) the antithesis of pragmatism is dogmatism; and (3) whatever truths it may or may not have discovered, law-and-economics is dogma. Law-and-economics does not violate the common law tradition by claiming to be objective or scientific. It violates the common law tradition by seeking to have the law conform to a grand theory.

An American Bench and Bar

When he visited America in 1831 and 1832, Alexis de Tocqueville was surprised to find how important the judicial system was in American governance. "Armed with the power of declaring the laws to be unconstitutional, the American magistrate perpetually interferes in political affairs. . . . Scarcely any question arises in the United States which does not become, sooner or later, a subject for judicial debate."[51]

Tocqueville recognized that one of the strong roots beneath the flowering of a distinctly American, and uniquely important, judicial system was the power of judicial review. But it is not the only root. The independence of the judiciary and its status as a coequal department of government were also strong roots. These features bestowed a prestige on the courts that no legal system had previously enjoyed.

Indeed, it might even be said that the founders created a bar and bench in their own image. Lawyers had been especially influential in creating the Republic. Twenty-five of the fifty-two signers of the Declaration of Independence and thirty-one of the fifty-five members of the Constitutional Convention in Philadelphia were lawyers. Many highly regarded—even revered—figures were lawyers, among them Thomas Jefferson, Alexander Hamilton, John Marshall, John Adams, and Daniel Webster. The legal profession began to attract a new breed; public-spirited men who were looking not only for a career by which they could advance in financial and social status but for work that would be socially meaningful.

The popularity of the law soared after the Revolution. In 1780, the large majority of America's college students went to divinity school and became ministers. Only twenty years later, only 9 percent of college graduates went into the ministry, compared to 50 percent who went into the law.[52] It says something about the kind of men and, later, women who have chosen the law as their profession that more than half of all members of Congress and more than 70 percent of all United States presidents, vice presidents, and cabinet secretaries have been lawyers.[53]

There was, at the beginning of the Republic, some question as to whether the American legal profession would become the province of the elite. The South leaned toward the aristocratic English model. Southern aristocrats sent their sons to study at the Inns of Court in London.[54] Perhaps *study* is too strong a word. The Inns of Court had no connection with any university; they were more exclusive residences and eating clubs than anything else.[55] At the end of eighteenth century, the only requirement for pupils at the Inns was to show up for a specified number of dinners. It has been said that the "English bar was becoming the only profession in the western world where the practitioners did not have to undergo any formal training at all."[56] Of course, the diligent could read the law on their own, observe barristers at work, and learn from table talk at dinner. But the main attraction that drew prospective young lawyers across the Atlantic probably had little to do with learning the law. A large number, perhaps 50 percent, of the barristers were members of the English landed gentry, most firstborn sons—that is, the heirs—of their families.[57] Those who were not landed gentry were nevertheless English "gentlemen." It was this social culture that Southern aristocrats sent their children to the Inns of Court to absorb.

America, however, was too egalitarian for the English model to prevail. Most American lawyers came from well-to-do families, to be sure. From the founding of the Republic until Tocqueville's visit, about 70 percent of American lawyers were college educated.[58] But this did not mean they came from an American aristocracy. Successful farmers also sent their children to become lawyers.[59] The development of law schools in the United States opened the profession still further. In 1784, Judge Tapping Reeve started the first school for lawyers, a proprietary institution in Litchfield, Connecticut. The Litchfield law school and its imitators were enormously successful until replaced by law schools affiliated with universities. This was a development resisted by the upper echelon of the American bar, who, through apprenticeships in their law offices, had been the gatekeepers to the top tier of the profession.[60] Nevertheless, the Harvard Law School was well under way when the University of Pennsylvania opened its law school in 1830. By 1850, fifteen university law schools were in operation.

By contrast, in England the courts were the exclusive province of the aristocracy. Only applicants from the right "condition of life" were admitted to the Inns of Court, and only barristers became judges.[61] It is no surprise, therefore, that even during revolutionary periods, English lawyers remained defenders of their class and of the status quo.[62] In America, however, the law became a favorite calling for children of successful farmers and merchants, families without pedigree who could afford law school tuition. Thus, while the English courts were the defenders of the elite, America's courts took a different path. Tocqueville believed American lawyers were a bridge between the elite and the people. "Lawyers belong to the people by birth and interest, to the aristocracy by habit and taste, and they may be looked upon as the natural bound and connecting link of the two great classes of society," he observed.[63] When he said that the American judge "perpetually interferes in political affairs," Tocqueville was hailing this role as a beneficial instrument of American democracy.

An American Procedural System

The English common law earned its name because it applied to all of England, not because it was intended for commoners.[64] Quite the contrary, it was an instrument of the English aristocracy. While in theory anyone could commence a lawsuit, the system was so arcane and expensive that in practice only the rich could afford access to the courthouse.

No litigant could expect to have his cause heard by an English court without the assistance of not one but two professionals. Only barristers could personally appear on behalf of parties in court, and therefore no litigant could go to trial without retaining one. The number of barristers was small and their fees were large.[65] But a barrister was neither the first nor the only expense. By the eighteenth century, a hypertechnical pleading system had developed. To begin a lawsuit, a plaintiff had to file requests that the court issue a writ for a specific form of action. There was a staggering number of different forms of action—more than sixty just for matters involving real property, for example.[66] The differences among the various causes of action were often obscure, and a party had to select exactly the right one or risk having his action dismissed. The pleading rules for defendants were also highly formalized.

Though essential for gaining access to the courts, pleading work was considered mechanistic and beneath the dignity of barristers. Pleadings were, therefore, drafted by attorneys, who represented a lower social and professional class. Attorneys were not members of the Inns of Court and learned pleading through apprenticeships. Although they had once been relatively inexpensive, by the eighteenth century attorney fees were also considerable. And on top of all of this, litigants were required to pay substantial court costs as well.

Much has been written about the merits of the common law pleading system. The argument is that through the process of choosing precisely the right cause of action with the right remedy, it forced parties to focus clearly on the nature of the dispute and on the relief the court would ultimately be asked to grant. This is poppycock. The English common law pleading system in eighteenth century was a petrified forest of arbitrary rules that did little to sharpen the thinking of either parties or courts about the issues in dispute. The rules had become ends in themselves. It was a system well described as "a miserable state of intricacy, expense and confusion."[67] The practical result was that the English civil courts were largely reserved for gentry and wealthy businessmen.

It has often been said that America did not replicate the English system because it lacked the resources—human as well as financial—to do so. There were, for example, simply not enough men trained in law to create a multitiered bar. This is true, yet there are other, equally important reasons why a distinctly American system developed.

In postfeudal England, commercial and social life probably did not much suffer if access to the courts was restricted. Business, social, and political arrangements were defined and regulated by class and custom as much as by law. Long-standing relationships probably often continued despite, and even during, disagreements. Most of the important commercial relationships were not between merchants or tradespeople but between commoners and gentry. For example, 75 percent of the farmland in England was owned by gentry, who leased it to tenants.[68] Litigation between these landlords and tenants was as unthinkable as it had been between nobleman and serf. Members of the aristocracy who found themselves in tussles with each other over matters involving money or property had access to the courts to resolve their disputes. Others relied not on the courts to enforce their contracts or provide retribution for injuries but on ingrained, reciprocal senses of duty. Commercial life remained predictable without widespread access to the courts.

America was a different place. It was a land of small, independent farmers, artisans, merchants, and tradespeople. Two-thirds of the white American families owned land, compared to only 20 percent of the English population.[69] Commerce was exploding. Commercial transactions were between equals and between strangers, or at least people without established relationships. There was not a rich body of law or commercial custom and practice to guide participants. Thus, the courts were essential to provide both security and predictability in commercial affairs. Americans contemplating business deals needed to know that courts were available to interpret or enforce contracts.

There are other reasons, as well, for why America could not afford a system choked with formalism. The American Revolution had not only been a political revolution. It had been a revolution in ideas.[70] The Revolution was a triumph of republicanism over monarchism, meritocracy over patriarchy, individualism over hierarchy, egalitarianism over classism. New rules had to be worked out for a new social and political order. The courts were needed not only to decide disputes on ad hoc bases but, in doing so, to write the laws for conduct, both business and personal, in a new society. The rules were to be the product of neither theory nor grand design. They were to be worked out piece by piece, as conflicts arose and parties came to the courts for assistance.

Even before the Revolution was completed, the American legal system had began to sweep aside the formalism inherited from England. Alexander Hamilton's personal notes, written in 1782, state that courts were acquiring a "more liberal" approach to pleading, one that would assist them "to Investigate the Merits of the Cause, and not to entangle in the Nets of technical Terms."[71] In 1799, Georgia enacted legislation declaring that a plaintiff could begin a lawsuit by filing a petition describing his claim "plainly, fully and substantially," and a defendant could reply by filing an answer that set forth "the cause of his defense."[72]

Reform did not always proceed smoothly. In Massachusetts, for example, the zeal of reformers bubbled over into proposals to abolish lawyers altogether.[73] Compromises were reached. Parties were allowed either to represent themselves in court or to be represented by persons not admitted to the bar; those wishing to be represented by attorneys could do so but were prohibited from engaging more than two attorneys per case. When the bar successfully pressured the courts to undo these measures, there was an explosion. In what is known as Shay's Rebellion, thousands of armed farmers surrounded the courts and forced them to adjourn.[74] Shay's Rebellion was crushed, but judicial reform, and procedural reform in particular, eventually succeeded. Judges began to ignore pleading errors and, when adversaries challenged them, freely allowed pleadings to be corrected. Massachusetts courts continued to move incrementally but relatively briskly toward doing away with the common law pleading system. "By the early nineteenth century," William E. Nelson writes, "the emerging concern in pleading was with substance, not with form."[75]

In the span of a few decades, American courts created a functional procedural system, one that helped make the courts relatively accessible and focus the litigants and the court on the merits of the case. In retrospect, this seems so obviously sensible as to have been inevitable. And in fact, by 1830, England itself began moving toward a modern pleading system. At the time, however, it was a genuine revolution. The common law system had been developed over centuries and was, for the most part, deeply revered by American lawyers and statesmen. Yet, over only a few decades, an integral part of the system was radically reformed. Moreover, the change was related to a new conception of the role of the courts and the common law.

The most distinguishing feature of the American common law system, however, is not procedural. It is the democratic feature of the system—citizens sitting as jurors, playing so large a role. It is to the development of this system of disciplined democracy that we next turn.

4

Disciplined Democracy and the American Jury

Legends

The jury system was both an ancient and a central feature of the common law heritage. Indeed, it is not too much to say that within the common law world, the jury is one of the institutions most closely associated with the development of civilized society.

Scholars debate whether the jury system was brought to England by William the Conqueror in 1066 or whether it previously existed in some form in England.[1] Either way, before trial by jury, disputes in England were resolved by trial by ordeal, trial by battle, or a process called "wager of law," where a litigant produced a prescribed number of friends of specified social rank to take an oath "with united hand and mouth" on his behalf.[2] Trial by ordeal was not fully extinguished until the church condemned it in 1215, leaving the jury system as the sole means of adjudication. By the time of the founding of the American Republic, therefore, the jury had been an element of the common law system for more than five hundred years.

Then relatively recent events caused the jury system to have a special resonance for the American founders. Four cases bear mentioning, not because they were all genuine legal landmarks but because the stories about them had become allegories that shaped the founders' thinking about the American legal system they wanted to create.

The first, known as *Bushell's Case*, occurred in 1670. William Penn and William Mead preached a Quaker sermon to an audience numbering several hundred in a public square in London. Quakerism was considered an effrontery to the king and to the Church of England, and consequently Penn and Mead were prosecuted for disturbing the peace. There was no question about what Penn and Mead had done; the only issue was whether their conduct constituted a crime. The judge instructed the jury that it did and ordered them to convict the defendants. A jury of twelve refused and acquitted Penn and Mead. Infuriated, the judge imprisoned the jurors. After several months, the jurors were permitted to win their release by paying a fine. Most did so, but four jurors, including a man named Edward Bushell, refused to pay the fine. Instead, they petitioned the Court of Common Pleas for a writ of habeas corpus, contending they were being held unlawfully. In a landmark decision, the chief justice held that a judge could fine or imprison a juror only for overtly corrupt behavior. The case marks the end of the English judge's authority to set aside jury verdicts or to coerce recalcitrant jurors into a particular result. The judge nevertheless retained a number of methods of attempting to persuade jurors, including the ability to comment on the evidence and on the credibility of witnesses and, under some circumstances, to set aside verdicts and grant new trials.[3]

The *Case of the Seven Bishops* came eighteen years later. King James II, an unpopular Catholic king of an overwhelmingly Protestant nation, issued a Declaration of Indulgence, purporting to abolish legislation enacted by Parliament that forbade Catholics from holding military or civil office and to grant religious freedom to Catholics and members of dissenting Protestant sects.[4] James ordered the declaration to be read in every church in the land during services on two consecutive Sundays. The archbishop of Canterbury and six bishops sent a petition to the king stating that they could not, in honor and conscience, read an illegal document in the house of God. The gist of this communication was that the king was acting unlawfully by attempting to abrogate the laws of Parliament.

James was stunned. "This is a great surprise to me" and "Here are strange words," he is reported to have said.[5] Clergy throughout England defied the king's order; it has been estimated that the declaration was read in no more than four hundred of the nine thousand churches in England. What upset James most was the challenge of his power to suspend acts of Parliament. He had the seven bishops arrested for seditious libel and imprisoned in the Tower of London, where they remained for a week until bailed out by twenty-one members of the House of Lords. They were tried in a proceeding described as "a travesty of justice."[6] Nevertheless, the jury returned a verdict of not guilty. It is said that when the verdict was announced to an assembled crowd of ten thousand awaiting the decision, they let out a cheer so loud that it cracked the oaken roof of the great hall.

The third case, that of John Peter Zenger, arose in America and is the only one of the four cases that remains famous in America today.[7] Zenger came to New York as a German refugee in 1709. He was twelve years of age at the time. One of his three siblings died during the voyage to America, and his father died shortly after arrival. Zenger's mother signed an agreement making Peter an indentured servant to a Quaker printer named William Bradford.

Bradford's story is a precursor to Zenger's. Bradford had previously owned a printing press in Pennsylvania. In 1692, after printing a tract accusing Quaker authorities in Pennsylvania of violating their faith by sending armed ships to fight piracy, Bradford had been prosecuted for seditious libel. He had argued that the accusations were true and that truth ought be a defense to a libel charge. Under English common law, however, anything encouraging "an ill opinion of government" was criminally libelous, regardless of whether it was true. Indeed, the old legal adage was that "the greater the truth, the greater the libel."[8] It is no surprise, therefore, that the judge rejected Bradford's theory that true statements could not be libelous.

Understanding all this, Bradford also argued that the jury should be the finder not only of the facts but of the law as well, that is, that the jury should decide whether truth should constitute a defense to libel. The court rejected this argument as well. Bradford was convicted, his printing press was confiscated, and he moved to New York.

After completing his agreed period of eight years of indentured servitude with Bradford, Zenger went into the printing business himself, first on the eastern shore of Maryland and later back in New York, where for a brief period he and Bradford were partners. In 1733, Zenger began printing a newspaper called the *New York Weekly Journal*. Almost immediately, the *Journal* began publishing articles and satirical fake advertisements that, in sum and substance, ridiculed William Cosby, the royal governor of New York, and accused him of corruption and abuses of power.

Cosby has been described as "dull," "mean spirited," and "spiteful." He is said to have been typical of colonial governors who were appointed to their positions because they were "members of aristocratic families whose personal morals, or whose incompetence, were such that it was impossible to employ them nearer home."[9] Cosby found the attacks on him intolerable. He wanted the responsible parties imprisoned for seditious libel and turned for help to a fellow member of the British aristocracy,

Chief Justice James DeLancey of the Supreme Court of New York, whom Cosby had appointed to the bench.

All the articles were either run under pseudonyms or unsigned. While there was no question that he had printed the material, no one believed Zenger to be the author. The articles were considered too literary to have come from his pen. DeLancey hinted at this when he ironically told the grand jury, "Sometimes heavy, half-witted men get a knack of rhyming, but it is time to break them of it, when they grow abusive, insolent, and mischievous with it."[10] The plan was to indict Zenger for seditious libel, then press him to reveal the author.

DeLancey asked a grand jury to indict Zenger, but despite the justice's strong urging, the grand jury refused to do so. DeLancey waited nine months and then tried again with another grand jury. Again the grand jury refused. Governor Cosby then instructed his attorney general to use the alternative method of commencing a criminal prosecution by filing an information with the court. The court dutifully issued a warrant for Zenger's arrest and set Zenger's bail at 800 pounds, despite Zenger's filing an affidavit stating his net worth was 40 pounds. In a transparent attempt to force him to talk, the court imprisoned Zenger for nearly ten months awaiting trial. He never revealed the identity of the author, however.

Zenger's trial produced one of the most dramatic episodes in American legal history. Before trial, Zenger's two lawyers requested that the judges presiding over the case (DeLancey and a second judge) disqualify themselves. They argued that the judges had been appointed by Governor Cosby without the consent of the New York Common Council and therefore served not during good behavior but merely at the governor's pleasure. The judges reacted to this challenge to their impartiality by disbarring Zenger's attorneys and appointing a green, twenty-five-year-old attorney to take over the defense. If this were not enough to demonstrate that Zenger was going to be tried in a kangaroo court, a jury pool was produced that—instead of having been drawn randomly from the list of freeholders—happened to include men who been appointed to government positions by Governor Cosby, as well as Cosby's baker, tailor, shoemaker, and candlemaker.

Zenger's novice attorney had the unexpected fortitude to challenge the jury pool. The attempt to rig the jury was so blatant that the judges were forced to order a new jury pool be selected in the usual manner. But they probably remained confident in the outcome of the case. All the other cards were stacked against Zenger. He was being prosecuted by the attorney general of New York, defended by a novice, and tried before judges determined to see him convicted.

The prosecutor made his opening argument. Then after making a few introductory remarks, Zenger's court-appointed lawyer sat down, and a new lawyer rose to announce that he was now representing Zenger. It was Andrew Hamilton, the most eminent attorney in the American colonies—a man "with so massive a legal reputation as to dwarf the presiding jurists."[11] At that moment, it must have become obvious to the prosecutor and the judges on the bench that the attempt to convict Zenger in a kangaroo court had collapsed. The judges were not going to be able to pull a stunt such as disbarring Andrew Hamilton, or intimidating him, or easily working their will with the jury. This was going to be a trial.

Or was it? Hamilton began by conceding that Zenger printed and published the statements in question. When Chief Justice DeLancey told the attorney general to call his first witness, the attorney general suggested the case was over. "Indeed, Sir, as Mr. Hamilton has confessed to printing and publishing of these libels, I think the jury must find a verdict for the king. For supposing they were true, the law says that they are not the less libelous for that. Nay, indeed, the law says their being true is an aggravation of the crime."[12] Further proceedings were unnecessary. "We have nothing to prove," as the attorney general put it.[13]

Hamilton continued to argue that falsity was a necessary element of the charge of libel, but the court would have none of it. In announcing his ruling on the point, Chief Justice DeLancey quoted prior case law. Excerpts from the trial transcript read as follows:

> Mr. Hamilton: These are Star Chamber cases, and I was in hopes that practice had been dead with the court.
> Mr. Chief Justice: Mr. Hamilton, the Court have delivered their opinion, and we expect that you will use us with good manners. You are not permitted to argue against the opinion of the Court.
> Mr. Hamilton: Then, Gentlemen of the Jury, it is to you that we must now appeal for witnesses to the truth of the facts we have offered, and are denied the liberty to prove. Let it not seem strange that I apply myself to you in this manner. I am warranted by both law and reason.
> Mr. Chief Justice: No, Mr. Hamilton, the jury may find that Zenger printed and published those papers, and leave it to the Court to judge

whether they are libelous. You know this is very common. It is in the nature of a special verdict, where the jury leave the matter of the law to the court.

Mr. Hamilton: I know, may it please Your Honor, the jury may do so. But I do likewise know that they may do otherwise. I know that they have the right beyond all dispute to determine both the law and the fact; and where they do not doubt the law, they ought to do so.[14]

Would the court treat this as insolence? Would it hold Hamilton in contempt? No one could be sure. "Pray, Mr. Hamilton, have care what you say, don't go too far," the attorney general warned him at one point.[15] Hamilton deftly turned away the threat. "Surely, Mr. Attorney you won't make any applications," he replied. "All men agree that we are governed by the best of kings, and I cannot see the meaning of Mr. Attorney's caution." It was a rejoinder with a triple entendre. Ostensibly, Hamilton was pledging his allegiance to the king and softening his defiance. "My well-known principles, and the sense I have of the blessings we enjoy under His Majesty, make it impossible for me to err, and I hope even to be suspected, in that point of duty to my king," he continued. At another level, however, Hamilton's words were a reminder that he—and the judges on the bench—had duties to a higher authority. At a third level, Hamilton gently implied loyalty to the state depended on "the blessings" bestowed by the state. Every mind in the room associated the word *blessings* with "the blessings of liberty," a phrase that had become so sacred a mantra among Americans that it would ultimately be written into the preamble to the United States Constitution.

The threat to liberty from abuse of power was the essence of Hamilton's defense, which he delivered in what is acknowledged to be one of the greatest jury speeches in American trial history. At times, Hamilton seemed to fly into the very teeth of the judges on the bench. For example:

I think it will be agreed that ever since the time of the Star Chamber, where the most arbitrary judgments and opinions were given that ever an Englishman heard of, at least in his own country; I say, prosecutions for libel since the time of that arbitrary Court, and until the Glorious Revolution, have generally been set on foot at the instance of the crown and its ministers. And it is no small reproach to the law that these prosecutions were too often and too much countenanced by the judges, who held their places "at pleasure," a disagreeable tenure to any officer, but a dangerous one in the case of a judge.[16]

Whether the judges—who had disbarred Zenger's two original attorneys for challenging the fact that they served at the governor's pleasure—thought of taking action against Hamilton we shall never know. Perhaps they would have done so with someone of lesser stature. Whether by virtue of his prominence, his indirect method of attack (never referring directly to the judges on the bench), or his sprinkling of small apologies here and there ("I hope to be pardoned, Sir for my zeal upon this occasion"[17]), however, Hamilton was permitted to deliver his closing argument to the jury without interruption.

It was one of the most masterful closing speeches ever delivered to an American jury. Hamilton's central theme—the role of the jury in protecting citizens from abuse of power—was delivered clearly yet just subtly enough to avoid his being held in contempt. Hamilton reminded the jury of *Seven Bishops*. The parallels were obvious; Hamilton could let the jurors draw their own conclusions without his expressly denouncing the judges as the governor's tools.

"Power," Hamilton said at one point, "may justly be compared to a great river."

> While kept within its due bounds it is both beautiful and useful. But when it overflows its banks, it is then too impetuous to be stemmed; it bears down all before it, and brings destruction and desolation wherever it comes. If, then, this is the nature of power, let us at least do our duty, and like wise men who value freedom use our utmost care to support liberty, the only bulwark against lawless power, which in all ages has sacrificed to its wild lust and boundless ambition the blood of the very best men that ever lived.[18]

At the end of Hamilton's speech, Chief Justice DeLancey tried one last time to assert himself with the jury. "Gentlemen of the Jury," he began:

> The great pains Mr. Hamilton has taken to show how little regard juries are to pay to the opinion of judges, and his insisting so much upon the conduct of some judges in trials of this kind, is done no doubt with a design that you should take but very little notice of what I may say upon this occasion. I shall therefore only observe to you that as the facts or words in the information are confessed, the only thing that can come in question before you is whether the words as set forth in the information make a libel. And that is a matter of law, no doubt, and which you may leave to the Court.[19]

The chief justice then repeated that it was the role of the court, and not that of the jury, to determine whether the printed words were libelous, and he sent the jurors out to bring back a verdict. It took them very little time to return with a verdict of "not guilty."

Zenger is today associated with freedom of the press, but that was not its contemporary lesson. As Daniel J. Boorstin observes, "[E]ven after the Zenger case, the question in New York was not whether the press should be 'well-regulated' but who should have the power of regulation."[20] Indeed, in 1798—sixty-eight years after *Zenger* and seven years after the Bill of Rights—Congress enacted legislation making it unlawful to write or publish "any false, scandalous and malicious" writings that brought Congress or the president "into contempt or disrepute" or to inspire hatred against them. The substance of the act was consistent with the common law principle under which Zenger had been prosecuted. The legislation expressly provided, however, that in any trial under the act the jury was to be the finder of both law and fact.

Zenger was immediately famous because it was considered a triumph of democracy over despotism. What was considered important at the time was not that Zenger enjoyed the freedom to publish what he wanted but that it was the jury—representing the community—rather than government officials who determined whether a particular act constituted a crime.

The fourth case arose in England in 1763, on the eve of the American Revolution.[21] A newspaper known as the *North Briton Review* published an anonymous article denouncing a speech King George III delivered to Parliament about the Treaty of Paris as "most unjustifiable" and "odious." The article suggested that the king had lied. King George instructed his ministers to prosecute the author for seditious libel. Since the article was unsigned, a general warrant was issued that specified neither the names of the persons to be arrested nor the places to be searched for evidence.

The king's men may have suspected whom they were after, a man named John Wilkes. Wilkes, one of the publishers of *North Briton* and a member of the House of Commons, was a colorful personality. He is described in various British histories as an "arrogant, uncomely, fulminating [man] who had more gall than talent";[22] a "thoroughgoing rake" who "had been well educated in the classics by a dim Presbyterian clergyman and in debauchery under his own instruction";[23] "charming and witty";[24]

and "a jester to the end."[25] It is said that when Wilkes was campaigning for Parliament, a voter told him, "I'd rather vote for the Devil," and Wilkes replied, "Naturally, but if your friend is not standing, may I hope for your support?"[26]

Wilkes is an unlikely character to have had a profound influence not only on the development of bedrock principles of the American jury system, which is our concern, but also on freedom of the press, protection against unreasonable searches and seizures, and the principles that legislative business should be conducted in public and that the people's elected representatives may not be deprived of their seats on political grounds. But in fact, Wilkes influenced all these fundamental principles of American democracy.

Wilkes was an inflammatory critic of the king's government, both on and off the floor of House of Commons, and the *North Briton Review* repeatedly excoriated the government. The paper was scathing and deliberately provocative. "The *liberty of the press* is the birthright of a BRITON, and . . . has been the terror of all bad ministers," the first issue declared.[27] When asked by Madame de Pompadour of France how far freedom of the press extended in England, Wilkes told her that was exactly what he was trying to find out.

Whether from the first the king's men suspected Wilkes as the author of the anonymous article is unclear. In any event, they needed proof, especially if Wilkes was their target, since he was a member of Parliament. In an embarrassingly blunderbuss fashion, the king's messengers arrested forty-nine people. Most were associated in some fashion or other with the paper, but some turned out to have nothing to do with *North Briton* at all. After a printer told the king's messengers that he had received the manuscript from Wilkes and that it was in Wilkes's handwriting, the king's men arrested Wilkes and dragged him off to the Tower of London.

At the request of several of Wilkes's friends, Chief Justice Charles Pratt of the Court of Common Pleas promptly issued a writ of habeas corpus, requiring the government to produce Wilkes in court and explain by what authority they were holding him. The king's ministers invalidated the writ, and the king's men then searched Wilkes's home, breaking open locks and seizing his personal papers.

An unrepentant Wilkes denounced the general warrant as "a ridiculous warrant against the whole English nation."[28] Chief Justice Pratt issued a second writ of habeas corpus and, after arguments in court, dismissed the case on the grounds that Wilkes enjoyed a parliamentary privilege. Wilkes and fifteen of the others who had been taken into custody then brought civil actions for false arrest, trespass, and assault against the responsible officials. Juries awarded 1,000 pounds to Wilkes and 300 pounds to a journeyman printer named Huckle.

These were enormous sums, far beyond whatever would have reasonably compensated them for the injuries suffered. Wilkes had been in the Tower for six days, but Huckle had been in custody for only six hours, during which time he not only had been treated civilly but had been fed beefsteaks and beer. The court estimated that perhaps 20 pounds would have been sufficient to compensate Huckle for his injury. Nevertheless, the jury awards were to stand. Writing for the court, Chief Justice Pratt said:

> [T]he law has not laid down what shall be the measure of damages in actions of tort; the measure is vague and uncertain, depending upon a vast variety of causes facts, and circumstances. . . . [T]he small injury done to the plaintiff, or the inconsiderableness of his station and rank in life did not appear to the jury in that striking light in which the great point of law touching the liberty of the subject appeared to them at trial; they saw a magistrate over all the King's subjects, exercising arbitrary power, violating Magna Carta, and attempting to destroy the liberty of the kingdom. . . . These are the ideas which struck the jury on the trial; and I think they have done right in giving exemplary damages.[29]

Moreover, Pratt continued, it was a "very dangerous thing for the Judges to intermeddle in damages for torts." Only when an award was so glaringly outrageous that "all mankind at first blush must think so" should a court grant a new trial for excessive damages.[30] *Wilkes* and *Huckle* were, in fact, the first recorded common law cases permitting punitive damages.

This was hardly the end of efforts by the establishment to get rid—one way or another—of John Wilkes. The House of Commons passed a resolution declaring Wilkes's writings to be "the most unexampled insolence and contumely towards his majesty" and undeserving of parliamentary privilege, and Wilkes was again prosecuted for seditious libel. The House of Commons expelled Wilkes from membership several times, only to see him repeatedly reelected. And, in an incident many believed to be a veiled attempt by the king's friends to murder Wilkes, Wilkes was seriously injured after being forced into a duel with a man who was a crack shot.

None of this stopped Wilkes. He argued that the Americans were right when they claimed that the king and Parliament were abridging their rights, and his allies organized a Society of Supporters of the Bill of Rights (though there was some question as to whether money raised for the society was skimmed to subsidize Wilkes's decadent lifestyle). Wilkes eventually became mayor of London.

But it is as a litigant that Wilkes left his greatest mark, at least on the western side of the Atlantic. The settlers of Wilkes-Barre, Pennsylvania; Wilkesboro, North Carolina; and Wilkes County, Georgia adopted his name. Parents named their children after him, too—a sort of curse, as it turns out, since one of these was John Wilkes Booth. Americans had even greater admiration for Chief Justice Charles Pratt. Pratt, who later became known as Lord Camden, had no fewer than seven U.S. cities and counties adopt his name.[31]

Bushell, Seven Bishops, Zenger, and *Wilkes* became powerful symbols of the importance of the jury system in a democratic society. *Bushell* stood for the proposition that jurors were free to decide cases as they saw fit—that the judge could not compel them to reach a particular result. *Seven Bishops* reaffirmed that proposition and illustrated the importance of the jury system in resisting governmental tyranny. Between the citizen and the Tower of London stood the jury; no one could be punished for a crime unless a representative body of citizens determined he or she was guilty of that crime. No decision by government officials, even by magistrates sworn to be impartial, was enough. *Zenger* was an American reaffirmation of that principle but contained another lesson as well—oppression can result from the misuse of power at many levels. This was not an instance of oppression being used as an instrument of government policy, as had been the case in *Bushell* and *Seven Bishops.* The villains, Governor Cosby and Chief DeLancey, acted for themselves, not for king and country. Wherever there is power, there is danger of its abuse; and the hand of power can more readily reach out and influence individual members of the governing class—such as judges—than it can a randomly selected group of citizens.

Wilkes took these principles further still. The jury system was not only a shield but also a sword. A citizen could strike back at those who wronged him, no matter what their station or rank. The law would not only prevent abuse or compensate the victim; it would also provide a mechanism for punishing the abuser and thereby deterring wrongful conduct in the future. This held even when a journeyman printer requested that punishment be inflicted on the king's messengers, to deter conduct by the king himself. Moreover, the decision about whether punishment would be inflicted and, if so, in what measure was ultimately to be made not by the elite—not by landed gentry educated at Eton or Harrow, Oxford or Cambridge, and called to the Inns of Court—but by a representative body of citizens.

It is the possibility not merely of failure but of punishment that provides the strongest deterrent. The king and his messengers had little to lose by arresting Wilkes if the worst that could happen would be the dismissal of the arrest warrant. It is the ability of the wronged to strike back that gives those who abuse power pause.

The Founders and the Civil Jury

Trial by jury took on special importance during the pre-Revolutionary struggle with England. When American smugglers who had been caught trying to avoid the hated English custom duties were tried before American juries, they were often acquitted. The British began to deprive these defendants of trial by jury by trying them in the admiralty courts, where all decisions were made by the judge.[32] Invoking a long-abandoned sixteenth-century law, Parliament directed that Americans agitating for independence should be tried before a special commission in England rather than before a jury in their colonies. Meanwhile, British officials indicted for capital offenses in the colonies were to be tried in Nova Scotia or England rather than before American juries.[33]

When the Constitution was being debated, the founders agreed that the right to trial by jury in criminal trials should be guaranteed. They disagreed, however, whether that right should extend to civil cases as well. As Alexander Hamilton put it in the *Federalist Papers*:

> The friends and adversaries of [the Constitution proposed by the convention in Philadelphia], if they agree in nothing else, concur at least in the value set upon the trial by jury; or if there is any difference between them it consists in this: the former regard it as a valuable safeguard to liberty; the latter represent it as the very palladium of free government.[34]

What Hamilton meant was that the Federalists, who were campaigning to have the states ratify the Constitution, believed that the jury system was important when liberty was at stake, that is, when one was being tried for a crime that could result in incarceration or execution. The anti-Federalists, however, argued that the jury system had a broader purpose—that it was an integral part of democratic government.[35] George Mason of Virginia complained that the Constitution established a judiciary that "will be a Star-chamber as to Civil cases."[36] It was, of course, part of a fundamental debate: to what extent should decisions be made by the people, to what extent by a more learned elite? Some of the founders feared that "excesses of democracy" threatened property interests, and they were loath to engrave a right to jury trials in civil cases into the Constitution.[37]

Although the Federalists temporarily won the point at the Constitutional Convention in Philadelphia, the anti-Federalist position ultimately prevailed with the adoption of the Seventh Amendment, which reads: "In Suits at common law, where the value in controversy shall exceed twenty dollars, the right of trial by jury shall be preserved, and no fact tried by jury, shall be otherwise re-examined in any Court of the United States, than according to the rules of the common law." Nearly all of the state constitutions contain similar guarantees.[38]

Another issue in dispute among the American founders concerned the scope of the jury's authority. The populist view was that the jury should be the finder of both law and fact; the conservative position was that, while the jury was the sovereign finder of fact, the authority to find the law belonged to the judge. *Bushell* and *Zenger* illustrate the issue. There was no question about whether William Penn and William Mead preached a sermon in a public place or about whether Zenger published the offending materials; the issues were whether preaching a sermon in a public place constituted a breach of the peace and whether a true statement could be libelous. Who had the authority to define the crime?

Jefferson was a member of the populist camp. He believed that while the jury usually restricted itself to finding facts and referred legal questions to the judge, this was entirely within the jury's discretion, and whenever liberty was at stake or the judge might be suspected of bias, the jury could decide the law as well as the facts.[39] Alexander Hamilton was in the other camp. Hamilton, who was always concerned about stability, constancy, and commerce, was afraid of unconstrained jury power. "Though the proper province of juries be to determine matters of fact, yet in most cases legal consequences are complicated with fact in such a manner as to render a separation impracticable," he wrote.[40] Hamilton suggested that when fact and law were inextricably intertwined, the judge should decide the matter. "I feel a deep and deliberate conviction that there are many cases in which the trial by jury is an ineligible one," he said.[41]

Hamilton ultimately prevailed on this issue, at least in significant part. Neither the main body of the Constitution nor the Bill of Rights declared the jury to have the authority to determine both law and fact; and, as research by my colleague Matthew P. Harrington has revealed, the jury's law-finding role was brought to an end in a surprisingly short span of time.[42] The development of commerce was critical in the young Republic, and a coherent body of law was critical to the development of commerce. Merchants, judges, lawyers, and legislators all came to believe that the law-finding power of juries deprived the system of a necessary level of predictability. Merchants needed a stable body of rules to know how to arrange their affairs; judges trusted themselves more than jurors; lawyers had increased value in a system where knowledge of the law mattered; and legislators did not want legislation effectively overruled from the jury box. Roscoe Pound has theorized that the times can demand a "reversion to justice without law . . . to bring the administration of justice into touch with new moral ideas or changed social or political conditions."[43] America went through a period of pure justice during the separation from England, but after the new nation was formed, America returned to a rule of law, governed by its own institutions.

America emerged with a distinctly American system. While the founders emulated the British system in many ways, in many ways they did not. America set off on its own path.

The Contemporary Civil Jury: England versus America

In England, the civil jury has all but disappeared.[44] Before 1854, all civil cases were tried before juries; then civil cases were tried without juries only with the parties' consent. In 1933, however, Parliament enacted legislation ending the right to a jury in civil cases except in a very few categories of cases, most notably defamation and false imprisonment. In all other civil cases, the right to a jury trial rested on the discretion of the court. So rarely did English courts grant a party's request for a jury that by 1966 only 2 percent of civil cases were being tried before juries.[45] Then the Court of Appeals of England effectively extinguished even that small cohort of cases by holding that a trial judge's discretion to grant a request for a jury trial was severely limited. The court launched a wholesale attack on jury trials. Its principal objections were three. First, jury trials are inefficient. Second, jury verdicts lack uniformity, which is inevitable since—unlike judges, who take awards in similar cases into consideration when determining damages—a jury is not told about other awards. Third, jury errors are difficult to correct on appeal. Judges explain their reasoning in written opinions, making it possible for appellate courts to find and correct errors. Such is not the case with juries. "They give no reasons," wrote the court. "They find no facts. Their verdict is as inscrutable as the sphinx."[46]

In 1981, Parliament restricted the right to civil juries still further. Now, even in those few categories of cases where there is a right to a jury trial, such as defamation, the judge may decide to dispense with a jury whenever a case requires a prolonged examination of documents, financial accounts, or scientific evidence.

Meanwhile, notwithstanding similar concerns, jury trials remain an integral feature of the American civil justice system. The Supreme Court has held that the Seventh Amendment guarantees a jury trial on every issue for which a right to trial by jury existed under English common law in 1791 (the year the Seventh Amendment was adopted).[47] That, however, is often exceedingly difficult to determine. The right to a jury trial depended on which court system a particular cause of action belonged to, which in turn depended on what the proper cause of action was. As previously discussed, the hyperformalistic categorization of causes of action was so prolix that few eighteenth-century English lawyers mastered it. Contemporary American lawyers and judges are well out of their element in attempting to make these determinations.

One might think all that is needed is a catalog of definitive, contemporary court decisions about which issues had a historical right to a jury trial. It is not that easy. Many contemporary causes of action did not exist two hundred years ago. Moreover, the modern American system is dynamic. It is not a collection of calcified forms of action. In ways large and small, it changes constantly, so that, for example, a "public nuisance" claim in the year 2000 may not mean precisely what it did in 1960. In fact, labels today are less important than substance, particularly in common law areas. Courts focus more on whether a claim is sensibly based on accepted principles of law than on whether the plaintiff's label fits an arbitrary system of classification.

In 1970, the Supreme Court gingerly suggested it might soften its adherence to the historical test. In a footnote to an opinion deciding whether parties had a right to a jury trial in shareholder derivative actions, Justice Byron White, writing for the Court, said that courts ought not merely to engage in an "extensive and possibly abstruse historical inquiry" but also should consider the type of relief requested and "the practical abilities and limitations of juries."[48] The last phrase sounded distinctly anti-jury. Would courts begin to whittle away the right to juries where judges thought they could do a better job? Was America beginning to head in the same direction as England?

Even thirty years later, the answer cannot be given: not yet, anyway. In the very case in which Justice White penned this footnote, the Supreme Court reversed a lower court decision and held that a right to a jury trial exists for most shareholder derivative actions.[49] And the Court has since reaffirmed the right to jury trial in a number of previously gray areas. Liberals on the Supreme Court often support the right to a jury because they believe in the democratic function of juries, that is, that juries represent the people and provide a check against the tendency of judges to favor the powerful. Meanwhile, conservative justices often support the right to jury because they favor strict construction of the Constitution. "The Court must adhere to the historical test in determining the right to a jury trial because the language of the Constitution requires it," Justices Anthony Kennedy, Sandra Day O'Connor, and Antonin Scalia stated in one opinion.[50] Moreover, modern American conservatives worry that the professional class is often more liberal than the population as a whole. Thus, for different reasons, they too may want juries available to balance judicial ideology. These dynamics—combined with the Seventh Amendment, similar state constitutional provisions, and a two-hundred-year American tradition—seem to guarantee that, even though the civil jury is under constant attack, its role will not be significantly diminished on the western side of the Atlantic.

Moreover, the right to a civil jury remains strongest in common law areas.[51] The Supreme Court has held that Congress can empower an administrative agency to hold adjudicatory hearings without a jury. The National Labor Relations Board, for example, can hold a hearing to determine whether an employee has been unlawfully denied back pay, and the Occupational Safety and Health Review Commission can hold a hearing to determine whether an employer is not providing safe working conditions, in violation of federal law.[52] The Court has drawn a line, however, between administrative fact finding regarding public rights—where the government is enforcing rights created by Congress—and private rights in the traditional common law areas of tort, contract, and property.[53] The Supreme Court has made it clear that the Seventh Amendment preserves the right to jury trials in common law areas.

Justice William Brennan proposed substituting a functional test for the arcane research in British legal history. Under Brennan's test, a right to a jury would attach to all issues relating to claims for money damages but not to those relating only to requests for equitable relief (i.e., a court order requiring or prohibiting a party to take certain action).[54] The rationale for the functional test is that it reaches the same result as the historical test in most cases while being far easier to apply. With some rather clear exceptions—most notably, admiralty and domestic relations cases, which were heard without juries—claims for money damages in eighteenth-century England were generally brought in courts of law, which had juries, while other claims went to courts of equity, which did not. The money damages/equitable relief dichotomy functional test is, therefore, a reasonable surrogate for historical research.

Yet, despite its obvious utility, the Supreme Court has not fully embraced the functional test. What almost certainly stops it from doing so, at least so far, is the concern that any modern substitute for a pure historical test—any backing away from strict construction of the Seventh Amendment—might produce a flexibility that ultimately leads to diminishing the right to a civil jury that the founders sought to guarantee.

Disciplined Democracy

Thus, unlike England, where lawsuits are heard and decided by judges, the core of the American civil justice system remains democratic. This does not mean that most cases are resolved by juries. Far from it. Less than 2 percent of all civil cases are resolved by a jury verdict.[55] A small number of the 98 percent of cases not adjudicated by jury are decided by judges, but the vast bulk of cases are resolved by the parties themselves by way of settlement. Nevertheless, the institution of the jury trial exerts a tremendous force on the entire spectrum of cases. Since the settlement value of a case depends on how a jury is likely to decide it, the jury system affects not only cases actually tried before juries but all those that might be tried before juries—including even potential cases that plaintiff lawyers decide not to file at all.

Yet, despite the jury's central position in the justice system, Americans are of two minds about a jury of the people. On the one hand, citizen participation is considered both a check on governmental power and a mechanism for bringing the people's voice into the justice system. On the other hand, there are serious misgivings about populism in the jury box. Therefore, the American jury system, and the civil jury system in particular, has been fashioned into a very particular kind of democracy. Citizen participation, though genuinely powerful, is nevertheless carefully circumscribed and controlled. It is a system of disciplined democracy.

There are no fewer than eight mechanisms that discipline jury democracy. They are: (1) the jury selection process; (2) rules of evidence, which control what information the jury hears; (3) procedural rules and practices that govern how the jury conducts its business; (4) the judge's discretion to bifurcate trials; (5) the judge's role in instructing the jury; (6) the judge's discretion to use special jury verdicts; (7) the ability of both the trial and appellate courts to order new trials when the jury's verdict is contrary to the weight of the evidence; and (8) the ability of trial and appellate courts to refashion verdicts.

Although the enunciated policy goal is to have juries "selected at random from a fair cross-section of the community," juries are far from randomly selected.[56] Juries are drawn from lists of either registered or actual voters, or in some states from property tax records. Courts using actual voter lists, for example, begin the selection process with the 49 percent of the adult population who actually vote.[57] Court personnel weed out individuals with prior convictions or pending charges and people who are not fluent in English or sufficiently literate to fill out a juror questionnaire. In a process called *voire dire*, potential jurors are then questioned by the judge or lawyers in the case. The judge excuses anyone whom she believes cannot be impartial or who is likely to disrupt jury proceedings or threaten the integrity of the proceedings.[58] The jury will include alternates so that jurors who present problems during the course of the trial can be replaced. Each side can exercise three peremptory challenges, allowing them to eliminate potential jurors without articulated reasons.[59]

Finally, the trial and appellate courts have a series of powerful devices allowing them to take clear cases away from the jury, to nullify a jury verdict and order a new trial, or to refashion a jury verdict.

It would have been possible to construct a system in which the jury heard all information either side chose to submit, together with arguments by the parties as to what weight to give various items of evidence. But that is not the common law system. Although in theory they are equally applicable to trials before both judge and jury, the rules of evidence were designed—and operate—principally as a jury control device. The underlying concept is that juries are not always capable of deciding what weight to give various evidence. Even if it is pointed out to them, jurors may not be able to appreciate the unreliability of hearsay. Or, for example, the jury's ability to consider rationally whether Upjohn should be liable for distributing Depo-Medrol to ophthalmologists might be destroyed if it heard evidence about Upjohn's conduct relating to its other product, Halcion. The rules of evidence are an elaborate and constantly refined means of attempting to ensure that the jury's reasoning ability is not overwhelmed by unreliable, irrelevant, or emotionally laden information.

There is a complex array of rules, customs, and practices that governs how the jury conducts its business. Are jurors allowed to take notes? If so, are they told they may do so or, further, given notepads and pencils? Are jurors permitted to ask questions? Again, if so, are they told they may do so? Must juror questions be submitted in writing, so that they may be screened by the judge and lawyers to avoid questions calling for inadmissible evidence? When can jurors begin deliberating? None of this is left to chance. These and countless other questions relating to every conceivable aspect of the jury process have been carefully considered—and are constantly being reconsidered, often in light of new research in jury behavior. Once again, the objective is to advance rational decision making.

Another procedural rule gives judges the discretion to bifurcate trials. A bifurcated trial is split into two parts. The first part deals with the question of liability, that is, whether plaintiff or defendant should prevail. Only if the jury finds for the plaintiff does the trial proceed to the question of damages, which deals with the extensiveness of plaintiff's injury and the sum to be awarded. The rationale often offered for bifurcation is efficiency, that is, a possibly unnecessary portion of the proceedings may be eliminated. But that is largely pretext. Bifurcation complicates many trials, since witnesses who need to testify about both liability and damages must be called to the witness stand twice, and there is often considerable legal argument about what evidence may or may not be offered in the first phase of a trial. The real objective of bifurcation is to ensure the jury is not so moved by sympathy for a severely injured plaintiff that it finds for her favor regardless of whether she is legally entitled to prevail. Similarly, courts may try the issues of liability and compensatory damages in the first phase of trial but reserve issues relating to punitive damages—and the defendant's allegedly outrageous behavior—for a second phase.

At the end of the trial, the judge instructs jurors about the applicable law. In federal court and a number of state courts, the judge may also comment on the evidence. This is a powerful tool. The judge's instructions come from the voice of authority and are the last words the jury hears before it retires for deliberation. Some jury scholars are urging judges to give preliminary instructions at the beginning of the trial to help the jury put the evidence it will hear in legal context.[60] The argument against doing this is that, to the extent a judge permits it, lawyers for the parties often give the jury a skeletal description of their legal theories in their opening statements, and this function is preferably done by the lawyers who, at the start of the trial, know better than the judge on what legal theories they are relying. This debate is one more illustration of the constant search—now informed by sophisticated research by social scientists—for ways to improve the jury system.

In civil cases, the judge has the discretion to require the jury to return a special verdict rather than a general verdict.[61] A general verdict may consist of the jury stating: "We find for plaintiff in the sum of $50,000." A special verdict requires the jury to answer a set of specific questions, called jury interrogatories. This tool forces the jury to consider the issues in a structured and sequential manner and provides the trial and appellate courts with information about the jury's analysis that may be useful in deciding whether to reshape the verdict. But, like most tools, special verdicts have their downside, as recounted in Jonathan Harr's best-seller, *A Civil Action*, about a case in which the judge's poorly constructed jury interrogatories misled the jury and resulted in internally inconsistent and irreconcilable answers.

Trial and appellate courts have a series of mechanisms that allow them to take cases away from the jury, set aside jury verdicts, and reduce jury awards. The theory underlying all these devices is that the right to a jury trial does not mean a right to have a jury decide a case on any basis it sees fit. It includes only the right to have a jury decide a case solely and rationally on the evidence.[62] Thus, the right to a jury trial exists only when there is sufficient evidence to give rise to an "honest difference of opinion over the factual issues in controversy."[63]

The most widely used of these tools is summary judgment. In any civil case where there is no genuine issue as to any material fact, the party entitled to prevail under the law may request that the court enter summary judgment in its favor without trial.[64] This is not discretionary. When a party—based on the pleadings, affidavits, depositions, and other materials—can demonstrate there is not a "substantial controversy" about the controlling facts, it is entitled to judgment without trial, regardless of whether the case is of a kind for which the right to jury trial is constitutionally guaranteed.

A second device is known in the federal system as "judgment as a matter of law." As the federal rule puts it: "If during trial by jury a party has been fully heard . . . and there is no legally sufficient basis for a reasonable jury to find for that party," the judge may decide the case.[65] Defendants commonly make requests under this rule after the plaintiff has rested his case. Plaintiffs (less commonly) make these requests after a defendant has completed her case. Under either circumstance, the court often defers decision until the jury has returned its verdict. This gives the court two advantages. If the jury reaches what the judge considers the right result, the judge can simply accept the jury verdict. If, however, the jury reaches the wrong result, the trial judge can set it aside, secure in the knowledge that should the appellate courts reverse that decision, the jury verdict may be reinstated without the case having to be tried again. In the terminology of most state courts, the court grants a directed verdict before the jury deliberates and a judgment notwithstanding the verdict, or "judgment *n.o.v.*," after the jury returns a verdict.

A jury verdict may be supported by substantial evidence yet nonetheless be "contrary to the clear weight of the evidence" or supported by fraudulent evidence. In such circumstances, the judge—though lacking the authority to enter judgment as a matter of law—possesses the authority to set aside the verdict and order a new trial.[66] The judge may also set aside a verdict based on false evidence, a power that is said to spring from the court's duty to prevent a miscarriage of justice.

Finally, courts may effectively refashion jury verdicts. "Where the verdict returned by a jury is palpably and grossly inadequate or excessive, it should not be permitted to stand," the Supreme Court has declared.[67] Judges reduce what they consider to be excessive jury verdicts through a device called *remittur*. The judge informs the parties that it will set aside the jury verdict and order a new trial unless the plaintiff agrees to remit the portion of the award the court considers excessive. Put bluntly, the plaintiff is given a choice: accept a lower judgment or try the case again to a new jury. The expense and inherent uncertainty of a new trial, which the plaintiff may lose entirely, places considerable pressure on plaintiffs to accept the lower amount.

It was generally considered a violation of the plaintiff's Seventh Amendment right for a court to reduce a judgment without giving the plaintiff this choice, and this is still the law with respect to compensatory damages. Some federal courts of appeals, however, hold that courts may reduce grossly excessive punitive damage awards without offering the plaintiff a new trial.[68] Their reasoning runs as follows: Grossly excessive awards of punitive damages are unconstitutional. When imposed by federal courts, excessive punitive awards violate the Eighth Amendment prohibition against excessive fines; when imposed by state or federal courts, they violate the right to due process. It is the responsibility of courts, not juries, to set constitutional limits. Therefore, when a court finds that an award is grossly excessive and thus unconstitutional, it may reduce the award to what it believes to be the constitutional ceiling, without the plaintiff's agreement.

Under this reasoning, a court has two ways to reduce punitive damage awards. It may unilaterally reduce the verdict to what the court believes to be highest constitutionally permissible sum, or it may give the plaintiff the option of accepting whatever the court believes is the appropriate sum—which, at least theoretically, may be considerably lower than the highest permissible amount—or of trying the case again. Not all federal courts believe courts have the power to lower punitive awards unilaterally, however.[69] The clash between the federal circuit courts on this issue arises from their differing interpretations of a 1996 Supreme Court case and will eventually have to be settled by the Supreme Court.

While judges have tools to adjust excessive awards, many courts give judges few mechanisms for dealing with the converse problem—inadequate jury verdicts. Federal courts are prohibited from offering the defendant the choice of accepting an increased award or trying the case to a new jury. The lack of symmetry comes from English common law, which recognized *remittur* but not the corresponding device of *additur.* In a 1935 opinion by Justice George Sutherland, the U.S. Supreme Court reaffirmed the common law approach. When a jury renders a verdict for a certain sum, reasoned Sutherland, it has essentially found that it is appropriate for the defendant to pay any sum up to the amount of the award, but "where the verdict is too small, an increase by the court is a bald addition of something which in no sense can be said to be included in the verdict."[70] This, of course, is nonsense. If a jury returns a verdict of $25,000, it may just as easily be said that the jury determined the plaintiff should receive no less than $25,000 as that it determined the defendant should pay no more than $25,000. In fact, both statements are wrong. The jury set a sum. Its verdict cannot be read as saying justice will be done if the defendant pays the plaintiff more or less than the amount of its verdict.

The 1935 Supreme Court decision prohibiting *additur* was a five-to-four decision, and the dissenters—Benjamin N. Cardozo, Louis D. Brandeis, Charles E. Hughes, and Harlan F. Stone—have shone more brightly through history than the majority group. Nevertheless, it still stands. Occasionally, a federal judge will employ *additur* anyway—and get away with it. Federal appellate courts hold that a party who consents to the court's changing of a verdict, whether by *remittur* or *additur,* may not then complain on appeal.[71] If the party doesn't agree, it gets the new trial, and the second jury verdict usually stands.

It is not mere chance that many of the jury disciplinary mechanisms favor defendants over plaintiffs. The English common law was an aristocratic system. It provided British citizens with law and justice, but it was also a defender of the status quo and a protector of the upper class. The American system is more democratic. Participation by the people is a sacred aspect of the system. The people must have a voice, even a strong voice, but not the only voice.

Is the Civil Jury Competent?

Although America has opted for a civil jury system, tension remains. The jury system is preferred, but it is not embraced without reservation. Several worries haunt confidence in the civil jury system.

The first worry relates to the jury's collective competence. How can a group of amateurs be as astute as trained professionals? Judges went to law school, practiced law, distinguished themselves in some fashion to rise to the bench, and, day in and day out, evaluate witnesses and lawyers' arguments. Shouldn't they be better at deciding cases than a group of bus drivers, accountants, homemakers, retail clerks, advertising executives, gardeners, short-order cooks, computer programmers? The answer of the American system is no. When it comes to finding facts—deciding what happened, why people did what they did, or who is the telling the truth—the collective judgment of laypeople drawing on their world experiences is better. It is better because a group of citizens with diverse backgrounds collectively possess wider experience and greater insight than a single individual, even someone with specialized expertise. And, in part, it is better because participation by the people is considered an essential check on power—both governmental power, as illustrated in *Bushell's Case, Seven Bishops, Wilkes,* and *Zenger,* and the power of elites.

Another worry concerns the jury's collective prejudice. The presumption is that juries are tenderhearted toward individuals, particularly the weak and injured, but insensitive—perhaps even antagonistic—toward the wealthy and powerful. If a sympathetic individual sues a large corporation, the jury will have a strong inclination to find for the plaintiff, regardless of the evidence and the law. That, anyway, is a popular image of civil juries. The next chapter takes up the question of whether reality jibes with popular belief.

There are considerable data about civil juries, much of these surprising. First, the data show an extraordinarily high rate of agreement between judge and jury in deciding cases. This was first studied in the 1950s. For more than four thousand civil trials, researchers asked the trial judges how they would have decided the cases, then compared the judges' opinions to the verdicts returned by the juries.[72] Judge and jury agreed on the issue of liability in 78 percent of the cases. During the same time, the researchers conducted a parallel study for criminal trials and found exactly the same rate of agreement, that is, judge and jury agreed on defendant's guilt 78 percent of the time as well.

These findings undercut the image of a pro-plaintiff civil jury in two respects. First, the fact that the judge-jury agreement rate was exactly the same for criminal and civil cases suggests that juries are not being influenced by pro-plaintiff sentiment in civil cases. Second, the 78 percent agreement rate is extremely high. It is unlikely that two judges hearing the same cases would agree more often. Moreover, for most of the cases in which they disagreed with the jury, the judges nevertheless said that they found the jury's verdict reasonable.

More recent data continue to reflect similar results. For example, in a 1987 survey of more than four hundred state and federal trial judges trying negligence cases in Georgia, 97 percent of the judges reported that they agreed with the jury at least 79 percent of the time.[73] In a separate survey of state and federal judges conducted nationally the same year, 61 percent of judges said they disagreed with civil juries less than 10 percent of the time.[74] A 1998 Arizona study of civil cases found an 84 percent rate of agreement between judge and jury.[75] And a survey of a thousand federal and state judges who spend more than half their time on general civil cases, conducted by Louis Harris Associates in 1987, found that 69 percent of state judges and 80 percent of federal judges do not believe that "the feelings jurors have about the parties often cause them to make inappropriate decisions."[76] The judges in the Harris poll were nearly unanimous in their belief that jurors usually make a serious effort to apply the law as they are instructed.

Jury verdicts have not only been compared to the assessments of judges. A number of studies comparing jury verdicts in medical malpractice cases with independent evaluations by physicians have found similar results—that is, a high rate of agreement between juries and physicians about whether doctors and hospitals were negligent.[77]

Comparison studies are not the only data relating to possible bias of civil juries. We know, for example, that juries find for plaintiff in 49 percent of all tort cases.[78] The plaintiff success rate varies significantly among different kinds of tort cases, however. Plaintiffs currently prevail in about 30 percent of medical malpractice cases, 40 percent of products liability cases, 50 percent of nonmedical malpractice cases (e.g., attorney and accountant malpractice), 60 percent of automobile cases, and 73 percent of toxic substance cases.[79] That product manufacturers and physicians are the most successful categories of defendants suggests that juries are not strongly biased against business enterprises or individuals with high status.

Data showing that the plaintiff win rate in tort cases where a business is the defendant is nearly identical (52 percent versus 51 percent) to the rate where the defendant is an individual suggest that plaintiffs are not benefiting from an anti-business juror bias.[80] (The difference between these figures and the earlier statistic that plaintiffs win 49 percent in all tort cases may be because intentional torts and defamation actions, in which plaintiff win rates are relatively low, were not included in this study.) And the fact that plaintiff win rates do not increase when their injuries are more severe indicates that juries do not throw law and evidence out the window to favor sympathetic plaintiffs.[81]

Win-rate statistics are not uniform. They vary not only by research methodology but by geography and over time as well.[82] Nevertheless, both a great deal of information and many different kinds of data about the civil jury—including experiments with mock juries and interviews with jurors in actual trials—collectively paint a picture of a civil jury that is far more conscientious, sober, and evenhanded than its popular image.

Are jurors overly munificent? The conventional wisdom has long been that jury awards are high—higher, at least, than awards by judges. The large-scale study in the 1950s, cited above, found that jury awards were, on average, about 20 percent higher than what judges would have awarded.[83] More recently, the war on the common law has included attacks on jury verdicts as being not only high but insanely high. W. Kip Viscusi, who is generally hostile to nearly all forms of regulation of corporate activity, suggests that jury awards are irrational, "explosive," and "escalating and random."[84] Viscusi argues that part of the problem is that "pain and suffering amounts are often the largest part of the damages award," and that juries have an "inability . . . to make reliable judgments" about these kinds of damages.[85] Neil Vidmar, a professor of law and psychology at Duke University, disagrees. Vidmar says the data show "that pain and suffering does not constitute the vast proportion" of jury verdicts, and that "the data on reliability suggest that juries are superior to judges."[86] Who is right?

According to Viscusi's own calculations, when adjusted for inflation, median jury verdicts in products liability cases rose 3.97 percent over a period of seventeen years (1971–88). This increase is not insignificant, but it is not "explosive" either. During the same period, however, the mean verdict increased 6.01 percent, a notably steeper increase. Other data also reflect a wide discrepancy between median and mean awards. A recent large study found that, for all tort cases, the median (midpoint) jury award was $52,000 whereas the mean (average) award was $455,000. The large discrepancy between these two figures appears to be due to a relatively small percentage of very large awards. About 8 percent of jury awards in all tort cases are for more than $1 million. This is not spread evenly among all types of cases, however; the percentage of million-dollar jury verdicts ranges from 4 percent in automobile cases to 25 percent in medical malpractice actions.[87]

There are gargantuan jury awards. Million-dollar awards are no longer uncommon, and there have even been a couple billion-dollar tort awards. The largest verdict in the history of personal injury litigation was handed down on July 9, 1999, when a jury awarded six people $107.8 million in compensatory damages and $4.8 billion in punitive damages.[88] Arguably, any award this large is far too great; still, one can understand the jury's motives. Patricia Anderson, her four young children, and a friend were severely injured when Anderson's 1979 Chevrolet Malibu exploded in flames after being hit in a rear-end collision. The jury heard evidence that General Motors (GM) knew the Malibu fuel tank was vulnerable to being ripped open in rear-end accidents. GM decided not to spend $8.59 per car to fix the problem because it calculated that would be more expensive than settling claims, which it estimated would require payments averaging $200,000 per person burned to death, or only $2.40 for every car manufactured.

GM claimed that the internal memorandum setting forth the calculation was not distributed to corporate decision makers, but the jury—which listened to the evidence in a trial lasting ten weeks—did not believe the company. "People who were well-qualified are not supposed to have instant amnesia. That is the way that most of the witnesses for the defendant reacted," the jury foreman told reporters after the case was over. "It was a business decision [GM] made to go ahead and fight lawsuits from fuel-set fires rather than fixing something that wouldn't have cost them much at all," concluded a librarian who served on the jury.

Assuming that GM was, in fact, as culpable as the jury believed, how large an award was required to deter it and other manufacturers from continuing with that kind of conduct? General Motors is the largest corporation in the world.[89] The jury's award, as enormous as it was, need not have affected company operations one whit. The company could have paid the entire award by depriving shareholders of dividends for one year. Of course, this would have resulted in furious shareholders. The jury may have remembered the very similar Ford Pinto case (which is discussed in the next chapter), considered the automobile industry to be a repeat offender, and concluded that shareholder outrage was necessary to teach corporate executives a permanent lesson. Whether the GM verdict was "excessive" is, therefore, something of a metaphysical question. The largest jury award in history may for many reasons be indefensibly astronomical, but it is hard to call it irrational.

It is, of course, a virtual certainty that the courts will drastically reduce the jury's award. In fact, the jury's award is so large as to become all but irrelevant to whatever sum the courts decide the final judgment ought to be. No one expects otherwise. GM's stock experienced the slightest hiccup on the day the verdict was announced, off about 2 percent. At the end of the next business day, GM's stock more than made up for the loss, and a share of GM stock was worth more than it had been the day before the verdict.[90]

In the final analysis, the questions of whether jury awards are excessive and, if so, whether they are becoming more excessive—although worth studying for sociological insights—have few public policy consequences. They do not matter because courts have ample mechanisms for dealing with excessive verdicts. And courts use those tools. Motions challenging jury verdicts are filed in about half of all cases, and courts grant 10 percent of these motions.[91] A study of nearly two hundred jury verdicts of $1 million or more revealed that, on average, plaintiffs recover only 43 percent of the jury awards.

The jury is a central feature of the common law, but it operates in a carefully crafted, self-correcting structure. The jury's verdict is subject to review by both the trial judge and the appellate courts to ensure it is supported by sufficient evidence and meets other legal standards. Large jury verdicts are themselves meaningless; the issue is whether the system is producing excessively large final judgments.

Many waging war on the common law ignore the difference between jury verdicts and final judgments. They run about clutching newspaper accounts of the latest astronomical jury verdict but ignore that verdicts deemed excessive by the trial judge or by the appellate judges are reduced. Some can be forgiven for their ignorance, but others should know better. Take, for example, the following statement by Harvard Law School's Kip Viscusi: "The proliferation of substantial products liability awards has made six-digit payoffs from a products liability suit much more frequent than comparable payoffs from state-run lotteries. The leading money winner in the products liability sweepstakes in 1987 received $95 million."[92] In fact, there was no "payoff" whatever in this case, and the plaintiff never "received" one nickel. A jury did return a $95 million verdict, but the trial judge eliminated the $75 million punitive damage award because he found it was not supported by sufficient evidence of outrageous conduct by the defendant, and the court of appeals eliminated the $20 million compensatory award because it found the plaintiff's expert scientific testimony did not meet the legal standard.[93]

The Civil Jury and Societal Values

Despite their high rate of agreement, juries and judges do not see things exactly the same way. Juries have certain beliefs, prejudices, and preconceptions that differ from the attitudes of judges, or at least from law created by judges. Researchers have discovered, for example, that juries hold corporations to a higher standard of conduct than they do individuals, even when the law subjects them to the same standard.[94] When, for example, a plaintiff is injured because of a dangerous condition on someone else's property, a jury is more ready to find the defendant liable when the defendant is a business than when the defendant is a homeowner. Similarly, a jury is more ready to find conduct to be negligent when performed by a corporate executive in the course of business than when performed by an individual in his or her personal affairs.

Researchers attribute this not to anti-business bias but to a belief, held by nearly half of individual jurors, that corporations should meet higher standards because their activities create greater risks. Although this may not yet have been explored by researchers, it seems likely that these jurors also believe corporations should be held to higher standards because their activities produce greater rewards, and because they have the resources and expertise to more easily meet higher standards.

Conversely, jurors harbor strong suspicions about plaintiffs. In surveys, more than 80 percent of jurors say they believe there are too many frivolous lawsuits, while only a third say that most people who file lawsuits have legitimate grievances.[95] Judges probably start a case more as agnostics: the plaintiff has the burden of proof, and the judge waits to see whether the plaintiff will convince her (judge) that he (plaintiff) has a legitimate claim. While the judicial attitude may be wary and questioning, however, juries start with feelings of hot skepticism bubbling over into outright antagonism toward the plaintiff.

What explains this level of mistrust? Probably two factors. The first relates to the belief in individual responsibility, which represents one the strongest social mores in America.[96] People should stand on their own feet, work for what they get, and accept the inevitable misfortunes of life stoically. Much of this is rooted in Judeo-Christian theology. The story of Job, for example, teaches that fate is a matter of God's will. Plaintiffs fly directly into the teeth of these deeply rooted beliefs. Plaintiffs come to court looking for money—money for nothing in the sense that it is not earned though work—and they seek to shift the burden of their misfortunes to others. Moreover, plaintiffs want the jurors to do these deeds for them. Many jurors, therefore, come to court with a semiconscious suspicion about the plaintiff's character, as well as some resentment for, in essence, being asked to become the plaintiff's accomplice.

The second reason jurors mistrust plaintiffs has to do with contemporary politics. The public, and thus jurors, has been affected by the war against the common law. In fact, jurors are not the only ones affected. During a ten-year span, from 1979 to 1989, the plaintiff success rate in products liability cases decided by judges fell from 56 percent to 39 percent.[97] When researchers looked at these data state by state, they discovered that plaintiffs' win rates dropped in states that did not enact tort reform legislation during the ten-year period, as well as in states that did adopt restrictive measures. Meanwhile, there was no drop in states that had enacted tort reform legislation before the relevant time frame. Researchers noted that drops may have occurred earlier, when tort reform efforts were underway in these states. Based on these patterns, the researchers concluded that "tort reform efforts are more important than the reforms themselves."[98] What this means is that the changes in legal doctrine were not as significant as the propaganda barrage—the coordinated campaign of planted news stories, op-ed articles, letters to the editor, public statements by politicians supporting tort reform—in the war against the common law. And if the war affects judicial attitudes, it affects the attitudes of the public at large, from which jury pools are drawn, even more.

It is easy to drown in a sea of statistics, but if there is one statistic that represents something of the bottom line about the continuing importance of the civil jury system, it is this: more than 75 percent of both federal and state judges agree "that for routine civil cases, the right to trial by jury is an essential safeguard which must be retained."[99] Why is this particular statistic so telling? The alternative to having cases decided by juries is to have them decided by judges, as has become the norm in England. Judges are preferring juries to themselves.

It is remarkable that professionals should endorse decision making by amateurs. What are they saying? First, the judges appear to be saying that juries are at least as capable as they at deciding cases. This conclusion is supported by the judges' responses to other questions in the 1987 Harris survey. For example, a majority of both federal and state judges said they believed juries rather than judges should determine not only liability but the amount of damages in all civil cases. Only 5 percent of federal and 7 percent of state judges thought that judges should determine liability in all civil cases. That is, judges overwhelmingly favor juries deciding damages in the first instance, subject to all the checks in the system. Forty-five percent of state judges and 73 percent of federal judges said they had reduced damages awarded by a jury at least once.

But the judges appear to be saying something else as well. The question asked whether the civil jury system is a "safeguard which must be retained." Safeguard against what? *Safeguard* was the pollster's term, not the judges', and it was not defined. What did the judges understand it to mean? What is it they believe society must be safeguarded against? What do judges see as the danger in judges deciding civil cases? There are two reasonable answers to these questions: judges believe the civil jury system is an important safeguard against either (1) judges, the professionals, losing touch with the values and mores of the people or (2) the long arm of the powerful.

The first may be illustrated by an example. In 1987, Jeanette Wilks, age thirty-five, and her older brother filed a lawsuit against the American Tobacco Company in Mississippi state court.[100] They alleged that their father, Anderson Smith, died as a result of smoking a pack and half of Pall Mall cigarettes per day for forty-five years. The trial judge held that cigarettes were unreasonably dangerous as a matter of law, and that because it had denied smoking was hazardous to health, under Mississippi law American Tobacco could not avail itself of the defense of assumption of risk—that is, American Tobacco was not allowed to argue it could not be liable because Smith voluntarily elected to assume the risks of smoking. The judge's ruling left the jury with only two main issues to decide: Were Pall Malls a substantial factor in Smith's death, and, if so, what amount of damages ought to be awarded? If anyone believed the judge's ruling meant the plaintiffs were sure to win, they were mistaken. It took the jury only two hours to decide that Smith died not, in substantial part, from either lung cancer or his pulmonary condition but because of a bladder infection.

There was no question that Smith had lung cancer and that it reduced his lung capacity 70 percent, was inoperable, and left him no hope of recovery. Smith suffered from chronic obstructive pulmonary disease as well, a condition so severe that it caused him great pain over the last several years of his life. The evidence was overwhelming that both conditions were caused by Smith's smoking. Dr. Robert O'Neal testified that Smith's immediate cause of death was a pulmonary embolism—a blood clot that lodged in the major artery of his lung. Dr. O'Neal explained that cancer caused blood to clot more quickly, and pulmonary emboli were strongly associated with lung cancer. American Tobacco's lawyer, however, asked Dr. O'Neal if it was possible that the blood clot that killed Smith resulted from surgery that Smith underwent for a bladder infection. O'Neal said it was possible but not common. That was all it took for the jury to decide, by a vote of eleven to one, that Smith's smoking was not a substantial factor in his death. (Unanimous verdicts are required in the federal courts and in most state courts, but some states allow civil juries to return a verdict supported by nine or ten members of a twelve-member jury.)[101]

How could a jury have gone after this red herring? The jurors may have thought they were persuaded that the plaintiffs had not met their burden of proof—the relatively light burden, in a civil case, of proving by a preponderance of the evidence, that is, that it was more likely than not—that smoking was a substantial factor in their father's death. But almost certainly what really motivated them was something deeper within them. The controlling force was their core belief that Anderson Smith chose to smoke and neither he nor his children should now complain that his choice turned out badly. They may have denied this, even to themselves. They may have believed that they decided the case entirely on the medical evidence. They may have convinced themselves that this man—dying of lung cancer, with an immediate cause of death strongly associated with lung cancer—may have just as easily have died from something possible but not common. But it was their deeply held belief in individual responsibility that made them swallow this nearly fantastical theory.

The irony is that the plaintiffs' lawyer, John W. (Don) Barrett of Lexington, Mississippi, understood that up until this point in time the tobacco companies had prevailed in one thousand cases in a row because jurors hold a passionate belief in individual responsibility.[102] Barrett believed this case had the potential to break the tobacco companies' streak. Anderson Smith had suffered from a schizophrenic-type condition and had spent much of his adult life in the psychiatric wards of Veterans Administration (VA) hospitals. To help keep him calm and occupied, VA personnel encouraged Smith to smoke. Smith functioned mentally at about a six-year-old level and could hardly be held responsible, morally or legally, for having chosen to smoke.

Barrett was prepared to prove all this, and he expected it to make the difference. But when the judge ruled that assumption of risk was no longer part of the case, defendants successfully argued that Smith's mental ability and how he had started smoking were irrelevant. When the judge ruled this evidence inadmissible, the case—though superficially appearing to be all but won—had, in reality, been turned into a loser. Barrett won too much in the pretrial maneuvering. His case became theoretically formidable but fatally wounded. After the case was over, jurors told reporters they were not convinced Smith died as a result of smoking. At the same time, Barrett suffered the indignity of having jurors tell him that they thought Smith should not recover because (they assumed) he voluntarily decided to smoke.

This case illustrates how the common law prevents legal doctrine from becoming detached from societal values. The judge could rule that the defendant had no assumption-of-risk defense and remove the issue from the courtroom by instructing the attorneys not to present evidence or make arguments relating to assumption of risk. But in the final analysis, he could not remove the issue from the case. The commitment to individual responsibility is too fundamental and too strong to be ignored. Barrett's original strategy was sound. The only way for the plaintiffs to win was to confront the issue directly and explain why they were not trying to avoid the issue of individual responsibility. No lawmaking authority—whether trial judge, appellate court, or legislature—can successfully tell jurors that a plaintiff who voluntarily elected to take a known risk should be compensated when his or her choice turns out badly.

Lawyers may tend to think of this case in terms of jury nullification, a controversial doctrine defined as "the act of a criminal jury in deciding not to enforce a law where they believe it would be unjust or misguided to do so."[103] This is not, however, the most useful way to think about what happened in this case. The jury probably neither consciously rejected the judge's ruling about assumption of risk (juries are generally not told about rulings of this kind) nor decided to substitute its own sense of justice for a law it considered unjust. It may have tried to follow the judge's instructions faithfully. Juries usually do; 98 percent of state judges and 99 percent of federal judges agree that "jurors usually make a serious effort to apply the law as they are instructed."[104]

A jury, such as the one in Anderson Smith's case, that has heard nothing about assumption of risk has no sense of having missed something. Nor may jurors be consciously aware that the judge's instructions are tugging them away from their own sense of fairness. Rather, jurors' preexisting beliefs and values form the prism through which they view the case. Jurors process the evidence, lawyers' arguments, and the judge's instructions in ways that allow them to decide the case in a manner consistent with their basic values. Cognitive dissonance plays a role. The jury in Anderson Smith's case may well have believed the plaintiffs had not met their burden of showing their father's smoking was a substantial factor in his death, but jurors came to this peculiar conclusion because, for them, the idea of compensating a man who voluntarily elected to run a risk was even more bizarre. In a sense, rendering a verdict in the plaintiff's favor was unthinkable, so the jurors took the only route open to them, namely, finding that Anderson Smith's death was not substantially related to smoking.[105]

The jury's importing of its own ideas of the law into a case can be disconcerting, especially when a jury's idea about the law is wrong. For example, in one case in which an elderly plaintiff was severely injured by a drunk driver, the jurors debated whether the defendant could be covered by insurance while driving drunk.[106] They had heard nothing about insurance during the course of the trial—as the law requires, so that jurors will not be tempted by an insurance company's deep pockets. There was no question that the defendant had caused the accident and should compensate the plaintiff for his injuries. Nevertheless, the jurors were concerned about the effect their verdict would have on the defendant, a young man who admitted his wrongdoing and appeared genuinely contrite. As a blue-collar worker with no more than an high school education, the defendant was not likely to ever earn much more than enough to help support himself and a family in modest circumstances.

The jurors worried that if they awarded the full amount necessary to compensate the plaintiff for his injuries, they would saddle this young man with a crushing, lifelong obligation. The jurors did not need to be told that automobile owners were required by law to have insurance, but during deliberations a juror said a driver cannot be covered by insurance while driving drunk. The jury debated this point and reached the erroneous conclusion that the defendant would personally have to pay the judgment. (Apparently, no one raised the prospect of the defendant discharging debts through bankruptcy.) The jury made a conscious guess about the law, got it wrong, and awarded the plaintiff considerably less than it would have if it had understood the law correctly.

The jury in this case made two errors. First, it guessed about a piece of information (one that the system thought it should not have), and guessed wrong. Second, the jury thought that being fair to both parties required it to consider the defendant's ability to pay, while under the law a defendant's financial capacity should not be taken into account when making an award of compensatory damages. Though the second of these is the more ambiguous, neither was necessarily caused by a clash between the law and the jury's values. Having had the experience of what went askew in this trial, the judge and lawyers might anticipate and—through more explicit jury instructions, the use of special jury interrogatories, or perhaps comments in the closing arguments—avoid a similar problem in the future.

That is not the situation with the Anderson Smith case. The verdict there was not an error in the sense that the jury would have reached a different result if it had been given additional information. If an omniscient being were to have told the jury that Anderson Smith's death was caused by his smoking Pall Malls, the jury might still have subconsciously searched for another route to finding in defendant's favor.

Juries certainly make mistakes. And a particular jury may be idiosyncratic in the sense that its values are not representative of the society at large. At the macro level, however—that is, looking not at individual cases but at a broad expanse of cases extending over time and geography—juries are, in one important sense anyway, never "wrong." Juries represent the voice of the body politic. The vast number of juries that, prior to 1988, consistently found in favor of cigarette companies in products liability cases reflected the will of the community. Plaintiffs in those cases may have had strong cases as a matter of legal doctrine, but the common law embraces more than the technical aspects of legal doctrine. Legal scholars may advocate that the common law take a particular path;

judges may attempt to place the common law on a particular path; but they can take the common law only so far without pubic consent.

Of course, community values shift over time, and the common law moves with them. A sea change in tobacco litigation is underway (as is discussed in chapter 8). No longer are tobacco companies unvanquished; products liability cases against tobacco companies are now producing mixed results.

The vector of change runs in both directions. Litigation is not only influenced by changing social conditions and mores; it helps change them. It is, moreover, a special arena in the debate over public policy. It is the one place in the system of American government that, in the words of Lon L. Fuller, "gives formal and institutional expression to the influence of reasoned argument in human affairs."[107] In the legislature, rational argument is often smothered by polemics—and all discourse may take a backseat to politics. Litigation provides a different mechanism for challenging accepted conventions, one that makes rationality its most important instrument. Democracy prevails, but in an especially disciplined way.

5

The American Common Law System

Is Proctor *an Example of System Failure?*

It is, of course, true to the point of banality to say that any large system will inevitably produce successes and failures. The health delivery system cures disease and saves lives, but it will inevitably cause illness and death; the safest transportation system is air travel, but some planes will crash; the educational system works well for some students but not for all. It is, therefore, not possible to demonstrate how well a system works by evaluating a single outcome. And just as it is not possible to prove that a school system is good or bad by pointing to a single student it served well or poorly, it is not possible to evaluate the common law system by examining a single case.

Yet, bearing this in mind, certain insights can be gleaned from a single example. This section returns to the case of *Proctor v. Davis*. As the reader will recall, this book opened with Senator John C. Danforth offering that case (albeit a rather distorted description of it) as an example of the failure of the products liability system. Danforth's object was to show that the system wallops defendants, especially corporations, with insanely large verdicts. He was trying to persuade the Senate that the tort system was producing jury verdicts that are both enormous and lacking in all rhyme and reason, and that the cumulative cost of these verdicts, together with litigation expenses companies are forced to spend to defend themselves from a plethora of lawsuits, is imposing a heavy financial burden on American business. This is an indictment with two counts. First, the system is irrational and produces injustices for parties who have the misfortune of being dragooned into litigation. Second, the system imposes heavy costs on business, resulting in higher prices for consumers, chilling the development of new products, and putting American firms at a competitive disadvantage in the global marketplace.

To some extent, the first count has been answered by the preceding chapter. Nevertheless, it is instructive to revisit *Proctor* and ask if the real case, rather than Danforth's miscolored sketch of it, supports the indictment. *Proctor* is a useful specimen for at least three reasons. First, it was proffered as an exemplar of a dysfunctional system. Second, the case is in some ways run of the mill yet in one respect—the gargantuan size of the verdict—highly unusual. The verdict was so large, in fact, that one wonders if the mere reporting of it through the media harmed the defendant. Third, what makes this case particularly interesting is that *Proctor* is, in many ways, somewhat ambiguous. Most detached observers will have a difficult time pronouncing the verdict right or wrong with a comfortable degree of certainty.

As the reader will recall from chapter 1, Meyer Proctor suffered from uveitis, a serious inflammation of the eyes. He was treated for this condition by an ophthalmologist named Michael J. Davis. Davis treated Proctor with Depo-Medrol, a steroid manufactured by the Upjohn Company that Davis injected near Proctor's eyes. Although Depo-Medrol had never been approved for periocular administration, it had become commonly used by ophthalmologists. Davis estimated that he had used the drug sixteen hundred times, and he believed ophthalmologists were administering Depo-Medrol about 1 million times annually. On the second treatment, Davis accidently injected Depo-Medrol directly into Proctor's left eye. Proctor underwent surgery three times in an unsuccessful effort save his eye, but his eye ultimately had to be removed. Davis testified that if Upjohn had warned of dangers associated with periocular administration, he would not have used the drug.

We may begin by asking whether the $127 million jury verdict in *Proctor* was rational. In this respect *Proctor* is atypical; this was one of the largest verdicts of the year, and in fact, one of the larger verdicts of all time. The judgment was ultimately reduced by more than 95 percent to about $9 million, a sum that is small in comparison to the original award but hardly insignificant. Even though Upjohn never had to pay the damages specified in the original verdict, let us nevertheless take up the question of whether the jury's decision was irrational.

It is the punitive damage award, which made up about 97 percent of the total award, that is at issue. One of the factors to be considered in determining punitive damages is the financial capacity of the defendant. Punitive damages are a form of punishment, and they must be large enough to sting. An award of $1,000 might impose a measure of financial punishment on an independent sidewalk news vendor, but it is not enough to punish the *New York Times*. Punitive damages are also designed to deter future conduct, and if that conduct is profitable, the award must be large enough so that the parties do not find it in their financial interest to continue socially undesirable conduct despite having to absorb legal costs from time to time. The evidence in the case was that Upjohn's net worth was $1.7 billion.[1] In 1994, Upjohn's revenue was more than $3.5 billion, on which it made a $491 million profit.[2] There is no formula for calculating punitive damages; it is a matter of judgment, taking into account both the nature of the conduct and the defendant's financial status. The jury's award of $124,573,750 represented about 25 percent of Upjohn's annual profit, 7 percent of its net worth, and 3.5 percent of its revenue. Although the jury did not explain how it calculated its award, the arithmetic suggests it intended to deprive Upjohn of one-quarter its annual profit, a sum that would presumably deny Upjohn much of its profit from promoting Depo-Medrol to the ophthalmologic market. Viewed through this lens, it is difficult to say that the $124 million punitive award was beyond all rhyme or reason.

The system may at times produce "right" or "wrong" results, but it is difficult for it to yield patently irrational outcomes. It is a system with powerful self-correcting mechanisms. In civil cases in federal court and in all fifty-three American jurisdictions (i.e., the fifty states, the District of Columbia, Puerto Rico, and the Virgin Islands), trial judges have considerable authority to reduce or set aside jury verdicts. While the standard varies somewhat among the states, the general rule is that the judge must set aside a verdict if "the verdict is against the clear weight of the evidence, or is based upon evidence that is false, or will result in a miscarriage of justice."[3]

The review is especially rigorous when punitive damages have been awarded. *Proctor v. Davis* was an Illinois case. Under Illinois law, punitive damages may be awarded only "for conduct that is outrageous either because a defendant's acts are done with an evil motive or reckless indifference to others' rights."[4] Punitive damages are not favored under Illinois law, and because they are penal in nature, the trial judge has a duty to ensure that punitive damages are not improperly or unwisely awarded.[5] In Illinois, a jury is not even permitted to consider punitive damages unless the judge finds there has been sufficient proof of aggravated circumstances; and after the jury makes an award, the trial judge may reduce it if, in his or her opinion, it is excessive. The appellate courts may eliminate or reduce a punitive award when they find the award resulted from "passion, partiality, or corruption."[6]

In *Proctor*, the jury, the trial judge, and the appellate court all agreed there was enough evidence not only to find Upjohn responsible but to warrant a large punitive award (though, of course, they disagreed about the amount of the punitive award). The appellate court expressly stated that there was evidence "that Upjohn not only knew of the adverse effects of periocular use of Depo-Medrol, but promoted and developed this off-label use through financial and technical assistance to doctors" and found that "Upjohn's conduct was sufficiently reprehensible to support an award of punitive damages."[7]

Even though Upjohn ultimately had to pay no more than 7 percent of the original award, the question deserves to be asked whether the mere handing up of so large an award, with its attendant publicity, caused Upjohn's stock to plunge, and if so, whether that was a normatively undesirable result.

The *Proctor* verdict was announced on Friday, October 18, 1991. Upjohn's stock had opened that morning at 44¾ per share and closed in the afternoon at 43⅝, off fifty cents per share. The jury verdict may, however, have been announced too late in the day to affect the market; the dateline of the wire service report of the verdict is Saturday, October 19, 1991.[8] Upjohn fell seventy-five cents per share on Monday, October 21, 1991, and lost another twelve and half cents on Tuesday, closing at 42⅞. Thus, within a period of three business days—from its close the day before the jury verdict was announced until the close two full business days after the verdict—Upjohn's stock lost $2 per share, or 4.5 percent of its value. Although the Dow Jones Industrial Average also declined during that period, Upjohn's loss was significantly more precipitous (the Dow lost 0.4 percent in value).[9] Two of the three largest pharmaceutical companies gained ground during the same time frame, so Upjohn's decline was not part of an industry trend.[10]

At first blush, therefore, it appears that the jury verdict did have an impact on Upjohn's stock, as at least one market analyst suggested at the time.[11] If the announcement of the $127 million verdict caused Upjohn's stock to fall then, however, all other things being equal, the announcement that the trial judge reduced the punitive damages portion of the award to $35 million should have caused Upjohn's stock to rise. It did not. Two full business days after the judge's decision to slash the jury verdict was announced, Upjohn's stock was fractionally lower (down 12.5 cents per share) than it had been at market close the day before the announcement.[12] And Upjohn's stock declined again after the appellate court of Illinois reduced the punitive award from $35 million to $3 million.[13] This suggests that the relationship between a legal judgment—even one of the largest judgments of all time—and the stock of a Fortune 500 company is a complex matter.

Putting the events in context helps. These were not good times for Upjohn. The company was facing serious problems related to another drug, a prescription sleeping pill called Halcion. Halcion (its generic name is trizolam, which is in a category known as benzodiazepine) was introduced overseas in the late 1970s and in the United States in 1983, following FDA approval in late 1982. By 1991, Halcion had become Upjohn's second most profitable product.[14] It was sold in more than ninety countries, and in the United States alone, physicians were writing half a million prescriptions for Halcion annually. But by 1991, Halcion was also a product with problems. It was associated with a number of serious side effects—anxiety, paranoia, amnesia, delusions, hostility, even verbal and physical aggression.

In 1979 the Dutch government suspended sales of Halcion. The next year Dutch regulators authorized Halcion in quarter-milligram tablets; but rather than lower the dosage, Upjohn elected not to distribute Halcion in Holland. In 1987, the FDA conducted a review and discovered that physicians in the United States were filing up to thirty times as many adverse-reaction reports for Halcion as they were filing for Dalmane and Restoril (two other benzodiazepine sleeping pills) combined, even though each of these other drugs was then out-selling Halcion. Under FDA pressure, Upjohn lowered the recommended dosage of Halcion to a quarter milligram and revised the package insert to warn that "bizarre or abnormal behavior, agitation and hallucinations" might be dose-related responses. European regulators were finding similar data, and by the summer of 1988, the half-milligram Halcion tablet had been banned in France, Germany, and Italy as well as Holland.[15] In 1989 another FDA review resulted in the addition of another warning, stating that amnesia "may occur at a higher rate with Halcion than with other benzodiazepine hypnotics."

By 1990, at least sixteen lawsuits had been filed against Upjohn claiming that Halcion had driven otherwise peaceful individuals to murder.[16] The one that received the most attention involved a fifty-seven-year-old Utah woman named Ilo Grundberg, who gave her elderly mother a birthday card and then, without any apparent motive, shot and killed her. Grundberg, who claimed she had no memory of the event, was arrested for second-degree murder, but after two court-appointed psychiatrists concluded Grunberg was intoxicated by Halcion and had not acted voluntarily, and prosecutors asked the court to dismiss the case. The Grundberg case received a strong burst of publicity when, in 1989, the popular ABC television newsmagazine *20/20* broadcast a story about Halcion titled "When Sleep Becomes a Nightmare."

The *Proctor* verdict was announced at a time when things had grown even worse for Upjohn and Halcion. In August 1991—two months before the jury award in the *Proctor* Depo-Medrol case—*Newsweek* published a four thousand–word article about Halcion. *Newsweek* reported, among other things, that the FDA had discovered that among 329 prescription drugs associated with hostile acts, Halcion ranked number one. (Xanax, an anti-anxiety drug chemically similar to Halcion and also produced by Upjohn, ranked number two.) The article quoted the head of psychiatry at Pennsylvania State University's Hershey Medical Center as saying: "This is a very dangerous drug. No other benzodiazepine has such a narrow margin of safety. The only justification for keeping it on the market is to ensure the company's profitability. From a public-health standpoint, there is no reason at all."[17] *Newsweek* also reported that Upjohn had just settled the Grundberg case. "Upjohn blinked" on the eve of trial, as *Newsweek* put it, to avoid a public trial scrutinizing Halcion's safety record—and, presumably, Grundberg's claim that Upjohn had "falsified and fraudulently misrepresented, concealed and omitted data" from the FDA.[18]

One month before the *Proctor* verdict, the U.S. Drug Enforcement Administration fined Upjohn $600,000 for keeping inadequate records of samples of Halcion and Xanax that Upjohn had distributed to physicians.[19] Less than two weeks before the verdict, both Britain and Finland ordered that Halcion be withdrawn from their markets.[20] British regulators said they acted after receiving new information, which, if they had known it earlier, would probably have resulted in the drug never having been approved. It appears some of these data were unearthed through discovery in the Grundberg case. When questioned by the press, a professor of psychiatry at Edinburgh University, who had been engaged as an expert by Grundberg's lawyers, said he had become privy to data involving early clinical trials of Halcion and considered them of public concern but could not comment further because the court had issued a confidentiality order at Upjohn's request. This raised eyebrows. "It is obvious why a company would want to keep secret its method of synthesizing its drugs. But it is less clear why clinical results should be kept secret," *New Scientist* magazine stated in an editorial.[21]

Then, one week before the *Proctor* verdict, the British Broadcasting Corporation (BBC) broadcast a story titled "The Halcion Nightmare" on its current-affairs program *Panorama*.[22] The story reported that Upjohn settled the Grundberg case after the court ordered the company to produce eight thousand pages of documents the company had fought not to release (with the hope that, by settling, the materials could remain confidential). Among these materials were data from a six-week clinical trial of Halcion, known as Protocol 321, that Upjohn submitted in support of its request for FDA approval. When it was ordered to produce this information, Upjohn announced that it had discovered that Protocol 321 data furnished to FDA contained "transcription errors." On camera, BBC reporters confronted Upjohn officials with the BBC's discovery that the so-called transcription errors resulted in an underreporting of serious side effects and that Upjohn did not give the FDA materials reporting some of reactions reported by their researches—including paranoia. Upjohn officials admitted the errors but seemed unable to answer the reporters' questions about the actual rate of paranoid reactions in the Protocol 321 clinical trial. The CBS program *60 Minutes* broadcast a similar show in December 1991. By then, Halcion sales had fallen 46 percent.[23]

The Halcion story continued to unfold over a period of years. Halcion stories appeared throughout the media, from the business press,[24] to medical journals,[25] to journals of sociology,[26] to legal periodicals,[27] to consumer magazines,[28] to journals of political opinion.[29] A series of new revelations and developments created a drumbeat of stories continuing over a period of years. From 1991 to 1996, *Newsweek* alone published eight articles about Halcion.[30]

This was the context in which the securities industry received the news of the *Proctor* verdict. Depo-Medrol was but a flea on the back of a Halcion elephant.[31] As the largest verdict of the year, *Proctor* received more than enough publicity to come to the attention of mutual fund analysts and major investors (and was disclosed in the company's annual report, which was filed with the Securities Exchange Council and was widely available to the investment community).[32] Sophisticated investors viewed *Proctor* through the prism of the still-unfolding Halcion story. At the time of the jury verdict in *Proctor*, Halcion raised questions about whether Upjohn ignored, suppressed, or manipulated criti-cal information regarding Halcion. *Proctor* now raised similar possibil-ities regarding a second drug. This had to give investors butterflies. Would Upjohn would turn out to be a company that—like the monkeys who see no evil, hear no evil, and speak no evil—deliberately avoided research that might reveal unwelcome information and concealed in-convenient information from regulators, physicians, and consumers?

It is not surprising that the *Proctor* verdict had a marked effect on Up-john stock. The more interesting question is why Upjohn's stock fell only 4.5 percent. The company had just been handed a $127 million verdict. This was, in effect, an enormous bill that would, should Upjohn have to pay it, put a significant dent in funds available for shareholder dividends or for new product development (then especially critical for Upjohn, which was shortly to have patents on four of its most profitable drugs ex-pire without having promising new products in the pipeline). And what if this verdict was only the first of a number of similar awards?

One might wonder, therefore, why, when the $127 million verdict was announced, Upjohn's shares did not go into free fall. While a con-tributing factor may have been the already depressed state of the com-pany's stock, the main reason was likely that analysts understood that Upjohn almost certainly would never have to pay that judgment. They know that punitive awards are subject to rigorous scrutiny by both the trial judge and the appellate courts and are often reduced. A twenty-five-year study of punitive damage awards in products liability actions found that defendants wound up having to pay the full award in only 40 percent of the cases.[33] Moreover, large awards are reduced more often than smaller awards.

Here, for example, are the ten largest jury verdicts of 1991, together with the final award in the case:

Case	Jury Verdict	Final Award
1. *Fineman v. Armstrong*[34]	$239 million	$0
2. *Proctor v. Davis*	$127.7 million	$9.1 million
3. *In re Apple Computer Litigation*[35]	$100–$175 million	$16 million
4. *The Narrows v. Underwriters*[36]	$85 million	$0
5. *Crown Point Center Ltd. v. Mellon Bank Corp.*[37]	$62 million	$10.8 million
6. *Waller v. Truck Ins. Exchange*[38]	$58 million	$0
7. *Santesson v. Travelair Ins. Co.*[39]	$57 million	$0
8. *Concise Oil & Gas Partnership v. Louisiana Intrastate Gas Corp.*[40]	$48.5 million	$22.5 million
9. *Ecks v. Nizen*[41]	$46.8 million	$25.9 million
10. *Abou Khadra v. Bseironi*[42]	$46.2 million	$23.6 million

Thus, seven of the ten largest jury verdicts handed down in 1991 were reduced by the courts, from a cumulative total of $869.5 million to $107.9 million, a reduction of more than 78 percent. Although this may be too small a sample to be statistically significant, it is consistent with a study that found 74 percent of all verdicts in excess of $1 million were reduced or eliminated.[43] These statistics do not capture the low order of probability that Upjohn would have to pay anything approaching the full verdict. *Proctor* was both a punitive damage award and a large verdict. Moreover, the defendant was a pharmaceutical company. While not everyone loves drug companies, courts are likely to be more generous to a company that produces medicines than, say, to a gambling casino or a used car dealer.

Upjohn's stock fell when the $127 million verdict was announced because the case seemed to confirm fears and forebodings growing out of Halcion. While it was the magnitude of the verdict that caught the media's attention, what was significant to the market was not the verdict's size (which was bound to shrink) but the implicit endorsement of the plaintiff's allegations. It is not that securities analysts and investors believed the jury verdict definitively established the plaintiff's position. They are more sophisticated than that; they know that other juries, presented with the same evidence, might well reach different conclusions. But if the verdict did not speak authoritatively about the ultimate truth of the plaintiff's allegations, it spoke powerfully about the potential strength of those allegations. At least one court had ruled that there was sufficient evidence for a plaintiff to have its case submitted to a jury, and that evidence was persuasive enough for at least one jury to reach a particular conclusion. A single jury might be right or wrong regarding whether Depo-Medrol was, in fact, unreasonably dangerous; and new facts confirming the safety of the drug might emerge. But the portion of the case concerning Upjohn's conduct was another matter. First, presumably no one knew—or would ever know—more about what Upjohn did, and why it did it, than Upjohn itself already knew. Upjohn's defense of its own conduct was, therefore, unlikely to get stronger, and it might well get weaker as regulators and future plaintiffs dug deeper into Upjohn's basket of dirty laundry. Second, the portrait painted of Upjohn in *Proctor* seemed to be the same unattractive picture being painted by the Halcion story. The two stories were mutually reinforcing.

What mattered to the market was the fact rather than the amount of the *Proctor* verdict. That is why Upjohn's stock failed to rise when the verdict was reduced. Upjohn's stock might have risen had the trial judge dismissed the punitive award; however, his finding that a $35 million award of punitive damages was appropriate only confirmed that there had, in fact, been persuasive evidence that Upjohn had engaged in heinous conduct.

Where the effects of the verdict desirable? "I can't punish the stockholders of this company to the extent that the jury did," the trial judge said when he reduced the award, adding, however, "I don't think [Upjohn] executives and leaders should get away" with their misconduct.[44] Ironically, the judge's action not only did not help Upjohn's shareholders but, if anything, reduced the value of their stock even further. The relationship between a single judgment—even the largest of judgments—and a company's stock is a complex one. The judgment will be evaluated by the market within the larger context of the market's understanding of the company. Most trial judges are not equipped to predict how their rulings will affect corporate stock, and perhaps they should not even try.

The judge thought Upjohn's shareholders should not be punished, or at least not punished too severely, for the conduct of corporate executives. He thought of the shareholders as innocent victims. He is indisputably right insofar as shareholders—qua their roles as shareholders—had anything to do with company conduct. In many companies, however, corporate executives and other insiders are themselves large shareholders. At the time of the *Proctor* verdict, for example, about 25 percent of Upjohn's stock was owned by members of management or the Upjohn family.[45] The tort system cannot punish the individuals who were directly responsible for the undesirable conduct; the best it can do is punish the company as a whole and hope that, in one way another, culpable officials will feel the sting.

It is an imperfect system. Many blameworthy executives escape unscathed. Some benefit from their own socially undesirable behavior. Their conduct causes the company's stock to rise, and they reap rewards in raises, bonuses (often in the form of stock and stock options), and increased stock value. These executives may then divest themselves of much of their stock long before injured people file lawsuits. There are often long lag times between an executive's decision and the external consequences that flow from that decision. Meanwhile, many blameless individuals may pay dearly.

The law need not always shed tears for shareholders. In large companies, most shareholders are more gamblers than owners. They bet that the company's stock will rise or that it will pay dividends. When they are right, they win; when they are wrong, they lose. In neither case do they "deserve" the outcome in some normative sense. Once they have made the decision to invest in a particular company, their fate depends entirely on the effort of others. The question is not whether shareholders deserve to be penalized when executives make decisions that jeopardize public safety in order to maximize corporate profit—any more than it is whether shareholders deserve to benefit when the executive calculus turns out to be correct and the company profits from socially undesirable conduct. Rather, the proper question is whether society at large benefits when the system imposes penalties on the company.

Was the process a successful search for truth? An ophthalmologist friend of mine tells me the jury got the case exactly wrong. He says periocular injection of Depo-Medrol is a safe and effective method of treating uveitis; and indeed, to this day it remains a widely used method of treatment when steroid eyedrops are not effective (as was the case for Meyer Proctor). Moreover, says my friend, a competent physician should never puncture the eyeball when making a subconjunctival injection, and if, for some extraordinary reason, that occurs—because of a sudden and unexpected movement by the patient, for example—the physician should not push the plunger and inject the medicine. My friend believes, therefore, that the jury should have found against Davis but for Upjohn.

Of course, my friend's opinion is based on my ten-minute description of the case, whereas the *Proctor* jury made its decision after a five-week trial at which they heard directly from Dr. Davis as well as from experts called and cross-examined by lawyers for Proctor, Davis, and Upjohn. Nevertheless, I do not dismiss the possibility that my friend may be right when he says Depo-Medrol is a safe and effective drug when properly administered, and a skilled physician should never wind up injecting it directly into the eye. Yet, if he is correct, why was Upjohn able to convince neither the jury nor the judge of its position?

The answer is that Upjohn itself did not know what level of risk Depo-Medrol posed in periocular use. Upjohn argued that Depo-Medrol posed no increased risk of blindness, that is, that Proctor lost his eye merely because his eyeball was punctured by a needle and not as a result of Depo-Medrol's special properties. Upjohn claimed it knew

of only three instances of patients losing vision after attempted periocular injections of Depo-Medrol, and in each case the physician had accidentally punctured the patient's eye.[46] But this tells us little or nothing of how many patients actually suffered adverse reactions. Upjohn
learned of the incidents only because the physicians reported the incidents by filing what are today called Adverse Drug Reaction (ADR) reports; yet ADRs are filed for only a tiny fraction of reactions actually
experienced. When surveyed, 61 percent of all physicians say they are
not familiar with ADR forms and guidelines; and among those who are
familiar with the system, some physicians simply do not want to be
bothered filing such reports, while others fear a report may somehow
reveal they committed malpractice.[47] It may be that well under 1 percent of all adverse drug reactions come to the attention of either the
FDA or the drug manufacturer. Upjohn's knowing of only three cases
of patients losing their eyesight after periocular injections of Depo-
Medrol tells us very little.

Risk must be assessed scientifically, and science requires methodically
sound study. Anecdotal reports will not do, either in the realm of science
or in the courtroom. While a pharmaceutical company cannot be expected to test its drugs for every kind of use physicians may find for it, periocular administration was not a rare use. Upjohn was selling 1 million
doses of Depo-Medrol annually to ophthalmologists, and the jury heard
a great deal of evidence about how Upjohn actively promoted its drug for
that use. Unlike most products liability cases, where the focus is on the
product, this case was more about Upjohn's conduct.

As a formal matter, the plaintiff had to show that Depo-Medrol presented certain risks and that Upjohn had failed to warn physicians
about those risks. It may well be that Depo-Medrol does not, in fact,
pose those risks. Or to put it another way: if our knowledge of chemistry, biology, and medicine were complete and perfect, we might know
that the loss of Meyer Proctor's eye had nothing to do with the chemical composition of Depo-Medrol. We might, then, know with certainty
that had Dr. Davis's syringe contained water instead of Depo-Medrol,
the effect on Meyer Proctor's eye would have been exactly the same.
But, of course, we are not omniscient, and our knowledge is neither
complete nor perfect.

Sometimes reality hits us over the head, as it did with respect, for example, to thalidomide. Thalidomide was sold as a tranquilizer and
sleep aid in Europe and Canada in the late 1950s.[48] It turned out that

thalidomide was an extremely powerful teratogen. About 1.5 percent of all children are born with congenital abnormalities, but nearly 20 percent of women who took thalidomide while pregnant gave birth to babies with birth defects, including grotesque abnormalities such as having flippers instead of arms and legs (a condition called phocomelia that is otherwise extremely uncommon). About ten thousand children with birth defects were born to woman who took thalidomide. Moreover, nearly half of pregnant woman taking thalidomide experienced miscarriages and stillbirths.

When something of this magnitude occurs, knowledge is thrust upon us whether we seek it or not. In most instances, however, knowledge is far harder to come by. The loss of vision by an elderly patient being treated for a serious eye disease will not get the same kind of attention as the birth of a child with flippers. In the former situation, neither the patient nor the physician will be as likely to demand an explanation, and reports of such events are far less likely to be made to the FDA or to come to the attention of the manufacturer or the medical community. If the periocular use of Depo-Medrol has not been tested in animals or monitored in carefully designed epidemiological studies, our knowledge is inadequate to determine whether, to a reasonable scientific certainty, the special properties of Depo-Medrol substantially contributed to the loss Meyer Proctor's eye.

It is the conventional view that, under such circumstances, the plaintiff should not prevail. The plaintiff must prove by a preponderance of the evidence that Depo-Medrol was a substantial cause of his injury, and if the plaintiff cannot marshal sufficient evidence to meet that burden, the plaintiff's case should be dismissed by the court. Nevertheless, *Proctor v. Davis* may have been both just to the parties involved and good for America, even if, as medical knowledge grows, we are able to say that injecting Depo-Medrol into Meyer Proctor's eye (instead of, say, a sterile saline solution) had nothing to do with Proctor's injury.

The civil justice system needs to seek pragmatic rather than absolute truth. Absolute truth is also referred to as the correspondence theory of truth; that is, something is true if it corresponds to reality. In this way of looking at things, the jury's conclusion was a successful search for truth if the jury would have reached the same conclusions if had it been omniscient. In *Proctor v. Davis*, the jury's verdict presupposed a finding that Depo-Medrol posed certain risks. That finding is true in an absolute sense only if the jury would have reached the same conclusion if its knowledge of chemistry, biology, and medicine were complete and perfect. Truth in this sense is eternal; when we know all there is to know, our conclusions are not affected by new knowledge.

The jury, however, did not know everything. In fact, it knew little about how periocular injections of Depo-Medrol affect the eyes. One way of looking at the case is to say that the plaintiff bears the burden of proof, and if, for whatever reason, the plaintiff fails to proffer evidence sufficient for a jury to determine that Depo-Medrol poses the alleged risks, the plaintiff has failed to meet his burden and his lawsuit must fail. Yet that is not the best way to consider this case. What we know about drugs depends on what the manufacturer has learned. Finding truth depends on our state of knowledge, and in the field of pharmaceuticals, our society depends on pharmaceutical companies such as Upjohn to learn as much as feasible about new drugs before making them available for widespread use.

The view from this perspective is that Upjohn was sanctioned not for distributing an unreasonably dangerous drug but rather for aggressively distributing a drug for a particular use while deliberately keeping itself in the dark about whether the drug was appropriate for that purpose. As the plaintiff's lawyers dramatically put it, the case was about "the substitution of human beings for laboratory animals."[49]

The Four Legs of American Common Law

The common law can be thought of in two different but related ways. Most often "common law" is defined in terms of who, how, and with what jurisprudential philosophy the law is made. Justice Harlan F. Stone, for example, wrote that the common law's "[d]istinguishing characteristics are its development of law by a system of judicial precedent, its use of the jury to decide issues of fact, and its all-pervading doctrine of the supremacy of law—that the agencies of government are no more free than the private individual to act according to their own arbitrary will or whim, but must conform to legal rules developed and applied by courts.[50] (This is, incidently, very much a description of American common law, where the jury plays a significant role, rather than the modern English common law system, in which the jury has all but been eliminated.)

The term *common law*, however, is also used to refer to the "trivium of contracts, torts, and property"[51]—three areas of law that have traditionally been developed through judicial decision. The view that these three fields constitute the common law is widely shared but seldom examined.[52] To these three areas I add products liability. It is this meaning of common law—that is, what areas of law make up what we call common law in contemporary America, and why these areas are distinctive—on which I now focus.

One of the themes of this book is that American courts do and should handle common law cases differently from other matters. It is important, therefore, to be clear about what areas of law comprise a contemporary common law and what distinguishes them from other areas. We can begin by asking why contracts, property, and torts are the traditional common law areas. The short answer is that these are the areas concerned with relationships between private citizens, whereas areas such as taxation, for example, involve relationships between citizens and government. But that answer only holds up with some explanations.

Sometimes it is useful to define something in terms of what it is not. That may be the case here. Therefore, this section explores why a number of areas of law are not generally considered common law subjects. The next section continues the discussion by focusing directly on the four areas that, I argue, comprise the common law. I hope that, together, both sections explain not only what distinguishes these four legs from other areas of law but why the effort in making the distinctions is worthwhile.

I said that common law subjects are concerned with relationships between private individuals. Yet family law—which is, after all, probably the area most directly and intimately concerned with relationships between private citizens—is generally not considered a common law subject. Why is that the case? Part of reason has to do with English family law being the province of ecclesiastical rather than the common law courts. Another, more contemporary factor is that fundamental questions of family law have to be answered through the political process. Who is eligible to marry? Is a person permitted to have more than one spouse? Is a man permitted to marry his stepmother? Are homosexual couples permitted to marry? What are grounds for divorce? Is a single person permitted to adopt a child? If a woman turns her child over for adoption with the stipulation that the child be adopted only by Roman Catholics, may the child nevertheless be adopted by Buddhists?

The answers to these questions represent fundamental societal choices. In eighteenth-century England, the answers were given by the church. Even in a secular democracy, the questions raise religious issues and cannot be answered without intruding into religious practices, and therefore the answers are best given by the people's elected representatives. That does not mean the majority's decisions are unconstrained. Here, as in other areas, the courts must decide whether legislation violates constitutional rights. But with this important caveat, it is not difficult to understand why the field of family law passed from regulation by the church to regulation by the legislature.

Not everyone would exclude family law from the list of common law areas. Richard A. Posner, for example, puts family law on the list because it is a body of law "made primarily by judges."[53] That is true in the sense that the legislature creates the skeleton of family law and leaves it up to courts, rather than legislatively created administrative agencies, to put flesh on the bones. A similar argument can be made for antitrust law, a field where Congress established broad and flexible principles and left it up to the courts to weave the fabric of the law. As Judge Frank H. Easterbrook sees it, Congress authorized the courts to develop a full body of antitrust law through the common law process, and presumably he would include antitrust law on the contemporary list of common law subjects.[54] Similarly, in 1936, then United States Supreme Court justice Harlan F. Stone wrote that one could no longer consider "the contours of the ancient rules of property, contract, tort and succession, as constituting the warp and woof of the common law."[55]

The list of common law subjects, therefore, depends on how one defines the term—and how one defines it depends on the purpose one has for defining it. I don't mean to engage in a purely semantic exercise. My interest is in compiling a list of those areas of law that the courts, and perhaps to a lesser extent legislatures too, consider the special province of common law courts.

This is important because how courts view their role influences what they will do. When, in 1999, for example, the Vermont Supreme Court held that the state constitution required the benefits of marriage enjoyed by opposite-sex couples be afforded to same-sex couples as well, it refrained from stating how that should be done. "We do not purport to infringe upon the prerogatives of the Legislature to craft an appropriate means of addressing this constitutional mandate," wrote the court.[56] If this had been a matter of property, contract, or tort law, it is likely the court would have fashioned a remedy itself.

By contrast, the same year the Ohio Supreme Court wrote an opinion excoriating the Ohio General Assembly for intruding into areas reserved exclusively to the courts.[57] The showdown between the Ohio high court and legislature involved a series of so-called tort reform measures enacted by the General Assembly—and, after having previously been declared unconstitutional by the court, reenacted. The measures included caps for punitive damages in tort and products liability actions and for noneconomic damages in medical malpractice claims, as well as statutes of repose prohibiting the institution of various tort and products liability claims after prescribed periods of time from the date of the defendant's activity (even if, before then, the plaintiff could not have known she had been injured by the defendant). The court did not declare that the common law was the exclusive province of the courts. Its decision was based on state constitutional provisions, such as the right to jury trial and the right to remedy for injuries in the courts.[58] Nevertheless, the court was almost certainly influenced by the legislature's intrusion into the traditional common law area of tort law. The court would probably have had a more difficult time invalidating legislatively imposed damage caps with respect to actions involving labor or environmental law, for example.

Why is constitutional law not part of the common law? Constitutional law is principally developed through judicial decision. The U.S. Constitution is short and general, and most of what we understand it to mean comes not from the document itself but from the cases interpreting it. Nevertheless, when courts make constitutional law (and there is no need to be coy about the fact that *making* constitutional law is what courts do), they are interpreting a written document. All constitutional law flows from a document adopted through a political process. Courts cannot make constitutional law without direct reference to that document. Or put another way, courts may make constitutional law only to the extent that they can fairly justify that what they are doing is interpreting the Constitution.

There are, as well, two other reasons to leave constitutional law off the list of common law subjects. First, constitutional law is distinct because—unlike contracts, torts and property, which are principally concerned with relationships between private citizens—constitutional law deals with the structure of government and with relationships between government and citizens. Second, with the exception of freakish episodes such as the Ohio General Assembly reenacting legislation that the state supreme court previously declared unconstitutional, the right of the courts to be the ultimate arbiter of constitutional law is unquestioned.[59]

As strange as it seems from a contemporary vantage point, criminal law was once part of the common law. Indeed, in ancient England, criminal law and tort law were one and the same; either the state or the victim could prosecute an action against a wrongdoer.[60] The two areas began to diverge in 1166, when legislation required that felony prosecutions begin with indictments handed up by what later became grand juries. Still, courts continued to create and define crimes through court decisions.[61] This did not offend early American jurisprudence, since the jury was considered the finder of both the facts and the law. Thus, the jury decided not only whether the defendant did what she was accused of doing but whether such conduct constituted a crime. The jury was the voice of the community, and in theory, therefore, no one was convicted of a crime without a judgment by the community that the act was, in fact, criminal.

All this changed for several reasons. First, the authority to find the law shifted from jury to judge. In a society suspicious of authority, it was considered too dangerous to allow judges to decide whether conduct was or was not criminal. Second were the related problems of uncertainty, inconsistency, and retroactivity. Individuals could not be sure whether a particular activity in which they might want to engage would be declared criminal. How could one reliably predict what a judge and jury might decide? And having judges (or anyone, for that matter) make these decisions retroactively meant those determining criminality might be influenced by the identity or politics of the defendant.

In 1812, a case reached the United States Supreme Court in which defendants were criminally indicted for libeling the president and Congress.[62] The defendants allegedly had stated in a Connecticut newspaper that the president and Congress secretly paid Napoleon Bonaparte $2 million for his permission to make a treaty with Spain. Was libeling the president and Congress a crime? It violated no statute, but the attorney general argued the court could declare it to constitute a common law crime. The Supreme Court had never before addressed the question of whether federal courts had the power to convict individuals of common law crimes; nevertheless, said the Court, it was an issue "long settled in public opinion." "The legislative authority of the Union must first make an act a crime [and] affix a punishment to it," it wrote.

The Supreme Court's decision technically applied only to the federal courts. Some state courts continued to try defendants for common law crimes.[63] But the Supreme Court had it right when it said this was now at variance with public opinion, and in both the United States and England, the practice of creating new crimes by court decision became increasingly rare. In the nineteenth century, state legislatures began to enact criminal codes. For the most part, these were efforts to codify the common law; the list of crimes and the elements of those crimes were taken from case law. Some of these codes abolished common law crimes, and henceforth no one could be prosecuted for a "crime" not expressly included in the statutes. To different degrees, however, many states continued to use the common law to fill in the gaps. Some codes stated that if a crime were not defined by statute, the common law definition applied; some expressly retained common law defenses and other principles not inconsistent with the statute.

On a few occasions, common law courts created new crimes in the twentieth century. The best known instance is a 1932 English case involving a woman who filed a false report with the police claiming she had been robbed.[64] The police expended time investigating, and innocent people were placed under suspicion. At the time, the English statutes did not make filing a false police report a crime. The court created and convicted the woman on a new common law crime it named "public mischief." What is most significant about the case, however, is not that the court held this was proper but that the case is notorious. Fifty years earlier, a leading authority on English criminal law had written that the time when courts would create new common law crimes was over, and but for this one case, his prediction might have held to the present day. This single case is, therefore, the exception that proves the rule. Contemporary commentators now state more cautiously that "a new offense will be created by courts only rarely in England" and will be a misdemeanor, not a felony.[65]

A few American jurisdictions still theoretically leave room for creating new common law crimes. For example, Florida's criminal code contains a provision that reads: "The common law of England in relation to crimes, except so far as the same relates to the modes and degrees of punishment, shall be in full force in this state where there is no existing provision by statute on the subject."[66] The origin of this provision dates back to 1829, seven years after Florida was organized as a territory and before it joined the Union. Like many of the states before it, Florida, needing a ready-made body of law, adopted the common law of England as its own. In Florida's case, it adopted English common law as it existed on July 4, 1776.

In 1972, a Florida trial court dismissed an indictment charging a defendant with the common law crime of nonfeasance.[67] "The need and reason for common law crimes has passed and ceased to exist, and the necessity [for the statutory provision incorporating English common law] is finished," it wrote. The Supreme Court of Florida reversed, however. The legislature had the authority to adopt the law of any other state or nation as the law of Florida, it held, and thus only the legislature could abrogate its law adopting English common law. It also held that the statute was not too vague to pass constitutional muster and did not deny defendant due process of law. The court also took two additional steps. First, it endorsed the wisdom of the continuing validity of common law crimes. There are times when defendants slip through statutory loopholes, and the common law is necessary to bring them to justice, the court reasoned, citing as an example a 1960 Florida case where a person being held for civil contempt escaped. Florida statutes made it a crime only for someone confined for a misdemeanor or a felony to escape from prison, and without relying on common law, the court would have been unable to punish the offender.

It is what the Florida Supreme Court took as its second step that leads to a curious result. The contemporary Florida statute simply adopts the "common law of England." No reference is made to July 4, 1776, or to any other date. The Court wrote:

> The common law has not become petrified; it does not stand still. It continues in a state of flux. And, its ever present fluidity enables it to meet and adjust itself to shifting conditions and new demands. It has been described as a leisurely stream that has not ceased to flow gently and continuously in its proper channel, at times gradually and imperceptibly eroding a bit of the soil from one of its banks and at other times getting rid of and depositing a bit of silt. In view of our English heritage, it is unthinkable that judicial limbo should be its destiny.

Thus, Florida's common law of crimes continues to evolve, and presumably courts can create new crimes. It is quite peculiar, however, that it is not Florida's courts that declare new crimes in Florida but England's. This suggests how rare—even in one of the few states, such as Florida, that continue to recognize a common law of crimes—criminal prosecutions of common law crimes are. Florida, it appears, continues to want the common law available to fill statutory gaps when the need arises, but the need so seldom arises that the Florida legislature cannot be bothered to make the Florida common law of crimes, rather than England's, the law of the state.

One might ask whether the common law continues to exist at the beginning of the twenty-first century. Today there are few, if any, areas of law not composed of both case law and statutes. The law of contracts, for example, includes a great deal of statutory law, from the Uniform Commercial Code (UCC) to a plethora of consumer protection statutes; from the federal Consumer Credit Protection Act and motor-vehicle "lemon laws" to state laws regulating door-to-door sales, installment sales, and layaway sales, to name just a few areas. Nevertheless, the heart of contract law remains court created. Although the UCC was based on earlier statutes (the Uniform Sales Act, which in turn was based on the English Sale of Goods Act), those acts were based on case law. And although it was drafted through a directed project, the Code was not an effort in sweeping law reform. The drafters tried to take the best rules from existing statutes, case law, and proposals from scholars. The concept of the best rule was flexible. In some instances it might be the most widely accepted rule; in others it was what the drafters considered the wisest rule; in still others it was the rule most likely to work well on a uniform, national basis. Finally, the common law spirit is evident in how the drafters expected courts to apply the code. The official comments praise the courts for implementing "statutory policy [of the earlier Uniform Sales Act] with liberal and useful remedies not provided in the statutory text" and for disregarding that act's "statutory limitation of remedy where the reason of the limitation did not apply." "Nothing in this Act stands in the way of the continuance of such action by the courts," the comments state.[68] Despite the number and importance of statutes, American lawyers and judges have no trouble recognizing contracts as a common law area.

If the common law continues to exist—that is, if there are four bodies of law that are, in an important fashion, distinct from other areas—the question may be asked: Why is that so.

Why the Common Law Is Special

The view that common law areas differ from other fields can be traced to the earliest days of Republic. Gordon S. Wood captures this spirit when he writes:

> Men began to draw lines around what was political or legislative and what was legal or judicial and to justify the distinctions by the doctrine of separation of powers. As early as 1787 Alexander Hamilton had argued that [one could only be deprived of rights by "due process of law"], which said Hamilton in an astonishing and novel twist, had "a precise technical import": these words now "only applicable to the process and proceedings of the courts of justice; they can never be referred to an act or legislature." Placing legal boundaries around issues such as property rights and contracts had the effect of isolating these issues from popular tampering, partisan debate, and the clashes of interest-group politics.[69]

There are two intermingled concepts in this passage. The first is that private disputes should not be resolved by legislatures, where decisions are influenced by politics and the relative power of the parties, but adjudicated by courts. Though we take this for granted two hundred years later, the concept was hardly widely accepted in the eighteenth century. Colonial general assemblies served as both legislatures and courts (as well as the executive arm of government), and the line between legislative and judicial functions was blurry at best. Indeed, in some instances legislative determinations of private matters lingered; it was only in the mid–nineteenth century, for example, that the practice of legislatures granting divorces was finally snuffed out.[70]

A second concept is nevertheless present: that certain areas of law should be reserved to the courts. In eighteenth-century America, the founders put the law of property and the law of contracts into that category, as Gordon Wood notes. Today we would place two other areas of law, torts and products liability, in that category as well. American common law, therefore, has become a four-legged table. How did this come about, and why these four particular legs?

In post-Revolutionary America, the founders were plagued by twin anxieties. On the one hand, they worried about populism, about a suddenly empowered majority wanting to satiate its own material cravings at the expense of the propertied class. The founders were fearful of

Robin Hood legislatures enacting laws that disfavored wealth, investment, and commerce. They were horrified at Rhode Island's policy of
issuing paper currency so that farmers who had borrowed money during the war could more easily pay off their loans—a debtor relief policy
they considered not only unfair to merchant-creditors in Rhode Island
but a threat to commercial stability outside the state as well. "Nothing
can exceed the wickedness and folly" of Rhode Island, wrote Madison.
"All sense of character as well as right have been obliterated."[71]

At the same time, they were concerned about public officials pursuing self-interests. The founders were accustomed to the British model
and its American replica, where political leadership had been supplied
by an aristocracy—by men of wealth, breeding, education, and a sense
of noblesse oblige. Washington, Madison, Hamilton, and Jefferson all
considered themselves to fit this mold. Now they saw men without
these traits holding public office and using their positions for personal
gain.[72] The natural but unwholesome symbiosis between politicians
and the wealthy became readily apparent. These concerns, which were
at the forefront of the development of an independent judiciary, also
gave impetus to what perhaps was only a semiconscious idea that certain areas of law were better entrusted to courts than to legislatures.

Nothing fell more clearly within this rubric than disputes over private property.[73] Legislators might favor the common folk over the
wealthy or the wealthy over the common folk, and general assemblies
were therefore dangerous places for making rules about property interests. Judges, though not wholly without prejudice, were at least less influenced by personal interests than were legislators. This followed the
English heritage, which treated law of real property as "the kernel and
core of common law."[74] This core grew large; for as commercial activity expanded during the eighteenth century, the law of contracts—previously a small area of law—expanded as well. And on both sides of
the Atlantic, the law of contracts was written primarily by common
law courts.[75]

To some extent the American founders gave property and contract
law special constitutional status. The Constitution prohibited the state
legislatures from enacting any "Law impairing the Obligation of Contract," and it prohibited the federal government from depriving persons of property without due process of law."[76] Neither of these provisions, of course, even suggests that courts have exclusive authority over
these areas of law; and courts have never taken that position. The idea

that common law areas are primarily the province of the courts flows from tradition and custom, not from constitutional law.

One period of constitutional legal history is worthy of note. For a span of three decades at the beginning of the nineteenth century, known as the *Lochner* era, the Supreme Court adopted the view that legislatures had little power to regulate private contracts. The case for which this historical period takes its name concerned a New York State law prohibiting bakeries from employing a worker for more than sixty hours per week.[77] The United States Supreme Court found the statute unconstitutional because the state legislature had "no reasonable ground for interfering with the liberty of person or the right of free contract." The Court held that the state legislature did not have a sufficient reason for infringing on the right of employers and employees to enter into contracts on terms of their own choosing.

The *Lochner* Court did not ground its decision on the contract clause of the Constitution. Rather, it relied on the portion of the Fourteenth Amendment that prohibits states from depriving persons of liberty without due process, a theory known as "substantive due process." For our purposes, this makes little difference. Either way, the Court was in effect declaring that, absent compelling circumstances, legislatures should give contracts a wide berth. "This is not a question of substituting the judgment of the court for that of the legislature," said the Court unconvincingly, as it proceeded to explain why it believed the law did not protect the health or safety of bakery workers. The Court's concern about society being "at the mercy of legislative majorities" was more revealing. This was an area the Court found ill suited for majoritarian rule.[78]

I do not want to overstate the point. First, the *Lochner* era did not last long and represents an aberrant period in legal history.[79] Second, the *Lochner* Court did not even mention the common law. It based its decision on constitutional law, and moreover, on substantive due process rather than on the contract clause. Third, scholars generally attribute *Lochner*-era jurisprudence to a laissez-faire ideology or an anti–labor union bias.[80] Nevertheless, as Laurence H. Tribe notes, the pattern of *Lochner*-era decisions is probably too complex to be explained by a single theory and the underlying causes remain "at least partly shrouded in mystery."[81] Some of the impetus may have been a feeling—and I mean just that, a feeling, rather than an articulated doctrinal position—that property and contracts were areas properly reserved for common law regulation.

Lochner-era jurisprudence came to an end with the New Deal. Much has been written about how *Lochner* succumbed to the economic, political, and sociological forces of the time; but here, too, there may be another piece to the puzzle. Increasingly, what had been categorized as private disputes involving contracts or property were reclassified as falling within new areas of public law, such as labor law or corporate law. It may be no accident that labor and corporate law emerged as distinct areas of law in about the same time period that *Lochner* jurisprudence was waning.[82]

It is important to draw a distinction between the ideological and jurisprudential philosophies of the *Lochner* Court. On the one hand, the Court may have been motivated by a laissez-faire ideology that sought to insulate private property, contracts, and business from governmental interference. This political strand of thought—which continues today with libertarian and property-rights movements—disfavors governmental regulation in all forms. It does not matter whether regulation comes from the legislatures, from administrative agencies, or from common law courts. On the other hand, the Court may also have been influenced by a perception that the legislature was interfering with the common law area of contracts. For these purposes, it is the regulator (legislature or court) rather than regulation per se that is the issue.

Classification has consequences. More or less consciously, courts are willing to give legislatures greater deference when the courts classify the legislation as involving an area of public law than when it is classified as common law. Though courts rarely, if ever, put it quite that way, they sometimes come close. In a 1976 opinion, for example, the Supreme Court wrote:

> Legislation adjusting the rights and responsibilities of contracting parties must be upon reasonable conditions and of a character appropriate to the public purpose justifying its adoption. . . . As is customary in reviewing economic and social regulation, however, courts properly defer to legislative judgment as to the necessity and reasonableness of a particular measure.[83]

What the Court is saying is that it is appropriate for courts to closely review legislation regulating contracts and to invalidate restrictions that, in the courts' judgment, are not reasonable or not sound public policy. In public law areas, however, the courts should generally accept the legislature's judgment on those matters.

Areas of public law generally emerge from private law. New kinds of activities are originally dealt with as isolated transactions between private individuals. As disputes arise, the courts regulate new activity through common law rules. For some forms of activity this is sufficient, but from time to time it becomes apparent that something new has arisen that requires comprehensive regulation. Corporations, for example, were viewed as webs of private contracts among investors, directors, employees, and customers. Over time, however, the growth and increasing complexity of corporate activity required new areas of public law—corporate law, securities regulation, labor law, antitrust law, and environmental law. Industry-specific schemes of regulation—dealing with food and drugs, motor vehicles, aviation, health care, telecommunications, nuclear energy, and so on—were also developed. In this sense, contract law may be thought of as a seminal area of law, since it precedes and spins off public law; or perhaps, as Lawrence M. Friedman puts it, as a "residual" branch of law, since it deals "with those areas of business life not otherwise regulated."[84]

Property law may have been the kernel of old English common law, and contract law may have developed in tandem on both sides of the Atlantic, but tort law came into its own in America.[85] Though we think of tort law as a major branch of law in eighteenth-century England, if not earlier, that is not the case. Tort law existed, to be sure, but as Friedman puts it, negligence was "the merest dot on the law" and all of torts "totally insignificant," a "twig" rather than a fully developed branch of law.[86] Not a single treatise about tort law was published in America until 1859.[87]

It was the Industrial Revolution that caused torts to develop into a full and rich body of law. In significant part, tort law flowed from creation of the transcontinental railroad system. This was a project gargantuan in both scope and effect. In 1840, a total of three thousand miles of railroad track had been laid throughout America—a prodigious amount, considering that a total of eighteen hundred miles of track had been laid throughout all of Europe.[88] Within the next twenty years, a total of thirty thousand miles was laid as companies raced to complete the first rail system crossing America. The Union Pacific and Central Pacific railroads won when they connected their tracks at Ogden, Utah, in 1869. By 1885, there were at least four routes running from one coast to the other; by 1890, the United States had a railway system consisting of 199,876 miles of track.

In their haste to lay track—the companies received substantial federal loans for each mile of track laid—the railroads threw safety to the winds. Everything was sacrificed to economy and efficiency. Rather than invest in automatic air brakes, the railroads used manual systems that required brakemen to turn wheels while standing on the tops of speeding railway cars. To limit crew size, brakemen were made responsible for brakes on as many as six cars, requiring them to rush from car roof to car roof, sometimes in snow or driving rain. Many fell to their deaths.

Air brakes were but one of many areas in which the railroads sacrificed safety. Railroads used a cheap but equally dangerous coupling system and successfully resisted most legislative attempts to require automatic coupling systems. Safety was further compromised by workers being bone tired. Trainmen normally worked fifteen to twenty hours a day.

These factors combined to create horrific levels of carnage. In just a single year (June 1888 to June 1889), 1,972 railway men were killed and 20,028 were injured on the job. This means that in this twelve-month period alone, more than 3 percent of all of the 704,443 men working for the railroads were killed or injured.[89] And things got worse. By 1916, more than 10 percent of American railroad workers were injured annually.[90] This rate of mayhem was by no means inherent in railroad operations; the accident rates of American railroad workers were orders of magnitude higher than their European counterparts.

The railroads had become too large and powerful to be regulated by state governments. Legislators introduced bills that would have required railroads to install automatic air brakes, but the railroads—arguing that automatic brakes were too expensive or not yet perfected, or that railroad executives knew more about running railroads than did legislatures—successfully lobbied against most of these measures. When, in 1873, Michigan enacted legislation requiring air brakes, most companies ignored it.

Legislative efforts to require an eight-hour workday were somewhat more successful. A number of states enacted such legislation—but to little avail. A 1867 letter by the president of the Illinois Central to a director of the company illustrates the attitude of the railroads toward state regulation. The Illinois legislature had passed a bill "hurriedly and without our knowledge limiting the hours of labor to eight per day," wrote the president. Fortunately, the company was able to appeal to a higher authority: the railroads themselves. "The companys leading into this city have all decided to employ the men by the hour working ten hours a day," declared Illinois Central's president.[91]

The railroads wielded enormous power at the federal level as well. In 1884 they defeated federal legislation that would have prohibited railroad workers from working more than twelve consecutive hours in a twenty-four-hour period. It was not until 1907 that federal legislation restricting working hours for railroad employees was enacted, and even then the limit imposed was sixteen consecutive hours per twenty-four-hour period.

In the early stages of the rail system, the courts were extremely deferential to the railroads. Chief Justice Lemuel Shaw of the Massachusetts Supreme Court—a figure of sufficient stature to be called "the founder of an American system of law"[92]—fashioned new legal concepts that benefited the developing railroad system, including the ideas and phrases "eminent domain" and "public utility."

Shaw also shielded railroads—and other emerging industries—from personal injury actions by their workers. In 1837, switchmen working for the Boston and Worcester Rail Road Corporation made a mistake that caused a train to fall off the tracks. An engineer named Nicholas Farwell was thrown from the train, and his right hand was run over and destroyed by the wheels of a railroad car.[93] Farwell sued the railroad, arguing that he had been injured by its negligence. "It is laid down by Blackstone," wrote Shaw, "that if a servant, by his negligence, does any damages to a stranger, the master shall be answerable for his neglect." Should the same rule apply when the injured party was an employee rather than a third person? Shaw and his court decided it should not. "The general rule, resulting from considerations as well of justice as of policy, is, that he who engages in the employment of another for performance of the specified duties and services, for compensation, takes upon himself the natural and ordinary risks and perils incident to the performance of such services," he wrote. The employee knows the risks at least as well as the employer, and it is therefore up to the employer and employee to allocate risk of injury as they see fit, in compensation or otherwise. And Farwell, in fact, had a higher salary as an engineer than he had received in his prior job as railroad machinist.

"If we look from considerations of justice to those of policy," wrote Shaw, "they will strongly lead to the same conclusion." Sounding very much like a member of the modern law-and-economics movement, Shaw wrote:

Where several persons are employed in the conduct of a common enterprise or undertaking, and the safety of each depends much on the care
and skill which each other shall perform his appropriate duty, each is an
observer of the conduct of the others, can give notice of any misconduct,
incapacity or neglect of duty, and leave the service, if the common employer will not take such precautions, and employ such agents as the
safety of the whole party may require. By these means, the safety of each
will be much more effectually secured, than could be done by a resort to
the common employer for indemnity in case of loss by the negligence of
each other.[94]

This is a famous case for two reasons.[95] First, it is a quintessential
example of Shaw's policy-oriented approach to the common law. Shaw
derived the fellow-servant rule not from precedent but from public policy, contending it was beneficial because it would result in fewer accidents than the alternative of making employers liable for the negligence
of their employees. Daniel J. Boorstin states that Shaw's "common law
approach was to become a whole philosophy," that of American pragmatism.[96] Second, *Farwell* is considered the seminal case of the fellow-
servant rule, which barred workers from suing their employers if they
had been injured as a result of the negligence of a coemployee—a doctrine that insulated employers from the vast majority of work-related
injuries to their employees. Shaw did not originate the fellow-servant
rule. It previously had appeared in two court decisions, one from England and the other from South Carolina. Those cases, however, were
less than clear, and it was Shaw's decision in *Farwell* that most American courts adopted. Indeed, the only state supreme court to reject the
fellow-servant rule was Wisconsin's, which maintained that the risks of
accidents could be most effectively reduced by employers.[97]

It is not possible to know whether Shaw truly believed workers such
as Farwell could readily leave a dangerous job and find safer work elsewhere or that they could command wages sufficient to compensate
them for risk, or—most significant—whether Shaw believed that making workers, rather than the company, legally responsible for injuries
would create the greater pressure for safety. From the modern perspective, these views sound naive. Nevertheless, the point remains that
Shaw justified doctrine in terms of public policy.

Of course, there may have been an unarticulated policy consideration at work as well. Historians who have studied the full body of
Shaw's work (and a prodigious body of work it is; Shaw wrote twenty-

two hundred judicial opinions) conclude that Shaw was not anti-labor. He was, however, one of the early visionaries who believed that the growing rail system was crucial to the nation's commercial and cultural development.[98] Though Shaw wrote *Farwell* only eight years after the first railroad began operation in Massachusetts, railroad "futurists" such as Dr. Hartwell Carver of New York and former Missouri governor Lillburn W. Boggs were already advocating public support for a transcontinental railroad.[99] In short order, public support of the railroads became national policy, and the nation munificently subsidized the development of the rail system in a number of ways. Through the power of eminent domain (created by Shaw), railroads were granted vast amounts of land. "No other corporations in human history have been endowed in such a profligate manner by a paternal government," observes Paul Johnson.[100] Railroads were also given charters, special banking privileges, tax exemptions, bond loans, and monopoly protections. Questions were raised as to what extent the railroads bought these privileges with unsavory practices, such as giving legislators free railroad passes. Yet the policies were generally popular.[101] The social costs of developing a rail system were great, but the social benefits were perceived to be greater.

The workers, therefore, constituted another subsidy. It is not clear whether the rail system could have been developed if this emerging industry had been financially responsible for worker injuries. It may have been neither fair nor just to make the workers and their families pay— with their lives and mangled bodies—a significant share of the cost of building the railroads; but from a cold-blooded point of view, it may have been necessary. And to be fair, the courts may have adopted the fellow-servant rule before the full enormity of the worker injuries could have been foreseen.

After the transcontinental rail system was complete and railroads had become mature operations, the fellow-servant rule fell into disfavor. Courts created a variety of exceptions to the rule. In 1884 the United States Supreme Court (which then wrote federal common law) fashioned an exception large enough to swallow most of the fellow-servant rule.[102] In the case before the Court, the plaintiff, an engineer on a freight train, was injured when his train collided with a gravel train coming in the opposite direction on the same tracks. The accident resulted from the negligence of the conductors on the two trains. The conductor on the plaintiff's freight train received—but neglected to pass on to the plaintiff—a telegram advising that a gravel train would be coming in the opposite direction and instructing the freight train to wait at South Minneapolis station until the gravel train had passed. Meanwhile, the conductor on the gravel train allowed his train to be so overloaded that the train stalled. He had to detach six cars, leave them on the tracks while he pulled the other six cars to an intermediate station, and then return to fetch them. But for this delay, the gravel train would have reached its destination before the freight train began its run. Had either of the conductors not been negligent, therefore, the accident would have been avoided.

The district court refused to dismiss the plaintiff's action on the basis of the fellow-servant doctrine. The trial judge instructed the jurors that if they found that the conductor on the freight train was the plaintiff's superior within the company hierarchy, then the fellow-servant rule did not apply. That the trial judge even gave this instruction itself illustrates that the courts were looking for ways around the fellow-servant rule. The jury found for the plaintiff. In a five-to-four decision, the Supreme Court affirmed. Its opinion quoted the following language from a treatise on negligence:

> It has sometimes been said that a corporation is obliged to act always by servants, and that it is unjust to impute to it personal negligence in cases where it is impossible for it be negligent personally. But if this be true it would relieve corporations from all liability to servants. The true view is, that, as corporations can act only through superintending officers, the negligence of those officers, with respect to other servants, are [sic] the negligence of the corporation.[103]

The Supreme Court's decision was quickly applauded by commentators. A treatise published just three years later noted that sixteen states had already followed the Supreme Court's new rule and predicted that others would probably follow suit.[104]

In 1893, the United States Supreme Court had something of a change of heart and reinterpreted and limited its prior decision. The Court declared that the plaintiff could not escape the fellow-servant rule by showing he was injured as the result of the negligence of any employee occupying a superior position within the company. "[T]he various employes of one of these large corporations are not graded like steps in a staircase, those on each step being as to those on the step below in the relation of masters and not of fellow-servants," wrote the

Court.[105] Rather, a company was vicariously responsible only for the negligence of employees to whom it had given "entire and absolute control" of a separate branch or department of the company. Indeed, noted the Court, its earlier decision was by the slimmest of margins because four members of the Court did not think a train conductor, although in charge of a train, rose to the level of superintendent of a corporate department.

The Supreme Court's interpretation of the fellow-servant rule applied only to actions brought in the federal courts, however. Many state courts rejected the Court's reinterpretation and created alternative doctrines under which employers were vicariously liable for the negligence of any employee whose duties related in some fashion to plaintiffs' safety.[106] The shield of the fellow-servant rule had been permanently cracked, and an ambivalent Supreme Court could no more repair it than the king's men could put Humpty Dumpty back togther. Times had changed. What had been nascent industries just half a century earlier were now titans. Society and courts were distressed by the number of workers losing limbs and worse. Justice Shaw's expressed rationale for the fellow-servant rule—that workers were compensated for risk—was no longer taken seriously. A student editor of the *Harvard Law Review* did not hesitate to declare that "the old economic theory is at variance with the facts, that the workman even in very dangerous employments—like mining—does not receive extraordinary compensation, that the amount of the risk does not appear in the price of the articles produced, and that the burden of a casualty if placed primarily on the workman is borne by his dependents or by charitable neighbors or by public charities, and is eventually in one way or another thrust indirectly upon the public,—the general public, not the public peculiarly benefited as consumers or the like by the production of the goods representing among other things the work of the person injured or imperilled."[107] A political slogan put the same thought more succinctly: "The cost of the product should bear the blood of the workman."[108]

The railroads were not the only industry whose workers paid the price of development. The accident rate for coal miners exceeded that of railway workers, and in 1906, 46 men were killed and 598 injured in a single United States Steel plant in Chicago.[109] With its common law shields against worker litigation disintegrating, industry now looked to the legislatures for help. What many leaders of big business advocated was a worker's compensation system similar to those recently enacted in Germany and England. Under such a system, workers would be entitled to compensation for all work-related injuries, regardless of fault and without having to litigate in the courts. The compensation they would receive for injuries, however, would be considerably less than they might normally receive through the tort system.

At first the American Federation of Labor (AFL) opposed worker's compensation legislation, preferring the increasingly liberal tort system.[110] Though two decades old and boasting a membership of 2 million, the AFL was not yet able to stand toe to toe with big business in the halls of Congress and the statehouses. After Congress enacted a weak worker's compensation program for federal employees in 1908, Samuel Gompers, the AFL's charismatic leader, recognized that labor had to settle for trying to influence inevitable legislation in the states as best it could. A model state worker's compensation program was drafted by the National Civic Federation. Although the federation purported to be an association of leaders from business, labor, and the public sector, and although its board included union leaders (Gompers among them), it was nevertheless effectively controlled by big business.

In May 1910, the federation informally distributed its proposal—one modest enough that even conservative P. Tecumseh Sherman, who chaired the drafting committee, described it as "a half-way measure."[111] The proposal gained political momentum when Theodore Roosevelt endorsed state worker's compensation legislation in a speech at the federation's annual meeting in January 1911. By the end of the year, twelve states had passed worker's compensation acts, and within ten years, every state had done so.

Not all business leaders supported worker's compensation. The most reactionary denounced the concept as radical or socialist. Conversely, those in business who supported it portrayed it as a progressive social program designed to benefit workers. These business leaders not only would make the proposal more politically palatable but also would help convince workers that employers did, in fact, care about workers—making unions unnecessary. Though often hailed as progressive legislation and the beginning of the welfare state, historian Michael B. Katz concludes that, on the whole, "the worker's compensation laws reflected business interests."[112]

Actions against employers by injured workers lived *en masse* within the tort system only briefly. At the beginning of the Industrial Revolution, the courts closed their doors to injured workers in order to protect the developing industries. When the courts opened their doors, the legislatures—at the behest of business—directed injured workers into an alternative system. Nevertheless, litigation by injured workers played an important role in the development of the American tort system. For the first time in history, the courts, notwithstanding their ambivalence, had begun to open their doors to common folk. With the assistance of entrepreneurial lawyers, people without significant education, social standing, or financial resources—people unable to protect themselves through the political process—turned the common law into an instrument of social policy.

Previously, the common law system had existed to dispense justice in individual cases. One man struck another, and the offended individual struck back not with a fist but with an assault-and-battery action in court. One individual insisted on walking through another's front yard on his way to town every morning, and the offended individual stopped him not with force but with a trespass action in court. This adjudicatory function was critical to civilized society. Now something else was at work as well. The Industrial Revolution saw the birth of business enterprises with wealth and political influence previously unknown. These enterprises mass-produced goods—but mass-produced injuries as well. It was neither the market system nor, on its own initiative, the legislative system that forced improvements in safer workplaces for railroad workers, mine workers, and factory workers. It was the common law system. The common law was no longer merely a system for adjudicating individual disputes; it had become a regulatory mechanism.

Perhaps the courts functioned imperfectly at best. One may argue that the courts should not have insulated industry from worker injury. Reasonable minds may differ, however; it may be argued either that the half century of protection was socially necessary or that it was a terrible injustice (or both). Whether one considers worker compensation a progressive system or a mechanism of exploitation, the common law was the catalyst for at least this measure of compensation, with its attendant pressures for improving worker safety.

The story of early railroads demonstrates the regulatory role of the common law. There are, and are always likely to be, professions and industries that for one reason or another cannot be adequately regulated by the political branches of government. For example, because of its special place in our democracy and protections guaranteed by the

First Amendment, the press is relatively unconstrained by legislative or administrative regulation. Yet those who have been defamed, subjected to an unwarranted invasion of privacy, or otherwise injured by improper conduct of the media—such as through publication of a help-wanted ad for a contract killer, to name but one example—may seek redress in the courts. The courts must evaluate whether the conduct is protected by the First Amendment, and the courts have protected democracy by defining freedom of the press broadly. Nevertheless, when people are injured as a result of conduct by the press that falls outside the scope of constitutional protection, it is the common law that holds the press accountable.

It is the tort system, therefore, that provides the only meaningful regulation of the press. The occasional lawsuit sustains a continuing concern about being sued, and it is this concern that exerts a form of regulation. Sometimes the concern is exaggerated and may make the press too timid. Sometimes, when the system wrestles with controversial issues, one jury might impose liability where others would not. When investigative reporters for ABC television lied on employment applications to get jobs at Food Lion and to surreptitiously film unsanitary practices by the supermarket, a North Carolina jury found ABC had committed fraud and trespass and awarded Food Lion more than $5 million in punitive damages.[113] The widely publicized verdict stimulated a national discussion about news-gathering techniques and whether journalists are ever justified in lying to obtain information. The case will both appropriately give editors and producers pause when pursuing future stories and unduly chill some journalistic investigations. (As is often the case, the verdict was better reported than either the trial judge's decision to reduce the punitive award to $315,000 or the court of appeals' decision to eliminate the punitive award altogether.) But without litigation, the press would be answerable to itself alone.

Similarly, the practices of law and of medicine are largely free from government regulation. Lawyers and doctors are ever mindful of the possibility of malpractice actions—with ramifications that are not uniformly beneficial. Doctors often exaggerate the prospects of being sued and, worse, practice "defensive medicine" by ordering unwarranted tests or performing unnecessary procedures. (The best medicine against malpractice is practicing good medicine and keeping good records.) Malpractice actions may not be an unmixed blessing, but on balance, most of us would rather be treated by doctors and hospitals—or patronize lawyers, architects, engineers, builders, real estate agents, stock brokers, used-car dealers, and airlines—who know litigation exists.

The single greatest development of the common law during the twentieth century has been the creation of a new area of law known as products liability. Now only forty years old, products liability has saved countless lives. It has brought critical information to light, forced manufacturers to make products safer, and driven off the market unreasonably dangerous products when regulatory agencies or Congress lacked the political will to do so. It has made America safer. It has also represented an indignity to corporate behemoths, which are intent on stamping it out. This dramatic story will be told in two parts. Chapter 6 deals with something of a mystery: Great progress has been made in the field of automobile safety, but why? It may seem at first blush that much of credit belongs to federal regulation—Congress created an agency to regulate auto safety in 1966—but a closer examination suggests something quite different. Indeed, the story of auto safety reveals a great deal not only about regulation by administrative agencies and courts but about American democracy at the dawn of the twenty-first century. Chapter 7 focuses more narrowly on products liability law. There have, I argue, already been two successful revolutions in the field of products liability. Now we are on the verge of a third revolution—a revolution that is not well understood but lies at the root of highly visible litigation over tobacco and guns, with great public policy ramifications.

6

Who Regulates Auto Safety?

Administrative versus Common Law Regulation

My principal claim in this book—that lawsuits are good for America because the common law serves an essential regulatory function—will strike some as outdated. After all, since the New Deal we have been accustomed to thinking of the regulation of commercial activity to be, quite necessarily, the province of administrative agencies. We can eat in a restaurant confident in the knowledge that it is periodically inspected and licensed by local regulators, that it serves milk that comes from a dairy supervised by state regulators and meat that is approved by the United States Department of Agriculture (USDA). We rely on state and local agencies to regulate not only restaurants but hospitals, pharmacies, gas stations, elevators, bus and taxi companies, insurance companies, amusement rides, barber shops, and building construction. At the federal level, we rely on the FAA to regulate air travel, on the FDA to regulate pharmaceuticals, on OSHA to regulate workplace safety, on the EPA and state environmental agencies to regulate facilities that discharge pollutants into our air and water. These are but a few examples of the myriad commercial activities regulated by government agencies.

I do not argue that administrative regulation is not essential. Quite the contrary; administrative agencies are and must be the principal instruments of regulation in the modern state. The question is whether the common law plays a role too, and if so, what that role is.

At first blush the common law seems ill equipped for regulating complex commercial activity. What role can this antediluvian system play in the modern world? Perhaps it is still useful for resolving disputes between individuals, but regulation is another matter. A regulatory scheme requires central planning. It must be devised by experts, mandated by legislatures, and operated by bureaucracies possessing special expertise. The common law, however, has no central brain, no planning mechanism. It is a messy system. Indeed, perhaps it is too much to call it a system at all if, as the dictionary says, a system is "an assemblage or combination of things or parts forming a complex or unitary whole."[1] The common law seems more like a series of events that are never assembled or combined in a coherent whole. Someone injured with an allegedly dangerous product sues the manufacturer. The court decides the plaintiff has a valid cause of action, and the jury decides in the plaintiff's favor. A second injured party files a nearly identical case in the same court against the same manufacturer; but a different jury, which is told nothing of the first case, decides in the defendant's favor. Meanwhile, a court in a different state decides there is no cause of action at all and that cases involving this particular product should be dismissed without trial. This seems more like chaos than a system.

Manufacturers complain that the common law leaves them both confused and abused. A federal agency with statutory regulatory authority tells manufacturers their products must meet certain standards. A manufacturer designs its products to meet those standards, but then some court says it is not enough; the product is unreasonably dangerous because it does not exceed those standards in some fashion. Even worse, a manufacturer may even be blamed for following the legally mandated standards. In one case, for example, a woman fell and was injured when the escalator she was riding at a shopping mall came to a sudden stop because an unidentified child pushed the emergency stop button.[2] The woman sued the manufacturer of the escalator. Her theory was that the emergency button, located near the floor at the base of the escalator, was too attractive to kids. An experimental psychologist testified the button was an especially bright red, brighter than most other emergency buttons and unusually attractive to young children. The button also required very little pressure, making it easy for a small child to depress.

But the escalator manufacturer had designed its product to conform to legally established standards. Many municipalities (and presumably the one in which this mall was located) have building codes that require builders to meet standards set by the American National Standards Institute (ANSI). Standards promulgated by ANSI's Elevator and Escalator Committee required escalators to have a "red stop button . . . visibly located at the top and bottom landing on the right side facing the escalator." The buttons must be placed below the handrail and within a few inches of the floor and be "covered with a transparent cover which can be readily lifted or pushed aside." If the manufacturer had engaged psychologists who had advised that yellow buttons were just as visible to adults in emergency situations and far less attractive to young children and had therefore provided yellow rather than red buttons, it would have been out of compliance with ANSI standards, and the escalator would not have been approved by the building inspector. The manufacturer must also have thought: Had we colored the button a duller red and required that more force be necessary to depress it, and then an incident occurred in which someone got caught in the metal grate and yelled for help, and there was a moment's delay because a bystander did not immediately locate the button or successfully activate it on her first attempt, we would have been sued because the button was not exactly as it was in the real case.

There is more to say about both this case and escalators, and I return to them at the end of this chapter. At this point, however, the case illustrates the issue of administrative versus common law regulation. Designing something as simple as an emergency stop button is complicated and necessarily requires trade-offs. The button probably cannot be both maximally conspicuous to adults in emergencies and minimally enticing to small children. Who should make these decisions—experts or juries? That is, in fact, just how the court itself saw it. One judge referred to it as a "burlesque" of modern products liability law. "Why should escalator design be a question for juries?" he asked. "No one supposes that courts would design escalators well, even with the help of many experts, if given the task. Why then ask them to identify defects after the fact?"[3]

In this chapter, I try to answer that question. I have chosen to examine the issue of administrative versus common law regulation within the context of automobile safety for a number of reasons. Automobiles are both ubiquitous and dangerous consumer products. Automobile accidents kill more than forty thousand Americans annually and injure something like ten times that number, making them far and away the most frequent cause of accidental death and a leading cause of all deaths in the United States. Automobile cases comprise one of the largest categories of products liability litigation. So automobile products liability litigation is important in its own right, even if it were to tell us little about other categories of cases.

But automobile cases serve as a useful example of other types of cases, too. Like many products in a world of advancing technology, automobile design is complex and requires trade-offs between safety and other considerations. Indeed, this is arguably just the kind of product that should be designed by experts and regulated by an administrative agency with special expertise, rather than by judges and juries untrained in engineering. And automobile safety is, in fact, regulated by a federal agency.

Or is it? Another reason to examine auto safety is that it presents something of mystery. We have a long way to go—death or serious injury on the highway remains a disturbingly high prospect for all of us—but cars are far safer than ever before. The progress, in fact, has been extraordinary.

The Stunning Improvement in Auto Safety

In 1970, 54,633 Americans were killed in motor vehicle accidents. The resident U.S. population was then 203 million. Twenty-five years later, the population had grown by 28 percent and stood at slightly more than 260 million. During the same period, the number of motor vehicles in the United States had increased by 86 percent. Yet, amazingly, the number of motor vehicle fatalities had not increased over this period. It had fallen. In 1995, 43,363 Americans were killed in motor vehicle accidents—a drop of about 21 percent over the twenty-five-year period.

The drop in the motor vehicle deaths over the past fifty years has been nothing short of spectacular. There are many ways to consider the data—in terms of raw numbers, deaths per population, or deaths per number of registered motor vehicles, for example—but the most useful measure is deaths per vehicle miles traveled. This yardstick properly accounts for some potentially confounding effects, such as Americans driving less during the gas crisis in the 1970s. The graph below, which displays in five year increments the motor vehicle death rate per 100 million motor vehicles traveled, displays just how dramatic improvements in auto safety have been.

In 1997, the latest figures available at this writing, the rate had fallen another tenth of a point to 1.6 deaths per 100 million miles traveled. Much work remains, to be sure. The motor vehicle fatality rate is still thirty-two times greater than the commercial aviation death rate, which currently stands at 0.05 deaths per 100 million passenger miles.[4]

Death Rate per 100 Million Vehicle Miles

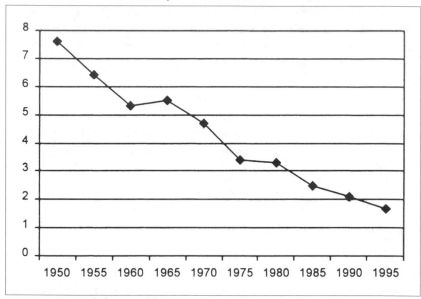

S O U R C E : *Statistical Abstracts of the U.S.* (1998 no. 1041; 1990 no. 1035; 1970 no. 856)

Nevertheless, the automobile fatality rate has fallen so far over the past fifty years, one cannot help but do a double take. The rate has been cut by 79 percent. But how much of an influence in this development was the common law, and products liability specifically?

A number of factors contributed to this dramatic increase in auto safety. Road improvements were one of the first contributors, starting with the development of the interstate highway system in 1956. Another factor was the national 55 mph speed limit, which Congress established in 1974 to save gasoline.[5] Despite data showing that it saved lives, Congress partially abrogated the national 55 mph limit in 1987 and repealed it entirely in 1995. (Hawaii is the only state retaining a 55 mph limit.) Whether the speed limit saved lives—and if so, how many—during the eleven-year period it remained in full or partial effect is a matter of hot dispute. Opponents of the limit have made much of the fatality rate continuing to fall after the limit was abrogated, but that does not tell us much, since the rate may have fallen further if it had remained in effect. A preliminary study by NHTSA suggested that the fatality rate may have risen by 9 percent when states reverted back to a 65 mph limit, and a 1999 study by the Insurance Institute of Highway Safety showed a 15 percent increase. But studies have gone both ways. There are so many variables that it is difficult to ascertain the effect with certainty. We do know, however, that the national limit had a pronounced effect on how fast people drove. In 1970, 44 percent of cars on interstate highways traveled faster than 65 mph; by 1980, that figure had fallen to 7 percent. The effect appears to be wearing off. The latest available figure (1993) is 24 percent. Because speed makes a difference in both reaction and stopping time, it is reasonable to assume that the national 55 mph speed limit did have a positive effect. Still, one must look elsewhere to explain the lion's share of the drop in the motor vehicle death rate.

A more significant factor has been the war against drunk driving.[6] This has been a four-pronged campaign involving legislation, enforcement, public attitudes, and common law litigation. One of the key issues on the legislative front involves the minimum drinking age. In the 1970s, thirty states lowered their legal purchase age from the traditional age of twenty-one to, most frequently, eighteen years of age. In 1984, Congress—lobbied hard by Mothers Against Drunk Driving (MADD), which had been formed four years earlier—enacted legislation requiring states to restore the twenty-one age limit as a condition of obtaining federal highway funds. All states complied, and over the following ten-year period the percentage of drivers aged sixteen to twenty who were involved in fatal automobile accidents and had a blood alcohol content of .10 percent or greater declined 47 percent. Current battles on the legislative front involve efforts to lower the blood alcohol limit to .08 percent. So far, fifteen states have done so, but MADD and its allies are encountering tough resistence in the remaining states.

MADD and its allies also have had mixed success in pushing law enforcement agencies to be more aggressive in apprehending, prosecuting, and jailing drunk drivers. Surprisingly, the most effective prong has probably been the effort to modify public attitudes. In 1986, Jay Winsten and colleagues at the Harvard School of Public Health met with 250 television writers and producers and asked them to help promote the new concept of "designated driver." The result was that the phrase was favorably mentioned in 160 prime-time shows over four television seasons, including in episodes of *Cheers, LA Law,* and *The Cosby Show.* In some episodes the term was spoken in a single line of dialogue, but in others it was a prominent feature of the plot. The term continues to appear in about a half dozen shows a season. The term *designated driver*—virtually unknown in the United States prior to this effort—has become part of the lexicon.

Common law litigation also played an important part in the war against drunk drinking. In the 1940s and 1950s, American courts began to allow "dram shop" litigation, that is, lawsuits against taverns and other commercial establishments that served alcohol to patrons who drove away drunk and injured an innocent party. Dram shop litigation grew exponentially in the 1970s along with the growing concern about highway fatalities. By 1985, courts in twenty-two states had recognized such actions, and legislatures in fourteen other states created such causes of action by statute. While most states allowed dram shop actions only against commercial establishments, a few states began recognizing liability against social hosts as well. Today a majority of states have dram shop statutes, although some have been enacted at the behest of the beverage industry and are subtly designed to make lawsuits more difficult.

Nevertheless, dram shop litigation made strong contributions to the fight against drunk driving, and thus to auto safety. First, it pressured insurance companies to require their tavern clients to train bartenders in techniques that would discourage patrons from becoming intoxicated and in helping patrons find other ways home. Second, it has both strengthened the stigma associated with drunk driving and helped create a secondary level of shame for others who fail to intervene when someone is about to drive drunk. Indeed, helping mold social mores is one of the things the common law does best. In masculine culture, at least, drinking and driving was acceptable, even macho, provided you could "hold your liquor" and not get caught. James Bond never had a designated driver. And even in their own minds, people who served alcohol took no responsibility for a drinker's conduct. Many were probably outraged at being sued. But when judges rule that plaintiffs have valid causes of action and juries hand up verdicts, in a very real sense the community has spoken.

The war against drunk driving has had a marked effect. The percentage of drivers who have been involved in fatal automobile accidents and had a blood alcohol content exceeding .10 percent has declined from nearly 26 percent in 1985 to about 19 percent in 1995. Nevertheless, the combined factors mentioned so far—better highways, the national speed limit, and the war against drunk driving—cannot collectively account for the lion's share of the drop in the death rate.

One of the most telling statistics is that motor vehicle *accidents* have not decreased at anything resembling the decrease in *fatalities*. In other words, there are fewer accidents but far fewer fatalities. There are only two possible explanations for this phenomenon. One is improvements in critical care. Although advances in trauma care have undoubtedly improved the automobile accident survival rate, the evidence that this is responsible for dramatic improvements is weak.[7] The other is improvements in crashworthiness of the vehicles themselves.

Here, finally, is a something of sufficient magnitude to explain the stunning decline in deaths on the highway.[8] The auto industry was almost completely unconcerned with safety. In 1965, the president of General Motors (GM) told Congress the company contributed $1 million for external accident research. It was a paltry sum, representing well under one-thousandth of GM's annual profit; moreover, the million dollars was supposed to cover a four-year project. The entire American auto industry spent an estimated $2 million annually on their own internal research and development relating to crash safety. "Safety doesn't sell," Lee Iacocca is reported to have said. The changes have been gargantuan. But how many of the improvements in auto safety have come from products liability litigation, and how many from administrative regulation?

Administrative Regulation

This will forever remain a mystery. It is impossible to unravel the individual causal factors, because three things happened simultaneously. First, as previously discussed, products liability came into being in the mid-1960s. It was included in the *Restatement (Second) of Torts* in 1964 and adopted by various courts throughout the decade. Second, in 1964, car safety and crashworthiness came to public awareness with publication of Ralph Nader's *Unsafe at Any Speed: The Designed-in Dangers of the American Automobile*. Nader received white-hot publicity the next year, when Senate hearings revealed that General Motors had hired detectives to spy on Nader in order to find out "whether he belonged to left-wing organizations, whether he was anti-Semitic, whether he was an odd-ball, whether he liked boys instead of girls," in order to discredit him.[9] This event seized public interest and propelled not only Nader and his book but, really for the first time, auto safety into public consciousness. And third, in 1966 Congress created a federal agency to promote traffic safety, the agency now called the National Highway Traffic Safety Administration (NHTSA). Incidentally, the same year the Great Society Congress established three other important regulatory agencies—the Consumer Product Safety Commission (CPSC), the Environmental Protection Agency (EPA), and the Occupational Safety and Health Administration (OSHA).

During its first eight years, NHTSA issued forty-five standards dealing with seat belts, fuel tanks, steering assemblies (which were to absorb energy in a crash and not skewer the driver in a collision), brakes, windshield wipers, and a host of other areas relating to safety engineering. Knowledgeable commentators report that this was not the dynamic agenda it appears, however. Many of the standards were preexisting in the sense that they had been previously established by federal agencies (in connection with government purchasing of cars), state and foreign governments, and organizations such as the National Bureau of Standards. In 1970, the National Commission on Product Safety concluded that only five of NHTSA's most recent thirteen standards were of even "moderate significance." Jerry L. Mashaw and David L. Harfst write that "this heyday of rulemaking was largely a testament to modest ambitions."[10]

Others disagree. Joan Claybrook, who was administrator of NHTSA from 1977 to 1981, argues that NHTSA standards mandating combined shoulder and lap belts and relating to steering assemblies, side-impact protection, head restraints, fuel system integrity, and other areas save more than one hundred thousand lives a year. But, amazingly, NHTSA largely stopped setting safety standards: it issued a total of forty-three standards from 1967 to 1972 but only two in 1973 and none in 1974. NHTSA's main focus turned to requiring manufacturers recall cars for safety corrections. Indeed, by the end of the 1980s, more cars were being recalled than manufactured. This was relatively small potatoes for the cause of auto safety, so much so that Mashaw and Harfst characterize NHTSA's shift from standard setting to recalls as "the abandonment of its safety mission."[11] Some knowledgeable observers believe that the NHTSA recall program withered as well.

What happened?

During the 1960s and 1970s, there was much concern about administrative agencies being "captured" by the industries they regulate. One tool of capture is information. Information is power, and most agencies are heavily dependent on regulated companies for information about research, product design, and accident experience. Another tool is staff relationships. Agency staff often become too cozy with their industry counterparts. Some come from industry and remain friendly with people in regulated companies; some try to ingratiate themselves with businesses in the hope of moving into the private sector. Or at least, these were the concerns. In fact, as was typical of agencies formed during the same time, Congress placed NHTSA under the direction of a single administrator rather than a commission to reduce opportunities for capture. Congress, the president, and the courts—which were considered less susceptible to capture—would have to remain vigilant to ensure agencies served the public interest.

Some observers believe that NHTSA has, in fact, suffered from these dynamics. A disturbingly high number of NHTSA managers, engineers, and lawyers have wound up employed by the automobile industry and by law firms that represent or lobby for the industry. At least two administrators and four chief counsels were subsequently employed by industry. Capture may be the least of NHTSA's problems, however. Its weaknesses have at least as much to do with being exhausted, starved, beleaguered, demoralized, and distrusted as with being captured. When it attempts to establish standards, NHTSA inevitably finds itself hammered from many sides.

First come the blows from industry. Auto manufacturers submit lengthy, detailed objections, forcing agency engineers to go through the exercise of defending their proposals from a plethora of complaints: the proposal is technically flawed, not technologically possible, not the best approach, not cost justified—and besides, NHTSA made a procedural glitch and must start the proposal process over again. Industry's armies of engineers, economists, and lawyers always outnumber agency personnel. NHTSA technicians must persuade agency managers at several levels that the industry objections are wrong. Then, if they are successful internally but government lawyers fail in court and the standard is overturned, agency managers feel publicly embarrassed and resentful.

And in fact, losing in court is commonplace. Courts ruled against NHTSA in half of the first dozen rulemaking cases that came before them. NHTSA is by no means unique. Starting in 1967, courts became increasingly rigorous in reviewing actions by administrative agencies and more ready to second-guess agency decision making. Thomas W. Merrill writes that "the period roughly 1967 to 1983 was characterized by widespread disillusionment with agencies, focusing in particular on the problem of capture."[12]

Although, according to Merrill, a new period began in 1983, it did not bring administrative agencies greater respect. Things got worse. The disillusionment with government regulation became deeper and more pervasive. Merrill relates this to the ascendency of public choice theory. Public choice theory holds that all actors in the political realm—not merely administrative agencies but also Congress, the president, even the courts—seek to maximize their self-interest by catering to various constituencies. Government is not a place where rational policymakers try to promote the public interest; rather, it is a bazaar where diverse groups maneuver to promote their individual interests, and where government officials promote *their* own interests by catering to their patrons. There is no point in trying to determine whether the Congress, administrative agencies, or courts ought to make particular decisions, since none of the actors are disinterested servants of the public interest. Rather, public choice theory leads to the conclusion that government should do as little as possible. It is best to let markets remain undisturbed. "In a word, those who have thoroughly assimilated public choice theory analysis tend to be libertarians," writes Merrill.[13]

Merrill may be attributing too much to theory, however. Although courts readily overturn administrative agencies, one wonders if they do so because judges are devotees of capture or public choice theories. What may have been far more influential is something that has been called judicial-centricism, more popularly known as "black robes disease."[14] This is something of a psychological occupational hazard. Men and women put on black robes, sit on elevated benches, are called "Your Honor," watch everyone rise when they enter or leave the courtroom. Law clerks treat them with genuine awe; luminaries of the bar bow and scrape before them. Sometimes savvy litigators exploit black robes disease; and attacking the actions of administrative agencies offers a splendid opportunity for doing so. Distinguished lawyers from large firms, representing great corporations, subtly belittle the work of the agency at issue. With just a touch of ridicule, for example, they lambaste the agency for failing to consider important data. That technique is always available, for no matter how much data an agency considers there will always be other data. Even when the information did not exist, the skillful lawyer can argue that the agency should have created it through research or tests before (so precipitously) proceeding with the rulemaking or recall at issue.

Other arguments can be made with the same effect. In 1971, NHTSA promulgated its famous Standard 208, which required that, however manufacturers elected to achieve it—whether by use of air bags, automatic seat belts, or other means—cars would have to offer a degree of crashworthiness that was defined in terms of what injury-like effects a frontal barrier crash at 30 mph would have on anthropomorphic dummies. This was an incredibly important rule for NHTSA. It inaugurated two new approaches, one substantive and the other procedural. Substantively, NHTSA was making a huge leap by requiring passive protection. That is, occupants had to be protected without their actively protecting themselves. This most directly related to seat belt usage. Cars had seat belts; the problem was that only something like 10 to 15 percent of occupants were buckling them. (Even by 1984, less than 15 percent were buckling up. It was not until 1992 that a bare majority of people used their seat belts. The figure presently stands at 69 percent.)[15] NHTSA's procedural leap was even bigger. NHTSA was making a considered decision to shift to performance-based regulation. That is, rather than specifying what features (e.g., a certain air bag) cars had to have, NHTSA would instead tell manufacturers how cars had to perform. Performance-based regulation would encourage manufacturers to compete to find the most economical, user-friendly way to make cars safer. It would stimulate the research and development of new technologies and the imaginative use of new approaches. Performance-based regulation would also keep both regulator and industry focused on the goals of saving lives and reducing injuries, which was more protective than focusing on whether a manufacturer's specifications matched NHTSA's specifications.

As one might expect for such a critically important piece of rulemaking, NHTSA gave Standard 208 enormous forethought. GM, which had invested more in air bag development than its competitors, announced it expected little difficulty in complying. Chrysler, fearing it might be at a competitive disadvantage, filed a federal court action attacking Standard 208 in myriad ways, large and small. It argued that NHTSA exceeded its statutory authority by requiring passive protection. It argued that the Standard was, in many ways, not practicable, and that NHTSA made numerous procedural errors in promulgating it.

The United States Court of Appeals for the Sixth Circuit upheld NHTSA on the big issues. The court held that Congress empowered NHTSA "to impel automobile manufacturers to develop and apply new technology to the task of improving the safety design of automobiles as readily as possible," and that NHTSA could properly promulgate standards that required the development of new technology.[16] But the court overturned Standard 208 nonetheless. The test dummies were not good enough. In some respects the specifications were not sufficiently detailed, which might allow different dummies that met the standard's specifications but performed differently in the crash test. This meant the standard was not "objective." Although congressional committee reports talked about standards being stated in "objective terms," the National Traffic and Motor Vehicle Safety Act itself did not mention objective standards. So the court created a definition. "Objective, in the context of this case, means that tests to determine compliance must be capable of producing identical results when test conditions are exactly duplicated," it wrote.[17]

One wonders about the wisdom of judges preferring their own views (or those of a regulated entity) about what constitutes a sufficiently described anthropomorphic crash dummy to those of specialists employed by a governmental agency. Even more important, however, is that the court's decision comes close to demanding that rulemaking be perfect. Any imperfection—the failure to sufficiently detail the dynamic spring rate for the dummy's thorax—warrants abrogation of the standard. Can any standard as complex as this be perfect? Would it not have been preferable for the court to hold that if Chrysler constructed dummies in strict compliance with Standard 208 that performed satisfactorily in the prescribed tests, Chrysler should be deemed to have complied with the standard? This is, I fear, an example of judicial-centricism—with judges being seduced by the notion that they are more careful, more analytically rigorous, and just plain smarter than bureaucrats.

The very same phenomenon occurred when the EPA tried to ban asbestos.[18] Asbestos, a natural mineral, is extremely poor at conducting heat and nearly incombustible. Beginning in the late nineteenth century, it was used to insulate boilers, steam pipes, and ovens and later was used in products ranging from hair dryers to brake linings. But asbestos is also extremely carcinogenic, something the industry learned from the experience of its own workers in the 1930s and 1940s but carefully concealed. The truth emerged in research published in 1964.

In fact, asbestos is both so carcinogenic and so omnipresent that, from 1967 to 1997, more than 170,000 Americans died of lung cancer from inhaling asbestos fibers, and an additional 119,000 will die by 2027.

In 1979, the EPA issued a formal notice that it would explore ways to reduce exposure to asbestos. Ten years later, after a laborious process, it issued a rule banning most asbestos-containing products. Based on an expert panel's review of more than one hundred studies, the EPA concluded that asbestos is carcinogenic at all levels of exposure and poses an unreasonable risk to human health. In 1991, however, the United States Court of Appeals for the Fifth Circuit overturned the ban because, it said, "EPA failed to muster substantial evidence to support its rule." The Fifth Circuit's EPA asbestos decision is very much in the same spirit as the Sixth Circuit's NHTSA Standard 208 decision, that is, the court claims to have found something less than perfect in the agency's action. The Fifth Circuit complained, among other things, that the EPA had not considered whether a less than total ban would be preferable. The court does not suggest what this more moderate approach might be. And in fact, any such approach would be impossible, for once asbestos is disbursed in the world, there is no way to stop asbestos fibers from being released into the air over time. Exhausted from a twelve-year process that came to naught, the EPA gave up. As one commentator put it, this episode shows how "a single unsympathetic or confused reviewing court can bring about a dramatic shift in focus or even the complete destruction of an entire regulatory program."[19]

Fortunately, the common law saved the day. Lawyers began filing products liability actions against asbestos manufacturers in 1964, and the more than two hundred thousand cases that have been filed on behalf of workers and others with asbestosis, lung cancer, and mesothelioma have effectively driven asbestos from the market.

The Fifth Circuit's asbestos decision also raises the issue of how politics affects the bench. The court's opinion was written by Circuit Judge Jerry E. Smith, who had been a long-standing member of the executive committee of the Texas Republican Party when Ronald Reagan appointed him to the federal court in 1987. Reagan's judicial appointments were the most ideological in history. What Reagan, and those selecting his judges, valued most in judicial candidates was a commitment to libertarianism. Though in other areas George H. W. Bush's appointments may have been less dyed in the wool, Bush's appointees were also pro-market and pro-business. Bush, for example, appointed a far higher percentage of millionaires to the federal bench than had any president before him.[20] Between them, Reagan and Bush appointed 548 district and appellate judges, 65 percent of the entire federal judiciary. This was a judiciary that respected business executives more than government officials and honored the free market above all else. In short, the judicial playing field had become even more heavily tilted against administrative agencies.

The composition of the federal courts did not change much during the Clinton administration, in part because the Republican-controlled Senate exercised unprecedented control over appointments during the Clinton years. It had long been part of the normal political culture for the Senate, whenever it was controlled by the opposition party, to slow down the process of confirming judicial nominees at the end of a president's term. During the Clinton administration, however, the Republican-controlled Senate took this to new heights. The slowdown was both longer—it occurred not only at the end of Clinton's two terms but throughout most of his presidency—and more extreme than ever before. The Senate went so far as to leave nearly 10 percent of federal court seats vacant for years, prompting Chief Justice William Rehnquist to publicly warn that the quality of justice was endangered. For a time, Senator Orrin G. Hatch, chair of the Senate Judiciary Committee, halted all confirmations until President Clinton acceded to his demand to nominate a Republican political operative and former Hatch aide to the federal bench in Utah. (Clinton finally nominated the operative, who was confirmed in record time, then proceeded to embarrass himself in his first trial by making so glaring an error that both the prosecutor and defense counsel asked for a mistrial.)

Perhaps the most scandalous part of the confirmation struggle was the Republican Senate's resistance to black nominees. Hatch did not even schedule confirmation hearings for two black nominees to the U.S. Court of Appeals for the Fourth Circuit, headquartered in Richmond, Virginia. Although there are more black residents in the Fourth Circuit than in any other, at this writing there has never been a black member of that thirteen-member court. As loathsome as are the racial politics, however, the most significant aspect of the story for our purposes is that, because Clinton had to compromise to move nominees through the Senate, and because Clinton was himself beholden to large contributors, federal judges appointed during the Clinton administration may be as pro-business and skeptical of regulatory agencies as Republican appointees. Clinton's judges are, for example, are heavy on millionaires (40 percent) and lawyers who spent their careers representing businesses in large law firms. In short, Clinton did little to temper the laissez-faire, libertarian, anti-regulatory disposition of the federal courts. This may not change as long as Republicans control either the presidency or the Senate; and because Democrats must raise large sums from the business sector too, it may not significantly change under any circumstances.

It should not be surprising, therefore, that regulatory agencies such as NHTSA suffer from "ossification," a phenomenon that occurs when, in the words of Richard J. Pierce, "agencies avoid rulemaking because of the fear that after years of effort and expenditure of millions of dollars, a rule will be struck down by the courts on judicial review."[21] Agencies experienced ossification well before the Reagan era and the Republican-controlled Senate. This came through in an unusually revealing exchange during oversight hearings in the 1970s, prompting Senator Vance Hartke (D–Ind.) to ask NHTSA's chief counsel: "Isn't it a lot better to get knocked down by the court than to concede before you start?"[22] The one word reply: "No." NHTSA's timidity was also evident in 1991 when, after years of the agency foot-dragging, Congress compelled it to mandate air bags. And because of the changed composition of the federal judiciary, agencies are, quite sensibly, even more gun-shy of litigation today.

Agencies such as NHTSA are also blown hither and yon by shifting political winds. Public choice scholars call this "cycling," by which they mean that agencies are driven around and around as different interests prevail for a period of time, then fall, then prevail again. One example relating to an important issue will suffice. The single most important way to improve crashworthiness is to ensure that vehicle occupants do not smash into the interior of the car in which they are riding—that is, to avoid the "second collision"—and the most effective and economical way to do that is with seat belts. It is no surprise, therefore, that in its first round of rulemaking in 1967, NHTSA required that all cars be equipped with seat belts.

But people were unaccustomed to using seat belts. Some repeatedly forgot to buckle up; some actively resisted doing so. An early study found that only 15 percent of people were using their seat belts. This presented NHTSA with a complex web of problems involving public attitudes, societal values, law enforcement, technology, and politics. Yet no one would have predicted how long and tortuous a road of inconsistency and self-contradiction NHTSA would travel. Repeatedly, NHTSA settled on one approach—ignition interlocks, buzzers, automatic belts, mandatory use laws, air bags, or some combination—then reversed course and chose another approach instead. When, in 1983, NHTSA was trying to rescind its own rule (requiring manufacturers, at their option, to install either air bags or automatic seat belts), the United States Supreme Court noted: "The regulation whose rescission is at issue bears a complex and convoluted history. Over the course of approximately 60 rulemaking notices, the requirement has been imposed, amended, rescinded, reimposed, and now rescinded again."[23] And the reversals have not stopped.

Some of the cycling resulted from changes in the Department of Transportation. In 1976, the secretary of transportation (who has final authority over NHTSA proposals) decided that public resistance to automatic seat belts would be tested by requiring them on five hundred thousand, but not all, new cars. Months later Jimmy Carter defeated Gerald Ford, and the newly appointed secretary of transportation decided that the demonstration program was unnecessary and that all cars must be equipped with air bags or automatic seat belts. Four years later President Reagan's secretary of transportation tried to rescind that rule. By the time the Supreme Court handed down an opinion saying the secretary had not presented an adequate basis for rescission and had to reconsider the matter, a new secretary of transportation had taken over, with a new approach: the standard would be rescinded if enough states passed laws requiring motorists to wear seat belts.

But it is not merely changes within the Department of Transportation that affect NHTSA. Elected officials intervene as well. A public firestorm erupted over NHTSA's attempts to force seat belt use by requiring manufacturers to install either ignition interlock or continuous buzzer systems. Many angry voters complained that this was an assault on freedom, and Congress abrogated the interlock rule and enacted legislation giving itself veto power over future NHTSA rules. When, during the 2000 election year, manufacturers lobbied the White House to stop NHTSA from adopting a 30 mph crash test standard for air bags—which, according to Public Citizen, would have forced manufacturers to redesign highly profitable SUVs—the White House forced NHTSA to keep the old 25 mph standard. During the same year, Congress stopped NHTSA from proceeding with two new programs it was about to undertake. At the request of Senator Richard Shelby (R–Ala.), Congress enacted legislation forbidding NHTSA from conducting static stability tests in order to rate SUVs on rollover hazards. And under the leadership of committee chair Bob Carr—a Democrat from Michigan, where GM, Ford, and Chrysler are headquartered—the House Transportation Committee quietly eliminated from NHTSA's budget $600,000 that had been earmarked for new and more stringent side-impact tests.

Sometimes changes are not merely the result of ad hoc pressure but are ideological and systematic. Ronald Reagan, who campaigned for president on a platform of reducing government regulation, forced NHTSA and EPA to rescind or relax thirty-four specific auto standards and regulations and cut NHTSA's budget in half. There is nothing nefarious in this. There are differing views about how much regulation is desirable in modern society. It is healthy for such issues to be publicly debated and for politicians to champion particular points of view; and it is appropriate for administrations to effectuate their own policies. Nevertheless, an agency such as NHTSA can never be sure how long a policy, once begun, may continue.

These phenomena did not only affect NHTSA's rulemaking program. NHTSA's recall program has also become ossified. In 1983, NHTSA alleged that rear brakes on 1980 General Motors X-cars—a class of more than 1 million cars sold under Chevrolet, Pontiac, Buick, and Oldsmobile brand names—had an unusually high tendency to lock prematurely, causing dangerous fishtail skids. After NHTSA's release of a dramatic film showing an X-car spinning out of control, broadcast on network television and seen by 53 million viewers, GM recalled X-cars with manual transmissions and a few early-production automatic transmission cars but refused to recall the rest of the 1980 models. NHTSA officials then discovered that GM had learned about the problem both in preproduction tests (an internal company task force recommended some design changes but decided against delaying production to fully remedy the problem) and from consumer complaints and accident reports but concealed this information from NHTSA. NHTSA sued to compel a full recall and to sanction GM from violating its obligation to inform NHTSA of a safety-related defect.

As a result of the publicity that NHTSA had chosen to give the issue, both sides had a large stake in the case. Vigorous litigation ensued; trial in federal district court consumed 113 days. GM won in the trial court, and NHTSA appealed. In 1988, the U.S. Court of Appeals handed down an opinion, written by Judge Kenneth W. Starr, then a recent Reagan appointee, finding that NHTSA had not established that X-cars skidded more than similar cars produced by other manufacturers.[24] Observers say that NHTSA's confidence was so badly bruised that still, twelve years later, it is so reluctant to litigate to compel recalls that the program has become essentially voluntary.

A regulatory agency often finds that the more energetically it pursues its mission, the greater the backlash—not only from the regulated industry but from Congress, the president, the public, and perhaps even the courts. This is not unique to agencies regulating health and safety. In recent years, the Internal Revenue Service (IRS) has been a particularly popular punching bag. Politicians curry favor with constituents by questioning how the agency has handled individual cases[25] and by lambasting the IRS generally in congressional hearings and on the stump.[26] The predictable result was revealed by a Syracuse University study, released in April 2000, showing that the IRS has become so gun-shy of powerful taxpayers—the kind that can litigate or, probably more important, purchase "access" to members of Congress—that it was auditing a lower percentage of returns by taxpayers making more than $100,000 per year than by those making less than $25,000. "Years of pummeling by Congress have so weakened the Internal Revenue Service—eroding its budget, staff, and spirit—that the agency has largely abandoned efforts to detect tax fraud among the rich and powerful, or even among ordinary taxpayers," the *New York Times* stated in an editorial.[27]

It is not difficult to see why, in his famous treatise about regulatory agencies, James Q. Wilson concluded that if the political branches gave an agency a great deal of discretion, the agency would come to use it in an "effort to stay out of trouble."[28] And NHTSA has found a program that does just that. NHTSA developed a New Car Assessment Program (NCAP) under which it crash-tests new cars and makes the results publicly available.[29] While manufacturers were not immediately happy with the program, they quickly learned to cope and, more, use the program to their advantage. NHTSA tells manufacturers exactly how its crash tests are performed so that manufacturers can conduct identical tests when new models are in preproduction. NHTSA rates cars on a five-star system familiar to readers of movie and restaurant reviews, and manufacturers are free to use the ratings in their advertising. NHTSA does not have enough money to test all models, and budget constraints have forced it to test fewer models each year for the past two years—down from seventy crash tests in 1998 to fifty-eight in 2000—but this, at least, is a program manufacturers are not lobbying to kill. General Motors requested that NHTSA test its 2000 Chevrolet Impala, then trumpeted the five-star rating.

In an effort to avoid provoking industry counterattacks and political backlashes—to "stay out of trouble," as James Q. Wilson put it— NHTSA is reduced to looking for programs that serve both auto safety and the auto industry. There is nothing wrong with programs that do both. Auto safety is not necessarily a zero-sum game; everything that is good for auto safety is not necessarily bad for the industry or vice versa. A regulatory agency that can only energetically pursue programs that serve industry has, however, in a very real sense, been co-opted by industry. At best it must serve two masters, industry and the public interest, rather than the public interest alone. Its dedication to its original mission is compromised and its potential effectiveness severely curtailed.

NHTSA has not only been captured, exhausted, besieged, ossified, cycled, demoralized, and co-opted but starved as well.[30] NHTSA has never fully recovered from Reagan's cutting its budget in half. In real dollar terms, NHTSA's budget in 2000 is 30 percent lower than it was in 1980; and NHTSA has fewer employees at the end of the Clinton administration than it had when President Clinton took office in 1992.[31] Congress appropriated a total of $367 million for NHTSA during its 2000 fiscal year—well less than 1 percent of the appropriation for the entire Department of Transportation and meager considering how central automobiles are to American society, the proportion of travel-related injuries and fatalities related to automobiles, and the size of the industry NHTSA is charged with regulating. Moreover, NHTSA keeps less than half of the appropriation for its own operations; the rest is distributed in block grants to the states.

NHTSA's budget constraints have consequences. In the fall of 2000, Congress held hearings to find out why Ford and Firestone knew for years that Firestone tires on Ford Explorers were failing at high rates but did nothing about it in the United States.[32] Firestone's internal company documents revealed that company was well aware of dramatically increasing warranty claims for tire separation. Firestone also realized that 64 percent of products liability cases alleging tread separation concerned tires made at just one of its ten North American tire factories, a factory that had been staffed with replacement workers during a labor dispute. But even after Firestone tires were replaced on Ford Explorers in three other countries, Ford and Firestone continued to hide the problem from NHTSA. Apparently, the companies calculated that the maximum fine NHTSA could impose for failure to notify ($925,000) was cheap compared to the cost of recalling 6.5 million tires.

Because companies conceal them, NHTSA needs to be able to recognize problems on its own. Through its Fatality Analysis Reporting System (FARS), NHTSA had collected information that, if analyzed, would have shown that fatal accidents involving Ford Explorers were associated with tire failure 2.8 times as often as for other SUVs. That analysis was not done, however, until after the scandal broke, and the *New York Times* was the one to do it. In the past, NHTSA might have been alerted to the tire problem through its program of collecting anecdotal information from garages and body shops, but budget cuts had forced NHTSA to discontinue that program.

In the wake of the Firestone Tire–Ford Explorer scandal, members of Congress bemoaned NHTSA's ineffectiveness and talked of increasing its budget—crocodile tears, considering how Congress treated NHTSA in the past. Neither NHTSA's limited resources nor its impairments were new. More than a decade earlier, Senator Slade Gorton (R–Wash.) described NHTSA as "a backwater where important safety initiatives are started and then disappear."[33]

The automobile industry's belief that it does not currently have to make large political contributions may be evidence of NHTSA's weakness.[34] In 1997, GM announced it would no longer make soft-money contributions to political parties. GM still contributes to individual candidates and finds other ways to win goodwill—by lending four hundred Cadillacs and SUVs to Republican officials attending the party's 2000 National Convention in Philadelphia, for example. And the increased concentration of the industry—Chrysler bought American Motors, then merged with Daimler, for example—has in many ways made it even more politically potent. What does it mean, however, that none of the automobile manufacturers currently ranks among the top fifty contributors to either the Republican or Democratic parties or was among the top patrons of any of the 2000 presidential candidates? Certainly it does not mean automakers have suddenly become shy about purchasing influence. Nor, in view of the unprecedented moneys other industries are contributing to politicians and parties, does it mean influence is no longer purchased in this fashion. What it may mean, quite simply, is that the automobile industry does not believe it needs to spend this money to protect its interests. Although the industry has multifaceted interests—it is concerned with EPA rulemaking, Defense Department purchasing, and many other government activities—NHTSA and automobile regulation remain a central concern. But it does not appear to be a concern that presently causes sweat to break out on the industry's brow.

The Bronco II Story

It is useful at this stage to consider one case study. I have selected the story of the Ford Bronco—a downsized SUV, nineteen inches shorter, nine inches narrower, and five inches lower than the standard Ford Bronco—that Ford introduced in 1983 to compete with the Chevy S-10 Blazer.[35] Ford produced seven hundred thousand units before replacing the Bronco II with the Explorer in 1989.

In 1988, after receiving reports of disturbing number of Bronco II rollovers, NHTSA instituted an investigation to determine whether the Ford Bronco II had a safety-related defect. On May 17, 1989, *Consumer Reports* reported that the Bronco II had fared poorly in its tests. The vehicle was unstable in sudden swerves and other accident-avoidance maneuvers, presenting a rollover hazard; and the June issue of the magazine included an article recommending against purchasing the vehicle. Nevertheless, NHTSA closed its investigation after receiving Ford's submission and without questioning Ford officials or conducting its own tests. NHTSA declared that further investigation would be unlikely to lead to a finding of a safety-related defect. Years later, Edgar F. Heiskell III, an attorney representing injured plaintiffs, deposed Ford officials and learned that Ford had deliberately concealed highly relevant information.

There had been reason to suspect that Ford knew the Bronco II might have rollover propensities even before it designed the vehicle. GM was in a rush to produce an SUV to compete with the Chevrolet Blazer. To speed up the design process, Ford used the Jeep CJ-7, a vehicle within American Motor Corporation's (AMC's) "Civilian Jeep" series, as an "image vehicle," which meant the Bronco II's dimensions and characteristics were patterned on the CJ-7. Ford knew—or at the very least had strong reason to suspect—that the CJ-7 had rollover problems. In 1979, NHTSA opened a defect investigation to determine whether the CJ-5 and CJ-7 had dangerous rollover propensities. Although NHTSA closed its investigation the next year, its rationale for doing so bordered on the nonsensical. NHTSA concluded that most rollovers occurred "under instances in which the limits of the vehicle are exceeded," which basically means that Jeeps were rolling over because drivers turned corners too quickly. But products must built for the real world and designed to be reasonably safe when used as people actually use them, not for some utopia where users strictly abide by instructions in the owner's manual. Moreover, it was obvious the Jeep had a certain panache that made it popular with young men who did not drive like their grandmothers. The image, in fact, was precisely the point. It was the image that made the CJ series extremely popular; ninety thousand were sold in 1979 alone. (The Federal Trade Commission would eventually charge AMC with misleading advertising for picturing the Jeep CJ as a safely zooming over rough terrain and down paved highways.) Therefore, NHTSA's decision settled nothing. And in fact, just months after NHTSA closed its investigation, the Institute for Highway Safety declared that the Jeep CJ had an "extremely hazardous tendency . . . to roll over in highway use." The institute reported that its tests showed the CJ-5 would overturn when performing a J-turn at just 22 mph. Ford selected the CJ-7 as an image vehicle because it wanted to copy its style and mystique, despite possible safety concerns.

What Edward Heiskell found out in depositions was that Ford's concerns about the Bronco II's rollover propensity were confirmed in its own testing. During preproduction tests on prototypes, Ford learned that the Bronco II was susceptible to rollover during lane changes and routine avoidance maneuvers, even at speeds no faster than 25 to 30 mph. In fact, Ford considered the Bronco II so dangerous that it suspended J-turn test drives out of fear of killing or injuring its own drivers. Some minor adjustments recommended by the engineers were incorporated into the vehicle, but the stability problem was far from cured. Ford engineers concluded that the track width would have to be increased two inches to achieve a minor improvement in stability and three to four inches to make a significant improvement. But this would have delayed production by several months, and Ford officials said no. Bronco II remained a vehicle with a center of gravity that was too high for the vehicle's track width. Moreover, passengers were seated so high that they raised the center of gravity; every time someone climbed on board, he made the vehicle more unstable. And making matters worse, drivers became accustomed to the fact that Bronco II generally understeered, but when it approached its cornering limit it would suddenly oversteer, thus exacerbating the rollover hazard.

At deposition, one Ford official admitted participating in a deliberate decision to conceal the preproduction tests from NHTSA. The excuse was that Ford feared NHTSA would misinterpret the data. Heiskell furnished this information to NHTSA. After an investigation, NHTSA admonished Ford for improperly withholding this information. But it took no further action against the manufacturer. NHTSA reasoned that although it had asked Ford for "all tests and analyses," in its response Ford had slyly said it was providing all data relating to *production* vehicles, which should have alerted NHTSA staff that Ford had not necessarily included tests on *preproduction* vehicles.

This kind of artifice does not work so easily in private litigation. Ford tried something similar in a products liability case involving a Ford Tempo. At issue in the case was whether, in an accident, the driver's seat had improperly broken loose from its track assembly, allowing it to fly backward and crush an infant strapped in a car safety seat in the rear of the car. An interrogatory propounded by the plaintiffs' lawyer asked Ford whether it had used "the same left front driver's seat and right front passenger seat tracks and seat backs" in other models. Ford answered that "the seat track assemblies used in the Tempo are unique to the Tempo/Topaz car lines only." The plaintiffs' lawyers were not so easily thrown off the track, however. They recognized the trick. As the Michigan Court of Appeals put it:

> What [Ford] did was craftily reformulate the question to ask only what it wanted to say, namely: that the seat track assemblies, not the seats themselves, were unique, thereby creating the misleading impression that the seats had not been used in any other vehicles. With that impression, plaintiffs would not expect to be told about tests and lawsuits involving the seats [in] other models, even though the seats were, it now turns out, the same. . . . Ford's answer was not simply a precise answer to a poor question; it was a dishonest answer, carefully crafted to mislead the reader.[36]

This was merely one of Ford's ploys in the case. The plaintiffs' lawyers had to litigate fiercely to get to the truth. They filed numerous motions to compel full disclosure. Ford repeatedly tried to mislead and stonewall, but the plaintiffs' lawyers continually pressed for complete and honest responses and eventually prevailed. When the deceptions were laid bare, the trial judge pronounced Ford's conduct "disgusting." "For over two years," he wrote, "Ford had concealed very significant documents and information, and, worse, had blatantly lied about those documents and the information in them." Unlike NHTSA, which found a foul but imposed no penalty, the court made Ford pay a price for its behavior. It ruled Ford had forfeited its right to defend the case.

Returning to the Bronco II story, there are other disturbing aspects. At deposition, a statistical expert witness, retained to help defend Ford in products liability litigation, told Edgar Heiskell she was aware of 5,672 Bronco II rollovers within six states during selected time periods. Heiskell furnished this information to NHTSA, together with his own extrapolation that, assuming the six states and selected time frames were representative, an estimated fifty thousand Bronco II rollovers would have occurred from the van's release in 1983 until the time of Heiskell's analysis in 1997. Heiskell formally asked NHTSA to conduct a new investigation and require Ford to warn Bronco II owners of the rollover hazard. NHTSA took no action.

During discovery, Heiskell also unearthed information that intensified concerns about agency "capture." Heiskell came into possession of an internal memorandum from one of Ford's Washington lobbyists to other company officials, reporting that the deputy director of NHTSA's public affairs office tipped him off that a CBS affiliate was working on a story about Bronco II rollover hazards. And Heiskell complained to NHTSA that two of its former officers—Jerry R. Curry, who, as NHTSA's administrator, had made the decision to close the Bronco II investigation, and William Boehly, who was director of NHTSA's National Center for Statistics and Analysis when NHTSA commenced its Bronco II investigation—were serving as Ford expert witnesses in Bronco II cases. When NHTSA questioned whether it was proper for Curry to work for Ford on Bronco cases, Ford dispatched two former NHTSA chief counsels, who were now both representing Ford, to discuss the matter with NHTSA lawyers. Curry ultimately withdrew as Ford's expert in Bronco cases; Boehly did not.

Though, in 1990, NHTSA decided against ordering Ford to recall the Bronco II, the same year Ford replaced the Bronco II with the Explorer, an SUV with a two-inch wider track. Ford denied rollover problems had anything to do with the change, but not everyone was convinced. *The New York Times* reported that seventy people per year were dying in Bronco II rollovers. Ford disclosed in a Securities Exchange Commission (SEC) filing that it was defending claims totaling $742 million in just thirteen Bronco II lawsuits. When asked by the press how many Bronco II cases Ford faced, the company said only that it had settled at least fifty cases and something fewer than a hundred cases and claims were still pending.

In an Indiana case in which two women were injured in a Bronco II rollover—one woman suffered brain damage that left her functioning at a thirteen-year-old level and with manic depression severe enough to cause her to attempt suicide; the other suffered facial deformities only partly remedied through multiple reconstructive surgeries and could walk with only an unsteady gait—a jury awarded plaintiffs $4.4 million in compensatory damages and $58 million in punitive damages. The trial judge reduced the punitive award to $13.8 million, which the state appellate court upheld. In Bronco II cases in Ohio and California, juries awarded verdicts that were reduced by the trial judges to $26 million and $7 million, respectively, although the latter remains under appeal at this writing. Other cases are pending, and injuries and lawsuits many continue as long as Bronco IIs remain on the road. Thus, despite the lack of action by NHTSA, Ford has paid and will continue to pay a substantial price for Bronco II.

Who Regulates Auto Safety?

There is nothing special about the Bronco II story. Bronco II was only one of a number of SUVs with rollover propensities.[37] The Isuzu Trooper II, Mitsubishi Montero, Nissan Pathfinder, Toyota 4Runner, and Jeep CJ-5 and CJ-7 all had stability problems, and *Consumer Reports* rated the Suzuki Samurai more dangerous than Bronco II. Rollovers have been a significant problem for SUVs generally; 47 percent of all fatalities in SUVs and light trucks result from rollover accidents, compared to 22 percent for passenger cars.

Moreover, rollover propensity is not the only problem with SUVs. In front-end crash tests conducted by the Insurance Institute for Highway Safety (IIHS) in 1996, five SUV brands could not be driven away after hitting an angled barrier at 5 mph, a performance so dismal as to have occurred only twice in hundreds of IIHS tests on passenger vehicles. Most disturbing of all, because of their mass, rigidity, and height, SUVs present unusually great danger for occupants of cars. One is three times more likely to die in a collision with an SUV than in a collision with a passenger car. Since 1996, more Americans have been killed in accidents between a car and a light truck (a category includes SUVs, vans, and pickup trucks) than in collisions between two cars.

But SUVs are getting less dangerous. Unstable models such as the CJ-7 and the Bronco II have been replaced with more stable models. On March 20, 2000, GM conceded for the first time that SUVs create greater risks for people in passenger cars and announced that at least some of its 2002 models would be redesigned to ameliorate this danger somewhat. On May 11, 2000, Ford publicly acknowledged that SUVs present heightened dangers for other motorists and disproportionately contribute to smog and climate change (current regulations allow an SUV to spew 5.5 times as much pollution into the air as a car). SUVs were then accounting for 20 percent of Ford's sales, and Ford did not intend to stop producing profitable models—even its Excursion, which weighed as much as ninety-two hundred pounds and weighed as much as two Jeep Grand Cherokees. But, Ford said, it would work to make its SUVs less dangerous and less polluting, and it equipped the Excursion with a bar below the bumper to try to stop the Excursion from overriding cars in collisions. DaimlerChrysler, Toyota, and Nissan are also modifying their bumpers and front ends to reduce dangers in collisions with automobiles.

The Bronco II and SUV stories are typical of the larger story of motor vehicle safety. SUVs have been getting safer, as have automobiles. The story of Bronco II parallels stories involving the Corvair, Vega, Pinto, and GM pickup trucks with side-mounted gasoline tanks. The progress in motor vehicles has been spectacular, though painfully slow. The graph near the beginning of this chapter, showing that motor vehicle fatalities have fallen by a whopping 79 percent, extends over nearly half a century. That progress could have been achieved much more rapidly. Very little of it results from new technologies that were previously unavailable. The patent on the first air bag was granted in 1953; GM conducted extensive research on air bags in the 1960s; and NHTSA believed passive restraints, including air bags, were within reach when it promulgated its ill-fated Standard 208, requiring passive restraint systems in 1973 models. The progress we have made to date

could have been made much earlier if manufacturers—and consumers—had not resisted it.

It is important to acknowledge that consumers have been part of the
problem. Manufacturers would have made safer cars if consumers had
demanded them. In 1956, Ford spent millions promoting an optional
safety package that included seat belts, safety door latches, and crash
padding, but only 2 percent of Ford's customers elected the seat belts.
Ford was punished for this attempt; it watched itself suffer a sizable
loss of market share to Chevrolet, which instead was marketing its
powerful V 8 engine and snazzy wheels. Lee Iacocca writes:

> Ever since the 1956 campaign, I've been quoted as having said "safety
> doesn't sell," as though I were offering an excuse for not making safer
> cars. But that's a severe distortion of what I said and certainly of what I
> believe. After the failure of our campaign to promote safety features, I
> said something like: "Look fellas, I guess safety doesn't sell, even though
> we did our damndest to sell it!"[30]

Twenty years later, GM took another stab at using safety as a marketing device by offering air bags as an optional feature on several
models. That effort also flopped.

When, in 1988, *Consumer Reports* declared that the Suzuki Samurai
was unsafe and prone to rollover and asked NHTSA to order a permanent recall (NHTSA took no action), Samurai sales slumped; but when,
in 1989, *Consumer Reports* made its announcement about Bronco II,
sales were not significantly affected. Analysts attributed this to Ford's
strong institutional image. Consumers apparently think the second
largest company in America does not make unsafe products. Moreover,
as SUVs illustrate, consumers can be almost as narcissistic as corporations. People buy SUVs because they like the image, and perhaps because believe they themselves are safer in SUVs, even though they may
know they are putting others at greater risk and polluting more.

The libertarian view is: let the free market reign. If consumers want
style rather than safety, let them have it. It should not be government's
role to force people to buy what they do not want. The market decides
whether cars have contiguous frames, shatterproof windshields, protected gas tanks, air bags or seatbelts, and what the height of SUV
bumpers ought to be. But of course, it is more complicated than that.
Someone who elects to buy an SUV puts others at risk. People who
elect to buy a car with an unprotected gasoline tank bear the health

consequences but not the financial consequences of that decision. After all, no one in America today pays his own medical costs. Most people are covered by insurance, either privately or through government programs such as Medicare and Medicaid. Someone without coverage will be treated when an ambulance delivers her to a hospital emergency room. The expenses will become part of the hospital's free-care/bad-debt costs, and must be made up through higher hospital charges paid by others. Therefore, society collectively has an interest in promoting auto safety, regardless of whether, at the individual level, consumers are demanding safe cars.

Yet, although it has been slow, there is no denying that spectacular progress has occurred. How can this be? If NHTSA is as beleaguered and weak as it appears, and other factors such as highway improvements and the war against drunk driving (though significant) cannot account for the full extent of the decline in highway fatalities, what is the rest of the explanation?

The paradoxical answer is that NHTSA, although weak, is part of a system that is far more effective than NHTSA alone. The system is like a four-legged stool. One leg consists of regulatory agencies, most visibly NHTSA but other agencies as well. We have been speaking of auto safety in terms of accidents, but motor vehicles kill and cause illness in less visible ways. The EPA and state environmental agencies make enormous contributions to auto safety by regulating emissions of carbon monoxide, volatile organic compounds, and other pollutants; by eliminating lead in gasoline; and by regulating the disposal of used motor oil and car batteries. The system's second leg is comprised of citizen advocacy organizations, including, notably, the Center for Auto Safety founded by Ralph Nader, Consumers Union, and MADD, but also including environmental groups.[39] The third leg is the press. Manufacturers have paid substantial prices in sales and institutional reputation when, for example, Mark Dowie's famous article "Pinto Madness" ran in *Mother Jones* magazine; *60 Minutes* broadcast stories about the dangers of the Pinto, the CJ-7, and all-terrain vehicles; and *Dateline NBC* broadcast its infamous report about GM sidesaddle fuel tanks. The fourth leg is the common law, and specifically products liability litigation.

The strength of the system flows not only from each of the four legs of the stool but from the architecture of the stool and the relationships among the legs. The common law system is a powerful ally of government regulators. That is, in fact, how the common law system is best thought of—not as an independent system but as an adjunctive mechanism. Agencies such as the FDA, EPA, OSHA, FAA, and NHTSA must always be the primary regulatory mechanisms in their respective fields. Yet, as the NHTSA example demonstrates, these agencies are vulnerable to attack and easily repressed. Yet somehow they succeed—not perfectly, to be sure, but still, as the progress in auto safety illustrates, surprisingly well.

Consider, for example, the NHTSA recall program. Many believe that NHTSA is so reluctant to litigate that its recall program is essentially voluntary. Since manufacturers know NHTSA is unlikely to go to court to compel recalls, one might imagine NHTSA has little to work with to persuade manufacturers to recall dangerous vehicles. But that is not entirely the case. Manufacturers face potential consequences even if NHTSA never draws its sword from the scabbard. NHTSA generally urges recalls when data collected through its Fatality Analysis Reporting System (FARS) show that a particular model is associated with unusually high fatality rates. These data are publicly available and can be potent in the hands of products liability lawyers. Manufacturers know the only way to reduce their exposure is to reduce injuries, and thus they have a powerful incentive to agree voluntarily to recalls. Indeed, one of the outrages brought to light by Ralph Nader in the congressional hearings in 1966 was that manufacturers sometimes conducted "secret recalls," that is, they had dealers correct defects during routine maintenance visits without telling the owners they had performed this additional work.

Today manufacturers have incentives both to recall vehicles in order to correct hazards and to take credit for doing so. Manufacturers know that in products liability litigation some courts will not hold them liable for a particular design choice even if it is associated with increased injuries. For example, the design choice may have been a deliberate trade-off of some degree of safety for a countervailing economic, aesthetic, or utilitarian consideration. Such trade-offs are made all the time, and appropriately so. After all, completely safe cars can be built, but they would probably be ugly, unwieldy, uncomfortable, inefficient, and prohibitively expensive. But if fatality reports demonstrate that the hazard is much greater than originally anticipated, or if the state of the art has advanced so that the hazard can feasibly be reduced, then some courts may hold manufacturers liable for failing to warn consumers of the danger or informing them that the danger can be reduced. These cases provide manufacturers with additional incentives to agree voluntarily to send recall notices to their customers.

Another aspect of the symbiotic relationship between government regulators and the private trial bar involves the exchange of information. Some states require that products liability plaintiffs do more than show that a product is unreasonably dangerous. To prevail, plaintiffs must also precisely identify the defect or design flaw that is responsible for the increased danger and show how the hazard could have been eliminated. This involves engineering work and may be very expensive. Sometimes this work is done by NHTSA engineers and is available to trial lawyers under the Freedom of Information Act. Sometimes experts retained by trial lawyers do this work. These lawyers may share the information with NHTSA informally or make it publicly available by using it at trial. Whichever way it flows, however, the information exchange strengthens both administrative and common law regulation.

While NHTSA and advocacy groups create and compile important information through, for example, crash testing and FARS, common law litigation is the single most powerful mechanism for prying information out of the hands of industry. Often regulatory agencies such as NHTSA are dependent on whatever information a manufacturer chooses to disclose. Agencies may have the power to compel production but often do not know when a manufacturer is hiding documents and, even when suspicious, may be too timid to challenge the manufacturer. But trial lawyers are not shrinking violets. They are congenitally suspicious. Because they litigate for a living, their antennae are sensitive to chicanery. When they suspect a manufacturer is concealing information, they need not ask superiors at several bureaucratic levels for permission to be aggressive.

Trial lawyers do not have to rely on whatever documents manufacturers turn over in response to written requests. They may summon company employees to testify under oath at depositions. This discovery device often shines a light into the otherwise impenetrable darkness of the corporate interior. Corporate witnesses may try to be evasive, but when skillfully interrogated by experienced lawyers, they are often faced with a stark choice: answer the questions honestly or commit perjury and run the risk that this will be discovered during depositions of other employees, who decide to protect themselves instead of the company. It was products liability litigation that brought to light that, even before it began

to sell those vehicles, Ford knew the Pinto was vulnerable in rear-end collisions and the Bronco II had a rollover propensity, and that GM knew its
1973–87 model light pickup trucks with side-mounted fuel tanks were
susceptible to exploding in side collisions.

Balancing Safety and Other Considerations

When is it appropriate to balance safety against competing considerations, and when is it not? Many fear juries are too unsophisticated to
evaluate such decisions intelligently, to appreciate that not every trade-
off between safety and other considerations is evil. Juries are too sympathetic to injured plaintiffs. Moreover, trials are public, and journalists who cover trials like to sensationalize stories and unfairly demonize
the big corporations. Those, at least, are the fears. As discussed in earlier chapters, the data do not provide much support for those concerns.
That is not to say these worries are entirely without foundation. There
are trade-offs in all things, however, including regulatory systems; one
must ask whether, on the whole, society is better off with these decisions remaining exclusively in the corporate back room or being
brought into the public courtroom, and via the media to the public at
large for discussion and debate.

This brings us back to escalators, which were discussed at the beginning of the chapter. The case mentioned at the beginning of the chapter
concerned the design of an escalator stop button. Before we return to
that case, consider another escalator case, one involving a mother who
rode an escalator at a Sears department store with her twenty-two-
month-old son.[40] The mother boarded the escalator on the same step as
her son, held the boy's right hand throughout the ride, and told him to
put his left hand on the handrail, which he did. When they disem-
barked, the boy screamed and blood spurted from the little finger on
his left hand. His finger had been caught in the space between the moving handrail and the escalator wall. The laceration was so severe that
the tendon had retracted into the palm of the hand and had to be su-
tured back in place while the young boy was under general anesthesia.
The boy underwent six months of physical therapy, but the last joint of
the little finger was left permanently immobile.

In compliance with the ANSI code, the escalator had pictograms
showing a woman riding an escalator while holding a young child's

hand, together with the words "Caution, hold handrail, attend children, avoid sides." And the escalator complied with ANSI standards in all other respects as well. Westinghouse Electric Corporation, the manufacturer of the escalator, regularly inspected the escalator to ensure it was working properly and in good repair. What else could Sears and Westinghouse have done to prevent this injury? Is a lawsuit over this matter a good thing, either in terms of dispensing justice or in terms of regulating escalators?

Many things are more complicated than they appear at first blush. Young children are routinely—and because of the nature of escalators, inevitably—injured on escalators. At trial, the manager of the Sears store conceded similar accidents had occurred in his store. And from both the court's own experience and a review of published cases, the Louisiana Supreme Court knew, as it put it, "that a multitude of children" are injured on escalators. The court cited a New York case where an escalator ripped an infant's finger from her hand; another New York case where an infant's hand was caught between the an escalator step and the bottom plate; an Arizona case involving a six-year-old whose hand was mutilated by an escalator; a case in Indiana in which a three-year-old's skin was caught between an escalator riser and the side wall. The list is much longer—so long, in fact, that a law review article published seven years earlier discussed 182 published court opinions involving escalator accidents.[41] That is a startling number when one considers that only a tiny fraction of injuries (perhaps no more than one in five hundred) give rise to litigation that results in a published court opinion.[42]

The Louisiana courts had themselves heard a disturbing number of cases involving just one category of escalator accident: small children whose sneakers were caught in the moving treads of escalators. Some of the children were sufficiently mangled to require amputation of portions of their toes. When, some years earlier, the Louisiana Supreme Court heard such a case, it reviewed a trial record in which the manager of the New Orleans department store where the accident occurred testified that he knew of "about four" similar accidents in his store; and a representative of Otis Elevator Company, which made the escalator, testified about how the friction of a moving escalator produces heat, which softens the rubber on sneakers, which he said was a factor in children's feet becoming caught in escalator treads.[43]

It is little wonder, therefore, that the Louisiana Supreme Court held that "escalators, for all their utility, are unreasonably dangerous to small children." The court was certainly influenced by the fact that principally it is the retailers who benefit from escalators. For shoppers, elevators might serve as well. But department stores and shopping malls prefer escalators because, as they move seamlessly from floor to floor, shoppers have open vistas of merchandise or stores, beckoning them thither. Department stores know that a price is paid, particularly with children's fingers and toes. Retailers reap the benefits, however, and escape much of the cost.

Earlier I hypothesized an escalator manufacturer who felt unfairly punished for designing a bright red, highly visible emergency stop button. Would he not be sued no matter what he did—whether the stop button was bright red and attractive to pranksters or less conspicuous or less accessible in emergencies? Perhaps. But with some background on escalators, this seems less unreasonable. Escalators, as it turns out, present significant hazards for the people who ride them. Emergency stop buttons are necessary to try to ameliorate those hazards; but to be useful, stop buttons must be readily accessible, and easy accessibility creates other hazards. The risk that pranksters will push emergency buttons, causing riders to fall and be hurt, is part and parcel of the inherent hazards of escalators. Retailers and escalator manufacturers have elected to expose people to a panoply of risks because it is profitable for them to do so.

Perhaps the emergency stop button could not have been better designed, but for these kinds of cases that should be beside the point. Escalators remain unreasonably dangerous despite the best possible design, construction, and warnings. While generally products are considered unreasonably dangerous if they are defective or if they fail a risk-utility test, escalators are an example of products that should be deemed unreasonably dangerous for another reason—because there is an unfair separation between benefits and costs. That is, without the law's intervention, those who enjoy the benefits are able to foist off significant costs of personal injury upon others. Escalators are unreasonably dangerous not because their risks exceed their benefits but because it is unreasonable to impose risk on people who are not deriving significant benefits.

The counterargument often offered is that consumers always pay the cost in the end. Escalator manufacturers pass on the cost of liability to department stores in the form of higher escalator prices, and department stores pass the costs on to consumers in the form of higher prices for merchandise. Yet this does not diminish the incentive to increase safety. A manufacturer that can make a safer escalator has a competitive advantage because it can sell its product for less than its rivals. Department stores that can reduce injuries and liability expense have a similar advantage over rival stores. Businesses have incentives to reduce every kind of expense, including liability costs.

Finally, the gripe of the hypothetical escalator manufacturer about being punished no matter how it designed the emergency stop button misses the mark. Unlike regulatory agencies, courts do not tell manufacturers how to design their products. It is surprising how often even sophisticated commentators seem confused about this. For example, John D. Graham of Harvard University writes: "In light of the unpredictabilities in the liability process, many auto engineers in the industry believe the legal process offers them limited information about how to improve the safety of their products."[44] But courts do not tell manufacturers how to design cars or escalators. All courts do is impose liability on unreasonably dangerous products, leaving manufacturers free to try to reduce injuries as they see fit. Moreover, the unpredictability of the litigation process is one of the system's strengths. Escalator manufacturers and department stores cannot fully protect themselves by complying with building codes or ANSI standards or by making an emergency stop button one color or another. They can reliably reduce their liability only by reducing injuries.

But, says the escalator manufacturer, under the present state of the art there is no way to make escalators safer. This is punishment without purpose. We do not know how to design an emergency stop button that is conspicuous and accessible in emergencies but cannot be pushed by pranksters. (One wonders: makers of emergency fire alarms addressed a similar problem with a device that sprays dye on the hand that pulls the lever.) We do not know how to make escalators safer for children's fingers and toes. Yet where there is a will, there is often a way. Without common law liability, there is little incentive for manufacturers of established and accepted products to continue to strive to make their products safer.

7

The Three Revolutions in Products Liability

Cardozo's Paradigm

On a clear and dry summer day in 1911, Donald MacPherson agreed to take a sick neighbor to the hospital.[1] MacPherson, who engraved and sold gravestones and other monuments in a small town in upstate New York, was successful enough to own a Buick, which he had purchased just two months earlier from Close Brothers, the local Buick dealer. MacPherson did not know it, but he was about to have an accident that would launch not one but three great legal revolutions, with profound implications for American society.

These were the early days of mass production of the automobile. A little over two hundred thousand cars and trucks were manufactured in 1911, increasing by almost a third the total number of motor vehicles then registered throughout the United States. Many companies were making automobiles, but two—Buick and Ford, each of which had sold its first car in 1904—were competing to become the industry leader. Cars were dangerous—so dangerous that insurance companies were reluctant to write policies covering automobile-related injuries. Drivers were part of the problem. There was appeal to being a daredevil—strapping on goggles and zooming down roads at speeds never previously experienced. America was, in fact, experiencing a speed craze. Paul C. Wilson describes how newspapers "carried stories of unidentified young men who were seen driving at terrific speed through towns, scattering chickens and terrifying the populace," and frustrating the local police, who "scarcely had a chance to blow their whistles as the machine rushed past."[2] Some were horrified at the speedsters. Police in Michigan even started shooting at cars rushing past. But others were enraptured and envious. There were powerful feelings in literally sitting in the seat of new technology, enjoying unprecedented freedom of movement, commanding enormous power, and experiencing the thrill of speed.

Automobile manufacturers exploited Americans' ambivalence toward their product. On the one hand, they encouraged the fascination. They boasted about the horsepower of their engines, competed to set speed records (in a publicity stunt in 1904, Henry Ford personally set a world record of 91.37 mph), sponsored car races, and incorporated streamlined designs that made consumer cars look like racing cars. On the other hand, manufacturers blamed reckless drivers for accidents and injuries, disclaiming any responsibility themselves. "The nut behind the wheel" became an expression manufacturers encouraged.

There was no question about reckless driving in MacPherson's case, however. MacPherson set out in his new Buick roundabout, a car with a bench seat for the driver and one passenger plus a rear rumble seat for a second passenger, with the sick man and the man's brother. The three men testified at trial that the car was traveling at 15 mph when, for no apparent reason, it went into an uncontrollable skid. They heard what sounded like wood breaking, looked down, and saw the left rear wheel collapse. Other witnesses testified that the car was traveling at 30 mph and that MacPherson lost control on a patch of loose gravel. In either event, MacPherson tried to stop the car or straighten its path, but to no avail. The car careened into a telephone poll and overturned. MacPherson was trapped beneath the axle and seriously injured.

Wheels were something of an issue in the automotive industry. One question was whether wheels should be wood or metal. Manufacturers of wire wheels contended that they were stronger and purported to demonstrate wire wheels' superiority by testing both types with hydraulic presses. Manufacturers of wood wheels, however, conducted their own hydraulic press tests that supposedly showed wood wheels were stronger. Another question was whether to use an open-spoke system—that is, using spokes to connect the central hub to the outer rim of the wheel—or to make wheels from a solid disk, which was clearly stronger. These two questions were being vigorously debated because MacPherson's Buick was far from the only motor vehicle to have a wheel fail. In the end, however, these and other issues were resolved by aesthetics. "Motorists preferred to have wheels of possibly inferior strength rather than spoil the looks of their cars," writes Paul C. Wilson.[3] Tastes would eventually change, but like most cars in 1911, the wheels of MacPherson's Buick were made from wooden spokes, a look still popular because it was similar to the wheels on horse-drawn wagon.

Undoubtedly, MacPherson did not believe he deliberately chose weaker but more stylish wheels. When he was well enough to do so, he consulted Edgar T. Brackett, a state senator who was considered the leading lawyer in the county, about filing a lawsuit against the Buick Motor Company. Brackett happened to have in his law office a bright young man named Harold H. Corbin, who had just graduated from law school and would later become a great trial lawyer. Between Corbin, who assisted with research and writing, and Brackett, who tried the case and argued the appeal, MacPherson wound up with an unusually formidable legal team.

"We will have to make some new law, but it's right and worth trying," Brackett is reported to have said to Corbin when he asked him to draft a complaint in the case.[4] Many would have considered this a fool's errand. Two sturdy legal principles stood in the way. The first, known as the privity rule, held that a manufacturer was responsible only to the person with whom he had a direct contractual relationship, that is, the person to whom he sold or leased his product. This long-standing rule originated in an 1842 English case known as *Winterbottom v. Wright*.[5] In that case, a horse-drawn coach used to carry mail collapsed, and the mail coachman was thrown to the ground and left permanently lame. The injured man sued the contractor who had both supplied the coach to the postmaster general and who had a maintenance contract to keep the coach under good repair.

There was no question that had the postmaster general personally been injured, he could have maintained an action against the defendant, for the contractor had direct obligations to the postmaster general. Of course, this was highly unlikely, as the postmaster general did not personally deliver the mail. Although everyone understood that the postmaster general employed mail coachmen and that these were the individuals at risk if the coaches were unsafe, the court held that the defendant had no responsibility to anyone other than the postmaster general. "There is no privity of contract between these parties," the renowned Lord Abinger had written in the court's opinion, "and if the plaintiff can sue, every passenger, or even any person passing along the road, who was injured by the upsetting of the coach, might bring a similar action. Unless we confine the operation of such contracts as this to the parties who entered into them, the most absurd and outrageous consequences, to which I can see no limit, would ensue."[6] All three of Lord Abinger's colleagues on the Court of Exchequer agreed.

It should come as no surprise that *Winterbottom v. Wright* was widely followed not only by British courts but by American courts as well. After all, Lord Abinger created the privity rule the same year that Chief Justice Lemuel Shaw of the Massachusetts Supreme Court created the fellow-servant rule in *Farwell v. Boston & Worcester Railroad Corporation*, and both rules protected newly developing industries. The privity rule had stood for more than half a century when MacPherson walked into Senator Brackett's law office. Like the plaintiff in *Winterbottom*, MacPherson had no direct contractual relationship—no privity of contract—with the Buick Motor Company. Buick had sold its car to Close Brothers, not to MacPherson. But times were changing. As was the case with the fellow-servant rule, courts were beginning to chip away at the privity rule. Some American courts recognized an exception when one furnished an article that he knew would be imminently dangerous to life or limb to someone who could not reasonably anticipate the danger.[7] Nevertheless, in 1911 the privity rule remained a strong obstacle to MacPherson's case.

There was a second obstacle as well. Even assuming that a court would allow MacPherson to maintain a cause of action against Buick, with whom he had no privity, MacPherson would have to prove not merely that the accident occurred because the car was defective but that the defect occurred because Buick had been negligent. This was far from self-evident.

Brackett's theory was that the left rear wheel collapsed and caused the accident. He had evidence to back up this claim: the wheel had been found lying on the ground some distance from the rest of the car, its spokes broken and scattered about. It appeared that the wheel broke and detached from the car before the accident. If this was so, it did not much matter whether MacPherson and his passenger's version of the accident or that of the other eyewitnesses was more accurate. The wheel should not have collapsed, regardless of whether the car was traveling at 15 or 30 mph, and of whether or not it encountered loose gravel.

But this did not necessarily mean that Buick had been negligent. Buick had not made the wheels. Like most automobile manufacturers, it purchased its wheels from a wheel manufacturer. Buick's argument was that this was sensible because wheel making was a specialty, and it could obtain better wheels from a firm with experience and expertise in wheel making than by making them itself. Buick purchased its wheels from the Imperial Wheel Company, a firm with a reputation as a reliable wheel manufacturer. To prove Buick negligent, Brackett and Corbin would have to show Buick's conduct fell short of an established standard—to be more specific, that it failed to use the degree of care that a reasonable automobile manufacturer would have employed. But what was unreasonable about Buick's relying on component-part manufacturers who had specialized expertise and an established record of reliability?

Dueling wheel experts became the most important witnesses at trial. Brackett called three local wheelwrights, all of whom pronounced the wheel in question to have been made from poor-quality hickory, "trash" as one of them put it. The poor quality was evident from how the wood broke. This wood broke squarely, showing it was weak and brittle; good-quality hickory slivered when it broke. More importantly, they testified that the quality of hickory was readily apparent from its grain. Strong hickory had a firm, close grain while inferior hickory had a coarse grain, as did the wood on MacPherson's wheel.

Brackett's suggestion that Buick was negligent in not examining the grain on the wheels it received from Imperial Wheel Company was complicated because the wheels were painted with a prime coat when Buick received them. One of the witnesses criticized this practice. "I never let a wheel come painted—so I can see the quality of the hickory used," he said. This man was a carriage maker, however, not a manufacturer of mass-produced automobiles. Brackett's strongest expert witness was probably his fourth, a man who worked for the Thomas Motor Car Company, then a major car manufacturer in Buffalo, New York. This witness testified that his firm individually tested each wheel by hydraulic pressure.

Buick's trial lawyer was William Van Dyke of Detroit. In selecting Van Dyke to represent it at trial, Buick opted for a lawyer who knew far more about the automobile industry than Brackett or Corbin but who would intensify feelings of a struggle by hometowners against the large, out-of-state corporation. Van Dyke's star expert witness was the director of the testing laboratory at Purdue University, who had a great deal of experience testing woods for the U.S. Forest Service. This witness dismissed the opinions of the local wheelwrights as myths. Grain meant nothing. The only way the quality of hickory could be determined was by measuring the interior rings, which was impossible by looking at the surface of the wood. Fast-growing hickory with five to twenty-five rings per inch was strongest; the spokes of MacPherson's wheel had fifteen rings per inch and thus were made from first-class hickory.

Van Dyke also presented representatives of other major automobile manufacturers. They dismissed the hydraulic test as worthless because it related only to how much weight a wheel could bear and said nothing about how wheels perform on a road. None of them performed pressure tests or scraped off paint to examine wood grain. In addition, Van Dyke presented wheel makers who agreed that little could be learned by examining wood grain. They evaluated the quality of the wood of MacPherson's wheel as fair. Finally, Van Dyke produced representatives of Buick itself, who testified that Buick had manufactured 125,000 cars, had obtained all of the five hundred thousand wheels from Imperial, and had never received even a single other complaint of wheel failure. Buick did not subject wheels to hydraulic tests, but it did drive each car over a ten-mile course on a country road, during which it accelerated the car to its top speed and took turns at 10 to 25 mph.

The jury brought in a verdict for MacPherson in the amount of $5,000, Buick appealed, and in due course the case was heard by the New York Court of Appeals, the state's highest court and one of the most respected tribunals in the nation. In 1916, that court handed down an opinion written by Justice Benjamin N. Cardozo.[8] It was a work of great craftsmanship and nearly a century later remains one of the most famous and influential opinions in the history of American jurisprudence.

First, Cardozo launched what he himself later described as an "assault upon the citadel of privity."[9] In counterpoint to Lord Abinger's decision in *Winterbottom*, Cardozo wrote:

> The dealer was indeed the one person of whom it might be said with some approach to certainty that by him the car would not be used. Yet the defendant would have us say that he was the one person whom it was under a legal duty to protect. The law does not lead us to so inconsequent a conclusion. Precedents drawn from the days of travel by stagecoach do not find the conditions of travel to-day.

Cardozo did not eliminate the privity rule per se. He expanded a previously recognized exception for imminently dangerous articles. Traditionally, this exception applied to things that were inherently dangerous in normal use—such as poisons, explosives, and weapons—which courts sometimes called things of danger. All Cardozo technically did was refine that term. "If the nature of a thing is such that it is reasonably certain to place life and limb in peril when negligently made, it is then a thing of danger," he declared. MacPherson's Buick was designed to travel up to 50 miles an hour, and "[u]nless its wheels were sound and strong, injury was almost certain."

One of the subtle elements of craftsmanship in Cardozo's opinion is its apparent moderation. The opinion does not announce a revolution in legal doctrine. Cardozo cited established precedent involving not only poisons, explosives, and the like but also anomalous cases in which courts had found that a defective scaffold and an exploding coffee urn were things of danger. He purported to take merely one more half-step, carefully justified by logic and the necessity of changing circumstances. Five of Cardozo's colleagues voted to affirm the judgment against Buick, only one dissented.

Cardozo launched attacks on two citadels, however. One was the attack on the privity doctrine. This was more or less an open attack; that is, Cardozo addressed privity directly, and although he purported merely to expand previously recognized exceptions, the implications are reasonably apparent. Cars are not the only mass-produced product that may turn out to be especially dangerous. Cardozo, however, also launched a second, far more subtle attack on a second fortress—the concept that one should be held accountable to another only if one has so agreed (e.g., by giving a warranty) or has done something wrong (e.g., by acting negligently).

Cardozo's opinion does not expressly say anything like this. This was a negligence case, and Cardozo's opinion stands only for the proposition that the manufacturer of a product that is "reasonably certain to place life and limb in peril when negligently made" is "under a duty to make it carefully" and owes this duty not only to the immediate purchaser but to anyone who reasonably could be expected to use the product. Or as Cardozo put it, "where danger is to be foreseen, a liability will follow." Yet by making the concept that a negligently made product may be "thing of danger" the heart of his rationale, Cardozo wrote an opinion that fell not only along a progression of cases involving exceptions to the privity rule but along a second axis as well—one where courts recognized an exception to the rule that one was liable to another only for wrongful conduct.

Common law courts had long held that one was responsible for harm caused by his animals, even if he had done everything reasonable to prevent such harm. This applied to barnyard animals such as cows, horses, hogs, and sheep. Someone who raised cattle and carefully fenced her animals in to prevent them from wandering onto adjacent lands would be held liable if, though through no fault of her own, those cattle escaped and trampled a neighbor's crops. Strict liability also applied to wild animals. The same year the New York Court of Appeals handed down its decision in *MacPherson*, for example, a lower New York court decided a case involving a woman who attended a vaudeville performance and was trampled by stampeding patrons when three performing lions escaped from their cages.[10] The law was well settled that the liability of an owner of a vicious animal was, as the court put it, "absolute, and he is bound to keep the animal secure, or he must suffer the penalty for his failure to do so," even if he had taken all possible precautions.

This case had a twist, however. The plaintiff did not sue the owner of the lions (who may have been difficult to locate, if he had a traveling act) but the theater. This was a defendant that neither owned nor controlled the wild animals. It had merely booked an act. The plaintiff did not claim the theater had been negligent but argued that it should be subject to strict liability. The court agreed. "Just as the owner could not under these circumstances relieve himself of liability by proof of due care in securing the animals, so the defendant cannot relieve itself of liability by showing that a third party owned and had the actual physical care of the animals."

The court also went on to say that the defendant's "wrong" consisted of bringing dangerous animals onto its premises, but it did not really mean this. There was nothing wrong in having dangerous animals in a circus act. It was not unlawful, and it did not violate social norms. What the court meant was that if, for profit, someone allows dangerous animals on his premises, then it is fair to hold him liable to any injuries that result, regardless of why they result. The defendant's liability stems from participating in a dangerous enterprise. And there is nothing "wrong" in doing that either. Dangerous enterprises are not necessarily bad; some are socially desirable, even necessary. But a rule of strict liability exerts pressure on those conducting dangerous enterprises to ensure maximum safety. It also recognizes that since some degree of harm may be inevitable, those who benefit from the activity must be prepared to shoulder this cost.

Beyond the wrinkle of deciding whether the rule should be applied to a theater owner, none of this was new in 1916. Moreover, animals were far from the only instances were strict liability applied. The leading case was still *Rylands v. Fletcher,* decided by the House of Lords in 1868.[11] The defendants in that case needed water for their mill. They hired competent engineers and contractors to construct a reservoir on their land. No one had any reason to know that, some time in the long-forgotten past, coal mining had taken place on that land, and vertical shafts, now fully concealed by soil, lay under the surface. When the reservoir was filled, an underground shaft gave way and water rushed through a maze of tunnels, flooding coal mines operated by the plaintiffs some distance away. The House of Lords held that "plaintiff, though free from all blame on his part, must bear the loss" and declared the principle that one "who for his own purposes brings on his lands and collects and keeps there anything likely to do mischief if it escapes, must keep it in at his peril, and if he does not do so, is prima facie answerable for all the damages which is the natural consequence of its escape."

During the same era, American courts decided that liability would generally be based on fault, whether intentional unintentional, the most common species of which is negligence. Chief Justice Lemuel Shaw of Massachusetts looms large once again; he is credited for being the first, in an 1850 case, to make fault and its subcategory of negligence the generally applicable standard.[12] Following Shaw, American courts made fault the default standard, applying in all circumstances except where specifically displaced.

Courts in both England and America in the same period developed a general concept as to when strict liability would apply instead of fault: one who engaged in an enterprise that exposed others to an abnormal danger would be strictly liable for resulting injuries. Keeping wild animals is one example. Others included storing, transporting, or using large quantities of gas, inflammable liquids, or explosives; blasting; pile driving; fumigating or crop dusting with dangerous chemicals; setting open fires; emitting smoke or dust in populated areas.

Judicial thinking was often muddled about whether it was the size or the unusual nature of the risk that mattered. Language was part of the problem. Courts often described danger with adjectives—uncommon, abnormal, excessive—that could be understood either way. Over time, this led some commentators to conclude, perhaps erroneously, that both factors were necessary.

The special-danger theme emerged not only from activities courts placed on the strict liability list but also from those they took off it. American courts tended to reject the rule of *Rylands v. Fletcher* as enunciated in that case; that is, they did not apply strict liability whenever something stored on A's land escaped and invaded B's land. Many courts took barnyard animals off the list. Some commentators have suggested that this was because courts, especially those in western states, were persuaded it was more efficient for crop growers to fence wandering cattle out of their land than for cattle owners to fence them in. Some suggest it was because grazing cattle had become common in these areas, and thus the risk ceased to be unusual. But another factor was probably present, if not dominant: American courts tended to find strict liability more appropriate for risks of personal injury than for property damage alone.

All of this was well underway when Cardozo wrote *MacPherson*. Thus, when he said an automobile was "a thing of danger" when negligently made, Cardozo employed a rationale with two implications, one relating to the privity rule, the other to the question of when negligence should be displaced by strict liability. Cardozo mentioned only the former. "The charge is one . . . of negligence," he stated at the beginning of the opinion, and he never raised the question of whether strict liability should apply instead. The legal mind, however, turns naturally to analogical reasoning. The expressed analogy was to privity exceptions, yet the analogy to strict liability jurisprudence stares one in the face. It is unlikely that someone as astute and deft as Benjamin N. Cardozo did not understand that the logic of his opinion ran down two tracks, or that he did not so intend.

At first blush, *MacPherson* seems like a poor vehicle for launching bold attacks. It was, notwithstanding the jury's verdict, a weak case. Plaintiff's claim was negligence; yet Buick had relied on a firm with both recognized expertise and an established track record of making high-quality wheels. Plaintiff argued that Buick should have inspected the wheels itself—but how? Experts disagreed about whether it was useful to scrape off the paint to examine grain or to place wheels under hydraulic pressure. Under these circumstances, would it have been sensible for Buick to second-guess the judgment of a specialist that had supplied Buick with tens of thousands of apparently high quality wheels? Or put the other way around: Was Buick negligent in relying on someone with greater expertise than Buick itself possessed? Generally, one is not negligent for relying on expert advice, even if the expert turns out to be wrong.

Yet it was the very weakness of the negligence claim that suited Cardozo's purposes. "We have put aside the notion that the duty to safeguard life and limb, when consequences of negligence may be foreseen, grows out of contract and nothing else," Cardozo wrote. "We have put the source of obligation where it ought to be. We have put its source in the law." Though he was careful not to question it, the concept of negligence recedes in Cardozo's opinion. It is considerations of public policy that come to the fore. If we substitute the term *product failure* for *negligence* in the above passage, no harm is done to Cardozo's reasoning; indeed, it stands on even firmer legs.

That, of course, is what *MacPherson* is all about. At bottom, it does not matter whether the wheel broke because it was made from the wrong kind of wood or because of some anomaly in this particular unit. It does not matter whether Buick made wheels itself or subcontracted them. It does not matter whether Buick should have independently examined the wheel. It matters only that the wheel broke. It is not a negligently made automobile that is a thing of danger; it is an automobile careening out of control, for whatever reason inherent in the vehicle itself that is a thing of danger. That is the inescapable logic of Cardozo's opinion.

Cardozo helped create a new paradigm in American law and thought. Lord Abinger's paradigm was based on contract. Someone who sold a wagon had whatever responsibilities he voluntarily assumed as a result of that transaction. If a seller represented that his wagon was well made and suitable for traveling on the country roads, he would be legally responsible for compensating the purchaser in the event that the wagon was not what he had warranted. The law's concern was setting straight the original bargain between buyer and seller.

This was the world of *caveat emptor*. To protect himself, a careful purchaser could insist on a warranty. The law, however, did not create obligations; it merely enforced promises voluntarily made and undertaken by businessmen (and I use the gender-specific term deliberately). Society's main interest was facilitating commerce. People were more likely to engage in commercial transactions if they knew there was a mechanism to enforce contracts, including warranties.

The class-based ramifications of Abinger's paradigm are obvious. Those with superior bargaining power—generally, the wealthy and powerful—are in the best position to demand or, conversely, to refuse to give warranties. And of course, Abinger's paradigm has no room for an injured mail coachman, to whom no promise had been made.

Cardozo's paradigm was based on public policy. "We have put aside the notion that the duty to safeguard life and limb . . . grows out of contract and nothing else," he wrote. "We have put the source of obligation where it ought to be. We have put its source in the law." No longer is the law's gaze fixed only upon the bipolar relationship between seller and buyer. Its ken is wider. Under Cardozo's paradigm, the law takes account of the fact that society at large has a stake in wheels on mail wagons, on cars carrying sick neighbors to the hospital, on school buses. One may killed by the failure of a wheel she never selected, never purchased, and never used. Recognizing that manufacturers of mass-produced goods affect public safety in a way that artisans never did, Cardozo's paradigm gives manufacturers an incentive not to expose citizens to unreasonable risk.

The First Revolution: Strict Liability for Defective Products

In retrospect, Cardozo's paradigm seems all but inevitable. Yet it would be nearly four decades before the common law would adopt strict liability for unreasonably dangerous products, creating the field known as products liability. An important milestone along the way is the first *Restatement of the Law of Torts*, promulgated in 1938 by the American Law Institute (ALI), a private but influential organization. The *Restatement* stated that strict liability applied to ultrahazardous activities—or, as it put it, "one who carries on an ultrahazardous activity is liable to another [who] the actor should recognize is likely to be harmed by the unpreventable miscarriage of the activity." [13]

The first *Restatement* was important for a couple of reasons. It acknowledged that the doctrine that strict liability applied to ultrahazardous activities was a principle of general application. That is, strict liability did not apply merely to collections of individual circumstances, such as wild animals and blasting. The principle abstracted from particular enterprises now applied generically, to all types of ultrahazardous activities. The first *Restatement* made it clear that strict liability was not for instances when, for example, the actor was probably negligent but negligence was too difficult to prove. The degree of care used by the actor was irrelevant. Strict liability was often most appropriate when care could not ensure safety. "[T]he thing which makes the storage of dynamite ultrahazardous is the gravity of the harm which will result from its explosion together with the practical impossibility of making a magazine of high explosives absolutely explosion-proof," the official comments explained. This was a clean break with the fault principle.

The first *Restatement* did not apply strict liability to manufacturers. It associated strict liability with using products, not making them. If an airplane fell from the sky and crashed into a home, those injured would have a strict liability claim against the plane's operator, not against the manufacturer. Airplane flight was still considered ultrahazardous in 1938. Courts stopped applying strict liability to air travel as it became safer. By contrast, the *Restatement* did not apply strict liability to driving because, among other reasons, "the risk involved in the careful operation of a carefully maintained automobile is slight." It noted, however, that driving an unusually large and heavy automobile that created special risks for others would be subject to strict liability—an observation interesting today in light of the special risks of SUVs, a subject discussed in the next chapter.

Several dates might be used to mark the fall of the citadels. One might pick 1960 when, for the first time, a state's highest court held that a manufacturer is strictly liable to ultimate users, regardless of privity, when its products are not reasonably suited for their intended use and injury results.[14] But probably the best date to mark the fall of the citadels is 1964, when the ALI adopted the *Restatement (Second) of Torts*. The second *Restatement* stated in part:

> One who sells any product in a defective condition unreasonably danger-
> ous to the user or consumer or to his property is subject to strict liability
> for physical harm thereby caused.[15]

The rule expressly provided that strict liability applied regardless of whether the seller exercised all possible care, and regardless of whether there was any contractual relationship between seller and user. This *Restatement* section was to be cited in more than three thousand court opinions and, in one fashion or another, to become accepted by every American jurisdiction.

Through a quirk of history, however, the second *Restatement* was drafted in a fashion that has resulted in decades of confusion among judges, lawyers, and legal scholars. Moreover, it has been the worst kind of confusion—the kind that occurs when the confused are not consciously aware of their befuddlement. The story is worth telling.

The most basic question in products liability is: What is it about a product that calls for imposing strict liability? The second *Restatement* gives an ambiguous answer to that question. It states that a product is subject to strict liability when it is in a "defective condition unreasonably dangerous to the user." There is no preposition between the phrases "defective condition" and "unreasonably dangerous," and no other words expressing a relationship between those two concepts. It not clear whether a product must be defective *or* unreasonably dangerous, defective *and* unreasonably dangerous, or in a defective condition *that is* unreasonably dangerous to the user. Moreover, neither the phrase "defective condition" nor the phrase "unreasonably dangerous" is adequately defined. This has created a Tower of Babel in which courts and scholars use the same words to mean different things, often without realizing it.

How did this Tower of Babel get built? Part of the explanation is that the carpenters had different agendas. Part of it is summed up by the adage that a donkey is a horse designed by committee. And part is simply that people made a key decision when they were tired, bored, and hungry.

The most important individual in a restatement project is the person selected to be the reporter. The reporter both writes the initial draft and serves as sort of an official adviser during the process. The reporter for the second *Restatement* was William L. Prosser. Since publication of his classic treatise, *The Law of Torts*, in 1941, then in its second edition, Prosser reigned as the preeminent torts scholar in America. Prosser was also a man with considerable personal charm. In short, Prosser had the position, personal capital, and skills to exert great influence over the project. Prosser happened to be a forceful advocate for strict products liability. And though he was still formulating his views, there is little doubt Prosser unambiguously supported Cardozo's paradigm.

In 1958, Prosser produced a first draft of the products liability section. Prosser's draft did not speak of defect; it applied strict liability to food "in a condition dangerous to the consumer."[16] A subsequent draft presented to the council two years later contained the same language.[17] Some members of the council (a traditionally conservative group), however, sought to narrow the scope of liability, and they changed the phrase to "defective condition unreasonably dangerous to the user or consumer." When, in 1961, this language was presented to the ALI's full membership for final adoption, F. Reed Dickerson, a law professor at the University of Indiana at Bloomington, rose to his feet and addressed the Institute:

> Mr. Chairman, may I make a small point? In this discussion of substantive issues I hesitate to bring up a mere question of draftsmanship, but I think this may have some significance. . . .
>
> I had always thought that "unreasonably dangerous" was simply the best possible test for what was legally defective. It seems to me . . . that everything we might want to cover here is subsumed under the words "unreasonably dangerous."
>
> Now, the addition of the words "defective condition"—it would seem to me that this involves unnecessary questions of meaning. For example, in addition to "unreasonably dangerous," what would a purchaser have to show in order to make out a defective product? I would think that if he showed that it was unreasonably dangerous, it would be per se legally defective, and it is only gilding the lily to add the word "defective."
>
> For these reasons I move that we strike the word "defective."[18]

At this juncture, Prosser made a mistake. He said Dickerson's suggestion would restore his own—that is, Prosser's original language. Prosser then tried to explain why the council changed his original draft:

> The Council [raised] the question of a number of products which, even though not defective, are in fact dangerous to the consumer—whiskey, for example [laughter]; cigarettes, which cause lung cancer; various types of drugs which can be administered with safety up to a point but may be dangerous if carried beyond that—and they raised the question of whether "unreasonably dangerous" was sufficient to protect the defendant against possible liability in such cases.
>
> Therefore, they suggested that there must be something wrong with the product itself, and hence the word "defective" was put in. . . .
>
> Now, I was rather indifferent to that. I thought "unreasonably dangerous" on the other hand, carried every meaning that was necessary, as Mr. Dickerson does; but I could see the point, so I accepted the change.[19]

By the time Dickerson brought this matter up the ALI had spent more than two hours discussing the proposed explanatory comments to the section. The members were tired, and some may have been especially tired of hearing from Dickerson, who had spent much of the morning making lengthy criticisms about relatively minor matters.

Perhaps Dickerson sensed impatience in the room and thought it would be better to sound as if this was not going to take long. The understated introduction was unfortunate, however. No one was alerted to the fact that, rather than a small point of draftsmanship, Dickerson was raising the fundamental question of what it was about a product that would subject it to strict liability. Two other law professors spoke briefly in support of Dickerson's motion, but the matter was quickly concluded in a voice vote. "The noes seem to me to have it," the chair concluded, and no one took him up on his invitation to have the votes counted.

Even more unfortunate was Prosser's own confusion at this moment. Prosser told the members that the council previously considered and rejected the very language that Dickerson was suggesting. This was, in fact, not true. Prosser's original language applied strict liability to "dangerous"—rather than *"unreasonably* dangerous"—goods. The council's insistence on qualifying this further made sense. Strict liability cannot sensibly be imposed on all dangerous products. Many dangerous products are socially desirable. Some drugs present risks of serious side effects but are nonetheless essential to save lives, for example. Cars are certainly dangerous, but in our society they are necessary. But even more important, all products are dangerous to some extent. Boats, trains, and planes are safer than cars, but sometimes boats sink, trains collide, and planes fall from the sky. Someone may be cut with a knife or, if allergic, suffer a fatal anaphylactic reaction from a single peanut. Therefore, imposing strict liability simply on "dangerous products" does not work.

While it was appropriate to qualify Prosser's language, the council added not one but two qualifications: (1) *unreasonably* dangerous and (2) *defective* condition. As we have seen, the concept of special danger was historically related to strict liability. The concept was modernized by using the concept of unreasonableness, which implies that an evaluation must be made as to whether the risk is appropriate, rather than relying on adjectives such as *uncommon* or *abnormal,* which courts sometimes tried to apply mechanistically. This policy-oriented approach fits squarely within Cardozo's paradigm. The additional qualification of defectiveness, however, reaches back to Abinger. The comments state a product is defective only when it is "in a condition not contemplated by the ultimate consumer."[20] A consumer expectation test is contract oriented; it focuses on protecting a purchaser from hidden flaws or imperfections.

The products liability section of the second *Restatement* became the single most influential provision ever promulgated by the ALI.[21] Many states adopted products liability with specific reference to this provision; it has been cited in more than three thousand judicial opinions.

The first revolution in products liability, therefore, was strict liability for defective products. There is a tendency to assume that the early concept of defect was roughly equivalent to what we now call "manufacturing defects," that is, unintended flaws resulting from some miscarriage in the manufacturing process. A unit with a manufacturing defect differs from the manufacturer's own blueprints and specifications and from other units produced by the manufacturer. A bubble in the glass of a champagne bottle that turns the bottle into a grenade and a bad weld in an airplane fuselage are examples. The first revolution was not strictly limited to manufacturing defects, however. MacPherson's Buick collapsed either because the individual wheel that collapsed contained a flaw or because all the wheels on Buick automobiles were made from the wrong kind of wood. And *MacPherson* is by no means unique in this regard. The New Jersey Supreme Court first applied the doctrine in a case involving a car that crashed because of an undetermined problem in the steering mechanism. The California Supreme Court first applied it in a case involving a power tool that failed because the set screws were not adequate for the machine's vibration.[22] Both of these cases may have involved a manufacturing defect, a design failure, or some combination of the two. Why the product was defective did not really matter, only that it was defective.

While no single definition of "defective product" was adequate (the second *Restatement* lists seven alternative definitions), it is probably fair to say the concept was connected more to result than cause. That is, products were defective if they failed in performance, regardless of the reason for failure. This is not to say that all first-revolution cases are easy ones. Everyone would agree that MacPherson's Buick failed; but does a truck fail if, with seven thousand miles on the odometer and traveling on a blacktop highway at 50 mph, it hits a rock approximately six inches in diameter and, thirty-five miles later, spins out of control and tips over?[23] These questions pushed courts toward a second revolution in products liability—one more radical than the first.

The Second Revolution: Strict Liability for Nondefective Products with Unreasonably Dangerous Features

If MacPherson's Buick illustrates the first revolution, the Ford Pinto exemplifies the second.[24] In the late 1960s, Lee Iacocca, then executive vice president of the Ford Motor Company, decreed that within two years Ford would design and bring to market a subcompact that would weigh no more than two thousand pounds and sell for no more $2,000. This presented Ford engineers with an enormous challenge. Producing a car within the weight and cost constraints was difficult enough, but complicating the task was the time requirement. Never before had Ford produced a car, from drawing board to assembly line, so quickly.

The Pinto, as the car was named, had to be "thrifted" to meet the price goal, and to proceed quickly, engineers started with an existing design and essentially lopped off a large portion of the rear end. Engineers traditionally preferred positioning the fuel tank above the rear axle, where it would be protected in accidents, but this became difficult and the engineers put the tank behind the rear axle instead. To limit weight, the engineers eliminated reinforcing side and cross members from the rear structure, and the rear bumper was reduced to an ornamental chrome strip. There were only nine inches of "crush space" between the fuel tank and the rear axle, which meant that in a rear-end collision, the fuel tank could easily be driven into the axle and ripped open.

At about this time, the National Highway Traffic Safety Administration (NHTSA) made it known that it was considering new fuel-system integrity standards, including a requirement that fuel tanks in cars and light trucks be able to withstand a 30 mph rear-end collision. Ford engineers understood that this presented special problems for their new subcompact, so to determine whether the Pinto could meet the proposed standards, Ford secretly conducted more than forty tests on prototypes. The fuel tank ruptured in every test at over 25 mph. In all of these tests, fuel leakage violated NHTSA's standard, and in at least one test gasoline flooded the driver's compartment.

Ford engineers developed a menu of approaches to address the problem, such as lining the gas tank with a nylon bladder at a cost of $5.25 to $8.00 per car or reinforcing the rear structure with side and cross members at cost of $4.20 per car. But every penny counted in the effort to meet Iacocca's goals, and Ford executives rejected all of the engineering suggestions. They decided not to incorporate any of these features until at least 1977, when NHTSA regulations relating to side and rear impacts were scheduled to become effective.

The Pinto was an enormous commercial success; Ford sold nearly 1.5 million within five years. No one knows how many people burned to death as a result. NHTSA identified thirty-eight deaths resulting from Pinto fuel-tank fires, but other estimates run between five hundred and nine hundred fatalities. More than a hundred products liability lawsuits were filed, and eventually much of the Pinto information was unearthed through the litigation discovery process. The best known of the Pinto lawsuits arose out of an accident that occurred May 28, 1972, when a Pinto was struck from the rear by a Ford Galaxy. The Galaxy was traveling between 28 and 37 miles an hour at impact. Under normal circumstances, the occupants might have been injured, but not critically. The Pinto's gas tank was driven forward and punctured, however, and gasoline sprayed into the passenger compartment and ignited.

The driver died from burn injuries several days later. Her only passenger, thirteen-year-old Richard Grimshaw, was saved through heroic measures but lost several fingers and part of an ear and had major surgeries and skin-graft operations over a period of ten years. A jury awarded the driver's family and Richard Grimshaw a total of $3.5 million in compensatory damages and $125 million in punitive damages. No one familiar with the data will be surprised to learn that the trial judge reduced the punitive award to $3.5 million (an amount equal to the compensatory damages). The appellate court declined Ford's request to eliminate the punitive award entirely. Ford knowingly endangered the lives of thousands of Pinto owners, it said, and the reduced punitive award represented only about .03 percent of Ford's net annual income. At the same time, the court rejected Grimshaw's request to increase the punitive award, noting that Ford might have to pay punitive damages in other cases as well.

MacPherson's Buick and the Ford Pinto both imperiled their occupants, but they did so in different ways. MacPherson's Buick failed on its own accord. It was not mishandled or mistreated in any fashion. It was doing exactly what it was supposed to do, simply driving along, when it collapsed. It was the Buick that failed, nothing else. The Pinto, by contrast, exploded only when subjected to an external force, that is, another car smashing into it. Everyone understands perfectly well that cars should not be mistreated in this fashion. Thus, the Pinto failed only when its owner or some third party did something wrong, or, in the language of negligence law, only when there was an intervening cause.[25]

One may believe that Ford executives acted irresponsibly in selling cars with gas tanks that they knew were prone to explode in rear-end collisions. For what it is worth, their defense is that the Pinto was no more dangerous than other American subcompacts at the time—which was true, but only because other subcompacts had their own safety problems. Products liability is not a fault-based system, however. Products liability ignores the manufacturer's conduct and focuses on the product. There was a problem with the Pinto, to be sure, but it was not that the Pinto was defective. The Pinto was not mismanufactured, broken, or faulty; it was built and functioned exactly as intended. It is a large leap from the proposition that manufacturers should be liable for injuries caused by product failure to the proposition that manufacturers should be liable because their products did not protect users from their own or someone else's negligence.

Courts did not embrace the crashworthiness doctrine—which holds that vehicles should provide a reasonable degree of protection in accidents—easily. In a 1966 case, for example, the plaintiff argued that a station wagon should have had a rectangular steel frame protecting the cabin and its occupants. The court wrote:

> Plaintiff argues that the defendant's "X" frame permitted the side of the automobile to collapse against the decedent when his station wagon was struck broadside by another vehicle. Plaintiff does not assert the "X" frame caused the decedent's automobile to be driven into the path of the striking car or prevented it from being driven out of the path.[26]

The court held that there was no liability. "The intended purpose of an automobile does not include its participation in collisions with other objects," it explained.[27]

This way of looking at things could not last. Although, as previously discussed, it is not strictly accurate to say that the first revolution included manufacturing defects and excluded design defects, it is true nonetheless that manufacturing flaws were clearly included within concept of defect while design hazards were doctrinally more ambiguous. Yet the public is exposed to greater risks from products with unsafe features than from those with manufacturing defects. Design hazards make every unit in a product line dangerous, whereas manufacturing defects affect only occasional units; thus there are far more products with design hazards than with manufacturing defects. Any doctrine that takes surer aim at lesser risks than at greater ones will inevitably become unstable.

It is not surprising, therefore, that eleven years after it held that the plaintiff who challenged the X frame of a station wagon did not state a cause of action, the same court adopted the crashworthiness doctrine.[28] "[M]anufacturers must anticipate and take precautions against reasonably foreseeable risks in use of their products," it held.[29] And in language diametrically opposite to the reasoning in the earlier opinion, the court noted that "a collision is a foreseeable incident of [a vehicle's] normal use. Thus, to say that collisions are not within their 'intended purpose' is unrealistic."[30] The crashworthiness doctrine is now well accepted[31] and, as discussed more fully in the previous chapter, has paid large dividends in lower automobile fatality rates.

The second revolution has been obscured by nomenclature. There is not truly anything defective about a car with an X frame, or a machine that does not have an interlock device preventing it from operating if the guard is removed, or a drug that is reasonably safe for certain uses but is being promiscuously prescribed in situations where its potential side effects exceed its benefits. All these cases involve nondefective products with unreasonably dangerous features. The label "design defect" is a misnomer, a remnant of the first generation. The linchpin of liability is not a defect but an unreasonably dangerous aspect or feature of the product.

The continued use of word *defect* has hidden the radicalism of the second revolution. The first revolution—which was truly defect oriented—was premised on the idea that the consumer did not get what he bargained for and hence originally defined *defect* in terms of consumer expectation. It was grounded in contract law. The second revolution was concerned not only with the seller-buyer relationship but with how products affect society at large. The linchpin of liability is not defect but unreasonable danger, and consequently the consumer expectation has been largely replaced by the risk-utility test.

The Third Revolution: Strict Liability for Unreasonably Dangerous Products

The third revolution in products liability is strict liability that is imposed on products that are unreasonably dangerous despite the best possible design, construction, and warnings. To many that seems like a radical concept. But in fact, the third is the least radical of the three revolutions. After all, if strict liability attaches to products with unreasonably dangerous features, how can it not attach to unreasonably dangerous products?

Consider first the prosaic case of *Shetterly v. Crown Control Corp.*,[32] which involved eight workers who suffered sprained, twisted, and broken ankles while using a Crown Pallet Truck during the course of their employment in a grocery warehouse. This unique vehicle was especially designed to collect boxes of groceries from warehouse floors. The truck consists of a set of forks on which rest wooden pallets, which are used as a platform for stacking cartons of groceries. Unlike a forklift, which is used to raise and lower objects, the pallet truck is used to collect boxes stored at ground level, and the pallet cannot be raised more than a few inches above floor level. The operator controls the truck by using handles perpendicularly affixed to a control arm at the front end of the vehicle. These handles permit the operator to operate the pallet truck while either riding on the platform or walking alongside the vehicle.

One of the principal features of the pallet truck is a coast control device, which allows the truck to coast slowly to a stop. If the operator releases the handle when he is beside an item he wishes to pick up, the vehicle will coast to a stop so that the pallet is right next to that item. By eliminating the need to carry cartons even short distances, the coast control device cumulatively saves great amounts of time. Operators are not injured if they ride on or walk beside the truck. Plaintiffs, however, all released the control handle before they were beside cartons they wished to pick up and walked in front of the vehicle while it was coasting. The pallet truck struck them at ankle height.

The federal district judge who heard the case first considered whether there was a feasible alternative design that would have prevented the plaintiffs' injuries. Experts testified that the control handles could not be made longer without interfering with the operator's ability to ride on the vehicle. The platform could not be lowered or equipped with a rubber guard because the vehicle had to clear debris that inevitably litters warehouse floors. The coast control device could not be eliminated without destroying the pallet truck's *raison d'être*—its great efficiency. Thus, the court concluded there was no feasible alternative design.

Next, the court conducted a risk-utility analysis to determine whether pallet trucks are unreasonably dangerous. It found that pallet trucks have high utility. After the grocery warehouse started using pallet trucks, the productivity of workers such as the plaintiffs, who assemble orders by retrieving cartons of groceries from various locations in the warehouse, increased 53 percent. Pallet trucks reduced assembly costs for this one firm by more than $2 million annually. The court found that these savings ultimately resulted in lower food prices for consumers. On the risk side of the ledger, the evidence was that the foot injuries for assemblers working on pallet trucks occurred at a rate of only one injury per 400 work years. Meanwhile, pallet trucks resulted in fewer back injuries, which were more frequent and on average more severe than foot injuries. The court found, therefore, that pallet trucks were not unreasonably dangerous, and it dismissed the plaintiffs' action.

What was significant was that the court did not end its analysis after determining that there was no alternative feasible design; it went on to determine whether the product's risks outweighed its benefits, and presumably it would have imposed liability if they had. This is generic liability analysis. Generic liability is a form of products liability. When a product remains unreasonably dangerous despite the best possible design, construction, and warnings, we have a choice. One alternative is to decide that products liability ends at this point. Since there is nothing more the manufacturer could do to make the product safer, there is no purpose to holding it liable. The other alternative is to impose liability—not merely on defective units or unreasonably dangerous models or brands but on products that generically fail a risk-utility test. Another name for this concept is *product category liability,* since liability is imposed on an entire product category—all pallet trucks or all cigarettes.

Generic liability is at the cutting edge of products liability and is very controversial. Many judges do not yet know the term or are not even consciously aware of the concept. Nevertheless, *Shetterly* is representative of how courts are conducting risk-utility analyses to determine whether a wide array of product categories should be deemed unreasonably dangerous and, consequently, subject to strict liability.[33]

Generic liability is running toward the future on two tracks. The first track, which in many ways may be the more significant, consists of commonplace cases such as *Shetterly.* There is, however, a second, far more visible track involving politically controversial struggles over tobacco and guns. For decades, smokers unsuccessfully sued tobacco companies. Indeed, injured smokers filed more than a thousand lawsuits against tobacco companies—and lost them all. Nearly everyone understands that something significant is happening, and that whatever it is began with tobacco litigation and may be spreading to guns. But exactly what is happening is not yet as well understood. It is to this question, and the future, that the concluding chapter turns.

8

The Common Law and the Future

Tobacco and Guns

On January 8, 1998, the *Philadelphia Inquirer* reported that lawyers for the City of Philadelphia were prepared to institute an action against gun manufacturers.[1] It was, at least publicly, a new idea. According to the article, the complaint would claim that gun manufacturers had created a public nuisance by saturating Philadelphia with guns. "The approach mirrors that taken by a group of state attorneys general who negotiated a groundbreaking settlement with the tobacco industry," noted the newspaper.

This report that Philadelphia was considering such an action received national attention. Not only is Philadelphia the fifth largest city in the nation, but its mayor, Edward G. Rendell, was sufficiently prominent and popular at a national level to have earned the sobriquet "America's mayor."

Mayor Rendell never filed that action, however.[2] In fact, subsequent reports led some observers to wonder whether information contained in the January 8 article had been leaked to the press by people within the Rendell administration or its legal team who feared they were fighting a losing battle to convince the mayor to proceed with the lawsuit.[3] Rendell had reason to consider the political ramifications of such an action carefully. Between the cities of Philadelphia and Pittsburgh lie more than 250 mostly rural miles. Nearly a quarter of a million members of the National Rifle Association (NRA) live in Pennsylvania, and the conventional wisdom is that politicians with statewide ambitions cannot afford to cross the NRA.[4] In any event, Rendell decided against proceeding.

But the genie was out of the bottle. Other mayors were persuaded about the merits of suing the gun industry. By the time Rendell announced he had decided against filing suit, five other cities had filed actions against gun manufacturers.[5] Within a relatively short period of time, more than thirty cities and counties filed actions against gun manufacturers.[6] The attorneys general of New York and Connecticut announced they were considering bringing similar actions on behalf of their states,[7] and the Clinton administration announced it was preparing an action against gun manufacturers focusing on gun violence in the thirty-two hundred housing authorities.[8] Philadelphia filed an action after Rendell left office.

Actions by governmental bodies differ from other cases in that they represent government policy. This does not mean there is a single, unified government policy. On the contrary, the municipality gun litigation is the subject of vigorous political struggles within government. While, on the one hand municipalities have been filing suits against gun manufacturers, at least ten state legislatures, on the other hand, have enacted statutes prohibiting local governments from pursing such actions, and similar bills are pending in a dozen more states.[9]

Nevertheless, actions by major cities such as Atlanta, Chicago, Cleveland, Detroit, District of Columbia, Los Angeles, Miami, New Orleans, Philadelphia, San Francisco, and St. Louis represent powerful normative statements. With more than thirty cities filing lawsuits and state attorneys general and the federal government publicly considering similar actions, it is no longer possible to dismiss the notion of gun manufacturer liability as bizarre, extremist, or out of touch with mainstream thought.

Most of the debate about the new wave of gun litigation revolves around legal doctrine, about whether a plaintiff's theories—including public nuisance, negligence, and products liability—may properly be applied to guns. I use the term *guns* to refer only to two categories of firearms: handguns and long guns equipped with large-capacity magazines. Handguns comprise about half of all guns in America but account for more than 80 percent of all firearm murders,[10] and the special threat to public safety posed by rifles with large-capacity magazines—which can spew thirty or more rounds in a matter of seconds— has become all too obvious.[11] But in fact, the fate of gun litigation does not hinge primarily on doctrinal arguments. Most of the theories are broad and malleable enough to permit courts to apply or not apply them to these cases. Flexibility is one of the hallmarks of tort law. Indeed, it has been said that while there may be black-letter rules in many areas of law, in torts there are only gray rules. Consider, for example, what William Prosser says about the doctrine of nuisance:

> There is perhaps no more impenetrable jungle in the entire law than that which surrounds the word "nuisance." It has meant all things to all people, and has been applied indiscriminately to everything from an alarming advertisement to a cockroach baked in a pie. There is general agreement that it is incapable of any exact or comprehensive definition.[12]

I do not quote this passage to disparage the theory of public nuisance.[13] My point is that tort law is necessarily elastic. It must be able to be stretched to fit new situations as courts deem it necessary to do so. The same can be said for products liability doctrine. The courts, therefore, can interpret—or, if necessary, mold—tort law to fit what courts think it ought to fit. Hence, the future of gun litigation will not ultimately be determined by doctrinal argument but by something deeper. Though the courts may not think this through on a conscious level, the fate of gun litigation hinges on whether the courts think this kind of litigation is consistent with—and perhaps more than consistent, whether it supports—fundamental societal values.

The story of how values relate to gun litigation begins not with the cities' lawsuits against gun manufacturers but with lawsuits filed several years earlier against tobacco companies by the state attorneys general. While everyone understands that tobacco litigation has made gun litigation possible, few appreciate why. The general assumption is that the law somehow changed about government lawsuits against private parties, but this is not so. This is a story not about legal doctrine but about disciplined democracy—about the interplay between law and fundamental societal values.

From the 1950s to the mid-1990s, smokers who contracted cancer and other diseases filed more than a thousand lawsuits against cigarette companies.[14] With the exception of one case relating not to tobacco but to asbestos contained in Kent cigarettes' "Micronite" filter, the cigarette companies had won them all.[15] It is worth pausing just a moment to consider the significance of that figure. Different lawyers, many of them highly skilled, representing different parties filed more than a thousand lawsuits against tobacco companies. Most of these lawyers undertook these actions knowing many had tried before but had been unsuccessful. They did so because they believed they had sympathetic facts and sound legal theories, in short, that their cases were strong enough to succeed despite long odds. They deployed different theories and strategies. They litigated in different courts in different jurisdictions at different times, spanning nearly half a century. Of course, the tobacco companies had far greater resources than any of their adversaries and pursued a deliberate strategy of litigating so fiercely as to drive plaintiffs' attorneys into bankruptcy. It does not diminish the effectiveness of this strategy to note that, alone, it does not explain a win-loss ration of one thousand to zero.

The world of tobacco litigation changed on May 23, 1994, when the State of Mississippi sued the tobacco industry, seeking to recover moneys expended by the state's Medicaid program in treating smoking-related illnesses.[16] "In equity and fairness, it is the defendants, not the taxpayers of Mississippi, who should pay the costs of tobacco-related diseases," stated Mississippi's complaint.[17] Other actions were eventually filed by all the other states. By November 1998, the tobacco industry settled these cases, agreeing to pay the states (and in the case of Minnesota, Blue Cross and Blue Shield of Minnesota as well) a total of $242.8 billion.[18] About a year later, the federal government brought its own action against the industry.[19]

Meanwhile, there was a resurgence in garden-variety lawsuits by smokers against tobacco companies, the same kinds of lawsuits the tobacco companies had previously won for more than a thousand in a row—but now plaintiffs sometimes prevailed.[20] A sea change has taken place—but why?

The conventional wisdom is that what changed was the emergence of new evidence showing the tobacco industry had lied about knowing that nicotine was addictive. But this is only part of the answer. The public had long understood how enormously difficult it is to quit smoking, and it had discounted the industry's protestations about the addictive nature of its product, along with its denials about the adverse health consequences of smoking. For the most part, the internal memoranda that came to light demonstrated what everyone already assumed.

What was more important was that the lawsuits by the attorneys general had fundamentally altered how Americans perceived tobacco litigation. The shield that had so effectively protected the tobacco company for so long had to do with fundamental societal values.

What do I mean by fundamental values? Sociologist and political scientist Seymour Martin Lipset has written: "[T]he nation's ideology can be described in five words: liberty, egalitarianism, individualism, populism, and laissez-fare."[21] Lipset speaks about these five values comprising an American creed.[22] In one way or another, all five of these values may affect what we think about, say, gun liability, but for several reasons, the one most relevant to gun control and gun litigation is individualism—a strand that is perhaps stronger than some of the others. For example, both Lipset and sociologist Alan Wolfe suggest that individualism trumps egalitarianism; that is, when the two clash, Americans always chose individualism over egalitarianism.[23]

What do Lipset and Wolfe mean when they talk about the mores of individual responsibility? Consider this passage from Alan Wolfe's most recent book. Speaking of what he calls the "strong ethic of individual responsibility," Wolfe writes:

> The moral ideal of middle-class Americans revolves around the notion that people are responsible for their own fate; they reserve the seventh circle of their moral hell for people like the Menendez brothers who kill their parents but claim that it was because of abuse or those—"sue happy," as one of our respondents called them—who knowingly buy a flawed product and then pursue litigation when its flaws are revealed.[24]

This was the shield that protected the tobacco companies in more than a thousand lawsuits. Jurors had little sympathy for plaintiffs who chose to smoke because they made the individual decision that, for them, the risk was worth the benefit. An adult who makes a deliberate choice must be prepared to accept the consequences of that choice. The idea that one cannot accept the benefits and then be heard to complain about the consequences is expressed in a variety of aphorisms: "If you have made your bed, lie in it"; "One must take the bad with the good." "Who will pity a snake charmer bitten by a serpent?" asked Ecclesiastes (10:11). Or, as Cervantes declared, "Those who'll play with cats must expect to be scratched."

Plaintiffs, of course, tried in many ways to penetrate this shield. Plaintiffs who smoked before the Surgeon General's warning appeared on cigarette packages and in advertising in 1965 argued that they did not know about the health risks when they started smoking and that later they could not stop because they were addicted. It did not work. Juries knew that public awareness about smoking risks was much older. The *New England Journal of Medicine* published a study in 1928 suggesting that smoking appeared to be associated with cancers of the

mouth and lungs.[25] *Reader's Digest*, then the largest-circulation magazine in America, began publishing stories suggesting links between
smoking and illness in 1941. Medical researchers produced the smoking gun, so to speak, in 1950, when the *Journal of the American Medical Association* (*JAMA*) and the *British Medical Journal* published
three large-scale studies establishing a strong correlation between
smoking and lung cancer. In 1953, the journal *Cancer Research* published the famous "mouse house" studies. Researchers had a suction
machine "smoke" Lucky Strikes, then painted the shaved backs of mice
with the substance distilled from the smoke (diluted so the mice did not
immediately die from toxic shock). Of the mice that survived for one
year, 58 percent developed malignant tumors. Ten percent of the
painted mice survived twenty months, compared to 58 percent of mice
in a control group. In 1954, the American Cancer Society released another large study that showed someone smoking one pack a day had a
nine times greater chance of contracting lung cancer than a nonsmoker,
and the risk for heavier smokers was sixteen times greater.

Although many newspapers and magazines avoided reporting this
information out of fear of losing cigarette advertising, enough did so
to communicate the news effectively. *Reader's Digest,* which then did
not accept advertising, continued to publish articles about smoking
and health. Its 1952 story "Cancer by the Carton" made an especially
large splash. The *New Yorker* and *JAMA* stopped accepting cigarette
advertising so that they could publish freely without feeling compromised. The *New York Times* alone ran thirty-three stories about
smoking and health during 1953 and 1954. By this time, the public
was well enough informed that cigarette sales started to decline for
the first time in history. According to a 1954 Gallup poll, 90 percent
of Americans said they had heard or read that cigarettes might be one
of the causes of lung cancer. While not everyone considered the smok-
ing-cancer connection to have been proved conclusively, the public
was aware that smoking might cause cancer and that smoking therefore carried a risk.

Juries, therefore, have little sympathy for victims who began smoking after the early 1950s. Moreover, the argument that a plaintiff
started smoking in the 1940s, became addicted, and could not stop
upon learning of health risks has not been persuasive to juries either.
While jurors are aware that cigarettes are addictive, they believe someone who really wants to can quit. Polls show 69 percent of smokers

themselves believe they can quit (notwithstanding the paradox that 74 percent say they have tried to quit but failed).

But the shield of individual responsibility was not available to the tobacco industry in lawsuits by the states. The plaintiffs were not smokers who chose to smoke because they decided the risks were worth the benefits, but taxpayers. Moreover, what had been a shield protecting the industry in actions by smokers became a sword in the hands of the states. An important corollary to the principle of individual responsibility is the axiom that those who benefit from something should pay for it and not expect others to subsidize them. The state lawsuits drove home the point that those who benefited from tobacco—the industry and its customers—were not fully paying their way. Smokers were bearing the health consequences of their activity[26] but not the full brunt of the economic repercussions. An inherent consequence of widespread tobacco use is that many smokers become ill. Few people, if any, directly pay medical costs in modern America. One is generally covered by insurance, whether private insurance or a government program such as Medicare or Medicaid. While some private insurance programs may charge higher premiums to smokers, Medicaid beneficiaries do not even indirectly pay their medical costs.

Economists refer to this as externalization, which is sometimes illustrated with the following hypothetical case.[27] Imagine a factory that makes widgets. The factory uses a great deal of water during the production process. It draws the water it needs from a river on which it is located and discharges the water back into the river after it is finished with it. The water is badly polluted after its use, however, and the factory does not bother treating it. The result is that the river downstream is essentially destroyed; it is too polluted to drink or to swim or fish in. The factory has externalized the cost of water, which is a production cost in same way as are the costs of labor or electricity—that is, it has foisted that cost off on the people living downstream, who either have lost a resource or must themselves build and operate a water treatment facility.

The principle of individual responsibility and its corollary, that people should pay their own way, require that the factory bear the cost of water treatment. The factory should not escape its responsibility by arguing that the cost of water is too high and would drive the factory out of business any more than the factory could argue that any of the other production costs of widgets are too high. If widgets are sufficiently valuable to those who use them, users will pay the production costs in the price of the product. But if the production costs of widgets exceed their value, then it is reasonable that widgets will no longer be made. Such is the free-market system. (The system is flawed to the extent that the law does not stop factories from polluting.)

Perhaps as a technical matter the issue of cost externalization should affect only the assessment of lawsuits against tobacco companies by third-party payers, and not those by smokers. Public attitudes are necessarily compartmentalized, however. Though they may never have heard the term *cost externalization,* Americans assimilated the concept from the state lawsuits, and this affected public sentiment about imposing civil liability on tobacco companies generally. Previously Americans looked on cigarettes as a lawful product that should be treated like other lawful products. The state legislatures and Congress might regulate the sale of cigarettes in certain ways (e.g., prohibitions on sales to minors, advertising restrictions, mandated warnings); however, Americans did not believe courts should impose additional restrictions, because doing so would treat cigarettes differently from other products.[28] One of the lessons of the attorneys general lawsuits was that civil liability does not result in different treatment for tobacco. Rather, it is necessary to ensure similar treatment. Liability corrects rather than disrupts the free-market system. That is, the characteristics of cigarettes and the health care system combine to create an exception to the free-market principle that those who benefit from something should pay for it. Civil liability corrects this anomaly.

I am not arguing that the public views tobacco litigation solely through the prism of individual responsibility, or that this is all that has changed. During the same period, the public had other reasons to view the tobacco industry with increasing disapprobation. New information came to light that the major tobacco companies were deliberately using nicotine to lure and addict customers,[29] were deliberately promoting cigarettes to minors,[30] and were deliberately lying when they denied these facts.[31] Much of this came to be symbolized by a single image: that of the chief executives of the seven major tobacco companies, standing in a line, right hands held high, swearing to tell the truth.[32] The executives appeared before the Subcommittee on Heath and the Environment of the U.S. House of Representatives, chaired by Congressman Henry A. Waxman (D–Calif.), on April 14, 1994. Each was asked if he believed nicotine was addictive, and each testified he believed it was not. Some of these executives were soon to be contradicted by their company's own documents, and in the case of the Thomas E. Sandefur Jr., CEO of Brown & Williamson, by a former vice president of his own company, who testified that within the company Sandefur repeatedly referred to nicotine addiction and said that Brown & Williamson was "in the nicotine delivery business."[33]

Recent revelations concerning the tobacco industry have had an effect, but one somewhat different from conventional wisdom. Except in certain, discrete areas, there is little evidence of a dramatic shift in public attitudes about smoking and tobacco companies. For example, polls conducted in 1989 and 1998 asking who Americans thought was responsible for smokers' health problems—tobacco companies or smokers themselves—found virtually no change in public attitude.[34] In both polls, only 16 percent said the tobacco companies were responsible.

Why have recent disclosures not had a greater effect on public opinion? Why, for example, do they not result in more Americans blaming tobacco companies for smoke-related illnesses? Why did they not galvanize the public into demanding that Congress pass the tobacco bill in 1997?[35] I believe there is a two-pronged answer. The first prong is that the new revelations merely confirmed what Americans long had assumed to be the case—that tobacco companies have long known but lied about the health effects of smoking. Therefore, revelations did not really change anything because, in the view of most Americans, they only demonstrated the obvious.

The second prong relates directly to the value of individual responsibility. Consider, for example, a 1998 survey in which nearly three times as many respondents said they agreed with the statement "Everyone should have the right to make his or her own choice about whether to smoke" as with than the statement "Smoking is a bad habit and our society should do everything possible to stamp it out."[36] The belief that individuals should be able to choose for themselves whether or not to smoke and should take responsibility for their choices is not affected by the public's perception of the tobacco companies per se. That is, it does not matter whether the people who sell tobacco are saints or sinners; either way, citizens may decide whether they want to use the product (and accept the consequences).

Polling data do reflect changes in certain areas, however. Public attitudes about secondhand smoke have changed dramatically. In 1994, only 36 percent of Americans said they considered secondhand smoke to be "very harmful. Within only three years, this number had increased to 55 percent.[37] Another shift occurred with respect to cigarettes and children. Americans have long supported restrictions on sales to minors, but what may be new is that, as of 1997, 80 percent of Americans had come to believe that tobacco companies purposely target children in their advertising.[38] Both of these areas relate directly to individual responsibility, since secondhand smoke affects individuals who have not chosen to accept the risk and minors are considered too young to accept responsibility for their actions. Americans support regulations that will protect nonsmokers from exposure. They also support campaigns designed to combat smoking by minors, including educational programs and stricter enforcement of restrictions on sales. None of this, however, spills over into a desire to punish the tobacco companies for misdeeds.

What about public opinion with regard to tobacco liability? In 1991, 1996, and 1997, the Gallup Organization polled the following question: "Do you think cigarette companies should be held legally responsible if they are sued by the families of smokers who died of smoking-related causes, or, does the fact that the companies put warning notices on cigarette packs excuse them from the responsibility?"[39] In 1991, 13 percent of all respondents said cigarettes companies should be liable and 66 percent said they should not be. By 1996, 30 percent favored liability and 51 percent did not. This reflects a marked change over a relatively short, four-year period.

One wonders what the results would have been had the question not given respondents this particular binary choice. Part of the shift that is occurring stems from a more complex view of responsibility. The old paradigm that asks, "Who is responsible for smoking-related illness: the tobacco company or the smoker?" is beginning to disintegrate. The state lawsuits have taught that this is not necessarily an "either-or" proposition. Both smokers and the tobacco companies may be responsible. As noted above, when Americans were asked who was responsible for smokers' health problems—tobacco companies or smokers themselves—16 percent of those responding said the tobacco companies were responsible. When a 1999 poll gave respondents more choices, however, a total of 30 percent said tobacco companies were either completely (9 percent) or mostly (21 percent) to blame for health problems faced by smokers, while a total of 55 percent said smokers were mostly (31 percent) or completely (24 percent) to blame.[40] What is perhaps most significant is that one-third placed the entire blame on one party while 65 percent saw responsibility shared in some fashion between smokers and tobacco companies.

Polls also show that Americans supported the lawsuits by the states against the tobacco companies. When Americans were surveyed about their opinions of the terms of the then-proposed settlement of lawsuits between the tobacco companies and the states, 22 percent said the terms were too hard, 29 percent said they were too easy, and 46 percent said they were about right.[41] Thus, fully three-quarters of respondents thought it appropriate that tobacco companies reimburse states for the costs of treating smoking-related illness—a result achieved through litigation. Another poll showed that a majority of Americans supported the lawsuit against the tobacco companies filed by the Justice Department to recover reimbursement for Medicaid costs attached to smoking-related diseases.[42]

All of this shows how Americans view smoking through the prism of personal responsibility. Americans do not want to relieve smokers of the consequences of their choices (and Americans still see smoking as a matter of choice, the addiction factor notwithstanding). Americans do not, however, believe it is appropriate that smokers or the tobacco industry foist costs off on others. Americans also believe it fair to hold both smokers and tobacco companies responsible for externalized costs.[43] After all, both derive benefits from smoking. Manufacturers will pass some, if not all, of liability costs on to their customers by raising cigarette prices.[44] As between those who benefit from an activity and those who do not, however, this may not matter. It may be fair to hold tobacco companies entirely responsible for externalized costs, regardless of whether they can recoup them from their customers and, like the widget factory, regardless of the impact on the industry.

The externalization factor is magnified in gun litigation. That is, the principle of personal responsibility—and its corollary that costs should not be externalized—works more powerfully in favor of liability for guns than for tobacco. With cigarettes, monetary costs are externalized but, except for injuries from secondhand smoke, physical injuries are not. With guns, however, physical injury is also externalized.

For the most part, victims are not customers; they are people shot or held up at gunpoint, generally with someone else's gun. In 1998, 7,361 Americans were murdered with handguns;[45] more than 170,000 people were robbed at gunpoint;[46] and approximately 104,000 people were shot but survived.[47] Thus, guns impose enormous costs—economic and noneconomic—on both victims and the public at large. The public bears the cost of treating shooting injuries in the same fashion that it bears the cost of treating smoking-related illnesses. The public also bears substantial costs associated with lifetime care of shooting victims, many of whom are young (much younger on average than those suffering smoking-related diseases) and permanently disabled. In addition to monetary costs, however, is a factor generally absent from tobacco: the noneconomic costs of being shot or held up at gunpoint.

These costs are an inevitable by-product of having guns, and particularly handguns, distributed promiscuously throughout society. Guns are present in 46 percent of American homes.[48] Nothing can be this omnipresent without being readily available to psychotics, sociopaths, troubled teenagers, as well as the enraged, desperate, intoxicated, immature, and reckless. Gun-related injuries are an inherent, externalized cost of gun sales in exactly the same way that smoking-related injuries are an inherent, externalized cost of cigarette sales.[49]

I return to the issue of externalization shortly. Meanwhile, it is useful to focus on another issue affecting how the mores of individual responsibility relate to gun liability. Who should be responsible for misuse of a gun: the manufacturer or the person misusing the gun? This supposedly rhetorical question presents a major theme of the gun lobby, which is also captured in the slogan "Guns don't kill, people do." The underlying message is that people have a duty to behave responsibly, that all products may be misused, that it is the person who misused the product who should be accountable—and, therefore, that the manufacturer of a lawful product is not accountable for how the product is used by someone who commits an unlawful act.

This issue is raised doctrinally through the defenses of misuse and of intervening or superceding cause. That is, one argument is that a manufacturer of a product that is not unreasonably dangerous should not be held strictly liable because someone was injured when the product was misused. Another argument is that the injury was proximately caused by the criminal, or by the tortuous act of the person who pulled the trigger, which should be deemed to supercede any manufacturer responsibility. In the context of gun liability, these issues are additional surrogates for the value of individual responsibility. As is the case with other aspects of this litigation, parties and courts will discuss these issues in terms of doctrine. Yet it is not at the doctrinal level that the courts will ultimately be persuaded but rather at the deeper level of societal values.

Implicit in both of these defenses is the suggestion that responsibility must be placed with either the manufacturer or the criminal. It is, however, an implication that evaporates when expressly stated. Quite obviously, both may be responsible. Several models make this apparent. One is dram shop liability. As discussed in chapter 6, the common law now recognizes that both a drunk driver and the tavern at which he drank may be held liable to injured third parties. This flows from society's coming to believe that the bartender has independent moral responsibility and that there is a public policy purpose to imposing liability on him. A second, similar model is a landowner's duty to protect patrons from criminal acts by others. Who is responsible when a motel guest is raped in her room—the rapist or the motel that failed to furnish a peephole or door chain? Under common law, a landlord was not responsible to her tenant for criminal acts by third persons.[50] That, too, has changed. Landlords may now be held liable for failing to take reasonable precautions to prevent acts by others. A third model is the crashworthiness doctrine, discussed in chapters 6 and 7. The vast majority of automobile accidents are caused by negligence, but for good public policy reasons, the law encourages manufacturers to do what they reasonably can to protect us from the negligence of others or, indeed, even our own negligence.

The fourth model is tobacco. The lawsuits by the state attorneys general ended the notion that smokers alone are responsible for smoking-related disease. Those who manufacture and sell cigarettes are also responsible because their enterprise imposes large costs to society at large, including nonsmokers.

As *Wilks v. American Tobacco Company*—the case in which a man functioning at a six-year-old level was addicted to cigarettes in the psychiatric wards of VA hospitals, discussed in chapter 4[51]—demonstrated so well, liability is not going to be imposed without the acquiescence of juries. Generic liability is the ideal effective vehicle for persuading judges and jurors that liability comports with societal values. Juries can easily be confused about why, for example, they should find a manufacturer negligent for producing a lawful product and giving customers exactly what they want. The reasons for imposing liability are clearer when the focus is on the consequences of distributing a product and on who benefits and who pays.

The principle that those who benefit should pay and should not externalize costs, including the costs of injuries, reflects values that are accepted across the ideological spectrum. One of the great liberal judges of modern times, Henry J. Friendly, wrote that there is "a deeply rooted sentiment that a business enterprise cannot justly disclaim responsibility for accidents which may fairly be said to be characteristic of its activities."[52] One of the most prominent conservative jurists, Judge Richard A. Posner, has written:

> The baseline common law regime of tort liability is negligence. When it is a workable regime, because the hazards of an activity can be avoided by being careful (which is to say, nonnegligent), there is no need to switch to strict liability. Sometimes, however, a particular type of accident cannot be prevented by taking care but can be avoided, or its consequences minimized . . . by reducing the scale of the activity in order to avoid accidents caused by it. By making the actor strictly liable—by denying him in other words an excuse based on his inability to avoid accidents by being more careful—we give him an incentive, missing in a negligence regime, to experiment with methods of preventing accidents that involve not greater exertions of care, assumed to be futile, but instead relocating, changing, or reducing (perhaps to the vanishing point) the activity giving rise to the accident.[53]

One of the strengths of products liability is that it does not take sides on how the risks should be reduced. There is much argument about whether risks are best reduced by different distribution schemes, gun locks, so-called safe gun designs incorporating new technologies, or other means, or whether, as Judge Posner put it, risks can be lowered only by drastically reducing or eliminating the sales of certain products.

One of the advantages of products liability is its agnosticism on how injuries should be reduced. Manufacturers are neither directed to made their products safer nor told how to do so. They are simply made liable for injuries resulting from the unreasonably dangerous nature of their products and thus given an incentive to reduce injuries. Manufacturers know their business better than judges, juries, legislators, or the staff of administrative agencies. They best can figure out how to reduce injuries through product redesign, different distribution, consumer education, or some other method. Products liability leaves manufacturers free to decide, for example, whether it makes more sense—for both technological and marketing reasons—to develop a smart gun that may only be fired by its owner or a nonlethal weapon that stuns rather than kills.[54]

Manufacturers can only complain that liability costs are so high they will be forced out of business. That may be, but that is the case with all products that consumers consider too costly. People will continue to buy products as long as the benefits are worth the price. The market works properly when people do not buy a particular product because its cost exceeds its worth. With guns, moreover, liability costs equal externalized costs, and externalized costs are increasingly viewed as avoiding individual responsibility.

Handgun manufacturers try to deflect responsibility by blaming everyone but themselves—blaming criminals, blaming government for inadequate law enforcement, blaming parents and schools for not instilling proper values. The flaw in their argument is that we live in an imperfect world. It is irrelevant whether a product would be reasonably safe in a theoretical world where parents and schools raise only angels. Manufacturers must make products reasonably safe for in the world in which we live.

Common Law in the Twenty-first Century

The common law is needed as much as or more than ever before. One of the changes we are witnessing at the beginning of the twenty-first century is unprecedented corporate power. Mergers and consolidations have created national and multinational organizations of staggering size and wealth. The combined revenue of the twelve largest United States corporations exceeds the total revenue of all fifty state governments. Meanwhile, it has become increasingly expensive for politicians to mount serious congressional campaigns, not to mention presidential campaigns. To run one must directly purchase extremely expensive television time, benefit from time purchased by one's party or another ally with "soft money," or both. In 1996, the average direct campaign cost (not counting soft money) was $673,739 for the House and $4.7 million for the Senate. Few can raise that much money except from the very wealthy, and the very wealthy are generally corporate executives. It makes little difference that individual contributions are limited to $1,000 each, and therefore $4.7 million must be raised from at least forty-seven hundred contributors. Businesses bundle contributions from executives, their spouses, and their suppliers and present these fragrant bouquets to politicians, who of course know full well what is expected in return. We have already seen the limits of administrative regulation. This is only likely to get worse.

What about market regulation? Do manufacturers not have strong incentives to make their products safe? Will they not be at a competitive disadvantage if consumers can purchase safer alternatives? Do they not have incentives to build and protect brand names associated with reliability, safety, and integrity?

We have already seen that corporations sometimes consider other market factors to be more important than safety. When it produced the Pinto, Ford believed it needed to rush a subcompact to market in order to compete with Japanese manufacturers and arch-rival GM. Under the market conditions then existing, Ford believed the corporate benefits of rushing a subcompact into production exceeded the costs of selling a dangerous car. Ford later made similar judgments concerning the Bronco II, Firestone tires, and as we shall soon see, the thick film (TFI) ignition system. From a purely economic standpoint, these may have been rational decisions. A system that depends on the market to regulate safety makes marketing and corporate profit more important than public safety. This is a value choice and must be recognized for what it is.

It is a mistake, however, to view corporations merely as rational, profit-driven enterprises. While they may be that in theory, corporations are large collections of individuals with personal agendas. The Pinto was Lee Iacocca's brainchild and special project. We shall never know to what extent corporate executives made their Pinto in a rational attempt to maximize company profits (taking into account the potential damage to the corporate reputation from exploding Pintos) and to what extent Iacocca's personal agenda—and the desire of subordinates to ingratiate themselves to him—drove those decisions.

Another Ford example illustrates the effect of corporate culture. In the 1980s and 1990s, thousands of car owners told Ford that their cars were suddenly stalling, often when making left turns.[55] This left some cars stalled in the face of oncoming traffic, resulting in serious accidents and fatalities. Ford, we now know, knew of the problem before it sold any of these cars; the car had an ignition system—called the TFI module—that was prone to fail when it was overheated. Ford engineers thought about mounting the module inside the passenger compartment so that it would not be affected by engine heat, but ultimately Ford placed the module near the engine. Ford engineers were concerned about "quits on the road," as they called stalling, as early as 1982; two years later they projected that more than half of the TFI ignitions would fail during the warranty period (five years or fifty thousand miles). In 1984, Ford officials considered a recall but rejected the idea because it would cost more than $429 million. Nevertheless, Ford continued to produce cars—more than 22 million vehicles—with the TFI ignition until 1995. Over the years, NHTSA opened and closed five separate investigations into the problem. Ford repeatedly assured NHTSA it knew of no defect, even as it was conducting extensive studies showing exactly what caused the stalling. Alan J. Kam, who for twenty-one years served as NHTSA's chief counsel for defect and enforcement matters, said this was the greatest deception he had ever witnessed by the auto industry. Ford "concealed signs of failures that were occurring at an astronomical level," he said. Judge Michael E. Ballachey of the California Superior Court, who heard testimony in a class action lawsuit, said the cover-up resulted from a corporate culture where executives' careers could be ruined by delivering bad news to higher-ranking officials. It was, he said, like the story of the emperor's new clothes.

The blend of executives pursuing corporate profit maximizing goals and their personal agendas turns out to be something of a witch's brew. Sociological research suggests that people are more likely to engage in anti-social behavior when they are part of large organizations. One of the most extensive studies of corporate crime ever undertaken found that 60.1 percent of the nation's largest corporations violated federal law at least once during a two-year period, with an average of 4.4 violations per company. In another study, the same researcher interviewed 68 retired middle managers of Fortune 500 companies, who revealed that it was not uncommon to feel pressured into violating federal laws to satisfy demanding higher-level managers.[56] And these studies concern violations of criminal law. There is no reason to believe that *lawful* anti-social corporate conduct, such as selling unsafe products, occurs less often than *unlawful* anti-social corporate conduct that may result in corporate fines but is highly unlikely to inflict punishment directly on individuals. Corporate employees can rightly believe that their personal risk of being punished for violating the law to advance the company's interests is quite small. One study showed that only 1.5 percent of federal enforcement efforts directed at corporations resulted in a conviction of a corporate officer.[57]

Kermit Vandivier, a young engineer and data analyst for B. F.

Goodrich Company, has given an unusual insider account of how Goodrich ended up providing 202 brake assemblies for U.S. Air Force aircraft that Goodrich engineers knew would fail, endangering planes and pilots.[58] A high-level and respected Goodrich engineer designed the brake, and his ego would not allow him to accept the fact that his design was flawed. The surface area of the brake disks was too small for the job. During the first test landing, the disks reached 1,500 degrees Fahrenheit, so hot they threw off incandescent particles and nearly completely disintegrated. When told of the problem, the engineer told subordinates this was their problem to solve; then, with confidence they would make his design work, he told Goodrich's customer, LTV Aerospace Corporation, that the first test had been successful. Eventually, a junior engineer went over his superior's head to the executive who supervised all project engineers. But this man was plagued by his own insecurities. Although he supervised graduates of the nation's top engineering schools, he himself had never gone to college. He lacked the confidence or skill to evaluate the problem and felt too vulnerable to admit he could not do so. In a debate between a senior and a junior engineer, it was politically more expedient to side with the senior. Besides, based on what he had previously been told, the executive had himself already told LTV that the brakes were almost ready for shipment. After the junior engineer's attempt to address the problem failed, others were reluctant to get involved. Kermit Vandivier went to the head of his section and describes how he was rebuffed. "[I]t's none of my business and it's none of yours," the section head told him. "I learned a long time ago not to worry about things over which I had no control. I have no control over this."

Step by step, individuals led themselves and the organization deeper into denial and deception. When the brake failed on twelve separate attempts, panicking engineers came up with ways not of fixing the brake but of fixing the test. During the test, they cooled the brake with fans and reduced pressure within the brake by releasing the brake when the test wheel had decelerated to 15 mph and by allowing the aircraft to coast to a stop, instead of keeping the brake applied until the wheel stopped. Records were altered to improperly reflect that the tests had been conducted in accordance with military specifications and regular engineering practices.

Part of Vandivier's job was to prepare a draft of the final report. This was the conclusion he placed in that draft: "The B.F. Goodrich P/N 2-

1162-3 brake assembly does not meet the intent or the requirements of the applicable specification documents and therefore is not qualified." But somewhere in the higher echelons of the corporate hierarchy, the negative conclusion was transformed into a positive one. When the report was presented to the executive without a college degree for his signature—and he was told that engineers at three levels, including the man who had originally designed the brake, had refused to sign it—this seasoned player of corporate politics found a clever way out. "On something of this nature, I don't think a signature is really needed," he told his secretary. And so the report went without signatures. Only the organization took responsibility. No human being did so.

Within a week of the report being delivered, test flights took place at Edwards Air Force Base. During one landing, the brake became so hot that small particle pieces flew off in incandescent sparks, and what remained was welded together. That plane skidded nearly fifteen hundred feet before coming to rest. After several near crashes, further testing was suspended.

During an ensuing congressional investigation, the man without the college degree admitted the data in the report had been altered but testified: "When you take data from several different sources, you have to rationalize among those data what is the true story. This is part of your engineering know-how." Data were changed "to make them more consistent with the over-all picture of the data that is available." In the main, that approach worked. The congressional hearing ended without reaching a definitive conclusion. Goodrich kept the brake contract. The brake was redesigned. The man without the college degree and the section head who learned not to worry about things he could not control were both promoted.

This is, in some ways, a small story. No plane was lost; no one was injured. But it illustrates how human beings within depersonalized institutions wind up cooperating in schemes that no one individual has devised, and for which no one considers himself responsible, even though they know full well that others may be injured or killed.

The corporate pressure in this case came from a reluctance to tell an important customer that a new brake failed in tests, that a redesign was necessary, and that an order of twenty-two brakes would be delayed—even though the customer would inevitably find out and the company's goodwill would be damaged. Personal and corporate pressures involving mass-produced products can be orders of magnitude greater. Consider a second case, that of the Rely tampon.[59] Proctor & Gamble (P&G) wanted to seize a large share of the sanitary napkin market from arch-rival Kimberly-Clark, maker of Kotex, and Tambrands, maker of Tampax. As P&G was preparing a huge national rollout, in which it would mail 60 million sample packages of Rely tampons to 80 percent of all American households, P&G learned that some women who used Rely in smaller test markets suffered vomiting and diarrhea.

The potential consequences of distributing a possibly risky product to tens of millions of people, who are going to use this product internally, are enormous. But the potential consequences of derailing a project at this stage are enormous too, not to life and limb but to profit and career tracks. Undoubtedly, a number of P&G executives had invested large amounts of political capital in the project. Even the CEO of the company might have to explain to the Board of Directors why he decided to abort a project of this magnitude.

P&G did not abort. Instead, even as it was preparing the rollout, it began planning a public relations defense of anticipated claims about Rely making women sick. One internal memorandum that later came to light, titled "Possible Areas of Attack on Rely," discussed how to defend the company from (accurate) charges that Rely contained carcinogenic materials and that it changed the natural balance of microorganisms and bacteria within the vagina.

P&G started receiving consumer complaints soon after rollout, up to 177 per month. In the spring of 1980, the Centers for Disease Control (CDC) reported that fifty-five cases of toxic shock syndrome (TSS) had occurred within the past six months. Most of the victims were menstruating young women. CDC was trying to figure out what was going on. Knowing this, P&G nevertheless decided to go ahead with introducing a deodorant version of Rely—a product P&G knew created another and unnecessary health risk, since menstrual fluids have no odor as long as they remain in the body. (But it was a brilliant marketing ploy, since just advertising a deodorant tampon would make women anxious about odor.) Some time later, P&G also went ahead with a program to distribute 2 million free Rely samples to high school students. It was, after all, hard to pull back at this stage. Rely had captured 24 percent of the sanitary product market, and P&G had enormous incentives to stonewall and keep aggressively promoting its very successful new product.

Cognitive dissonance is a powerful psychological force. Executives probably persuaded themselves there was no real reason for concern. There are nervous Nellies on every project, they probably told themselves. So, some women developed high fevers and vomiting after using Rely. It was probably just coincidence; they probably had the flu; and besides, it was not as if Rely was killing people. In the summer of 1980, however, P&G learned that a woman had, in fact, died from TSS after using Rely. What should we do now? P&G executives asked themselves. An internal P&G memorandum gave the answer: "We should continue our planned activity to support this brand and build its share to leadership status." Another internal memorandum described how P&G representatives met with doctors and public health officials in Ohio to try to extinguish rumors "mistakenly" linking Rely and TSS. When, in September 1970, the CDC told P&G that it had just completed a study showing that among women with TSS who used just one brand of tampon, 71 percent used Rely, P&G tried to persuade the CDC not to release that information to the public.

The FDA was pressing P&G to recall Rely. P&G engaged lobbyists to try to get the Carter White House to stop further action by the FDA and CDC. But on September 22, 1980, P&G relented and announced a recall. It was an extremely expensive action. P&G placed advertisements warning women against using Rely tampons on six hundred television stations, on 350 radio stations, and in twelve hundred newspapers. Thousands of P&G workers were involved in the national recall effort. In addition to these formidable costs, P&G lost $75 million in posttax profits from discontinuing its profitable product line. (It was a financial sacrifice P&G could afford, however. Rely accounted for less than 1 percent of P&G's total sales, and the loss of profit on Rely was expected to reduce net earnings from $7.78 to $6.87 per share. And, incidentally, though the Rely brand died, P&G achieved its goal of obtaining a leading share of the sanitary product market by purchasing Tambrands in 1997.)

We know P&G executives made the decision to recall Rely reluctantly. Just days before, they sent lobbyists to politically snuff out action by governmental regulators. Even if P&G's lobbyists had been unsuccessful, P&G could have fought an FDA recall order, perhaps even successfully. What persuaded P&G to make a large financial sacrifice and recall the product? Perhaps P&G executives were genuinely worried about women's health; but if this was their controlling motive, one wonders why they did not act sooner. Company image was probably a factor, although one wonders how many consumers would stop buying Crest toothpaste, Ivory soap, Tide detergent, or other P&G brands because they did not like P&G's conduct regarding Rely tampons. History does not give us many examples of consumers boycotting irresponsible manufacturers.

Although no single factor may have been controlling, P&G must have considered its potential products liability exposure. Looming large was its inability to calculate what that exposure might be. In all likelihood, they believed that relatively small numbers of women would die from TSS—relatively small, that is, in comparison to tens of millions of customers. In 1980, for example, there were 522 reported cases of TSS and forty-two fatalities. If P&G was confident its exposure was limited to compensatory damages, it might have calculated it was more profitable to keep Rely on the market. But P&G attorneys undoubtedly advised company officials that the company would face punitive awards if it acted in ways juries considered grossly irresponsible—and that there was no way to estimate the amount of such awards. P&G executives were apparently worried that their conduct had already exposed the company to punitive damages, because shortly before ordering the product recall, they instructed managers to shred Rely documents. Although P&G executives denied that this had occurred, *Wall Street Journal* reporter Alecia Swasy writes that P&G employees, including one high-level former executive, told her that the document destruction took place and that those who carried it out call it the "Ides of September."[60]

Products liability does three things. First, it increases the manufacturer's cost of distributing unreasonably dangerous products. When considering how much profit it will make, the manufacturer must take into account potential liability. The objective is to change the calculus of rational, profit-maximizing corporate managers. The greater the potential safety risk, the greater the potential legal exposure. Manufacturers may or may not be able to pass all their liability costs on to their customers, depending on a variety of factors.

How much have costs imposed by the products liability system increased the cost of consumer goods? There is much dispute about this. Institutes funded by big business have published studies purporting to show that litigation costs have substantially increased consumer prices or bled away a significant share of the gross national product. The most reliable studies reflect a very modest effect. A 1991 study by the National Insurance Consumer Organization found that the cost of insuring products liability, including both insurance premiums and the cost of self-insurance, constituted only 0.21 percent of retail sales. Meanwhile, an analyst looking specifically at the auto industry estimated that liability costs do not exceed 0.2 percent of annual revenues of domestic automobile manufacturers.[61]

Second, the discovery process unearths facts that would otherwise remain within the dark recesses of corporations, spreading them across the public record in courtrooms, from which the media may communicate them to the public at large. When corporate executives are debating whether to distribute dangerous products, fear of exposure changes both corporate and personal calculations. No one wants the newspapers to portray her as someone who, through blunder or corporate avarice, endangered the community.

Third, not only does the products liability system bring into public view decisions balancing the utility and the hazards of the products we use and depend on, but it allows the people to pass judgment on those decisions. Decisions balancing risks and utilities can, indeed, be very difficult. Products cannot be risk free, and we must often accept considerable risks to enjoy important benefits. The law understands this; it imposes liability not on dangerous products but only on unreasonably dangerous products. A product is considered unreasonably dangerous when the cost it imposes on society at large exceeds its benefits.

When does that occur? How does one calculate social benefits? We know such judgments cannot be the exclusive province of manufacturers, insulated from review. We know, as well, that regulatory agencies cannot do the job alone. Some believe such judgments involve complicated economic valuations, too difficult for the lay public and best entrusted to economists. The data do not support the view that juries are unable to grasp complicated problems. But even that aside, it is appropriate that the people participate in these judgments. It is, after all, they who, in the end, benefit from, pay for, and are injured by products. It is not hyperbole to say that these can be, quite literally, life-and-death decisions. These are value judgments, and in a democracy it is the people's values that must prevail. The people may seek to work their will at the ballot box and the sales counter. We have seen, however, that in contemporary America both mechanisms, though critically important, are inadequate. The common law continues to provide America with another means—a disciplined means—in which the people participate in the affairs that affect them. It is not a perfect system, but it may be more needed today than ever before.

Notes

NOTE TO THE INTRODUCTION

1. Louis D. Brandeis, *Other People's Money and How the Bankers Use It* 62 (A. Stokes Co., 1914).

NOTES TO CHAPTER 1

1. Sidney Blumenthal, *St. Jack: The Good Republican*, New Republic, Oct. 17, 1991, at 13 ("figure of moral stature"); David Johnson, *Danforth Says He'll "Answer the Dark Questions" on Waco*, New York Times, Sept. 10, 1999, at A19 (Waco appointment quotes). See also David Jackson and Sam Attlesey, *Bush's VP Choice Still Anyone's Guess*, Dallas Morning News, July 23, 2000, at 1A; Rick Pearson, *Danforth Re-Emerges as Bush's Potential VP*, Chicago Tribune, July 23, 2000, at 14; and Neil A. Lewis, *Back in Public Arena: John Clagett Danforth*, New York Times, Sept. 9, 1999, at A17.

2. 140 Cong. Rec. S7672 (daily ed. July 27, 1994). Statement of Senator Danforth.

3. Guido Calabresi, *A Common Law for the Age of Statutes* 5 (Harvard University Press, 1982).

4. See Susan B. Glasser and John Mintz, *Bush's Capital Plan to Woo Big Business*, Washington Post, Aug. 1, 1999, at A1.

5. See John B. Judis, *Taking Care of Business*, New Republic, Aug. 16, 1999, at 24, 26.

6. Charles Lewis and The Center for the Public Interest, *The Buying of the President 2000*, at 215 (Avon Books, 2000). For information about Bush's use of tort reform in his presidential race, I rely on: M. Charles Bakst, *Ragged Bush Visit*, Providence Journal, Sept. 9, 1999, at B1; Maria L. La Ganga, *Bush Has Right Message for Silicon Valley*, Los Angeles Times, July 2, 1999; Thomas W. Waldron, *Bush Praises Contributions on Faith-Based Institutions*, Baltimore Sun, July 15, 1999; Jim Yardley, *Bush Approach to Pollution: Preference for Self-Policing*, New York Times, Nov. 9, 1999, at A1; Jill Zuckman, *N.H. 5th-Graders Toss a Few Softballs to Candidate Bush*, Boston Globe, Sept. 8, 1999, at A4.

7. See Robert Dreyfus, *The Real McCain,* Arizona Republic, Jan. 9, 2000, at J1; Stephen Tuttle, *Arizona Politicians Know All, See All,* Arizona Republic, May 28, 1995, at E3.

8. See *Battle Stations,* National Law Journal, Feb. 12, 2000, at 454; Alison Mitchell, *Bush and McCain Exchange Sharp Words over Fund-Raising,* New York Times, Feb. 10, 2000, at A26; Don Van Natta Jr. and John M. Broder, *With a Still-Ample Treasury, Bush Builds a Green Fire Wall against McCain,* New York Times, Feb. 21, 2000, at A21.

9. The facts of this case are drawn from the appellate briefs by the parties and from the three published court opinions: *Proctor v. Davis,* 656 N.E. 2d 23 (App. Ct. Ill. 1997), reversing the judgment of the trial court against Upjohn; 677 N.E. 2d 918 (Ill. 1997), vacating the prior decision on procedural grounds; and 682 N.E. 2d 1203 (App. Ct. Ill. 1995), affirming judgment against Upjohn as to compensatory damages and reducing punitive damage award.

10. See Brief and Argument of Plaintiffs-Appellants, Separate Appellees/ Cross-Appellants in the Appellate Court of Illinois, *Proctor v. Davis,* Nos. 92-3151 and 92-3513, Appellate Court of Illinois (hereafter "Appellate Brief of Plaintiffs"), at 232.

11. Telephone interview with Barry Goldberg, Esquire (July 31, 1998).

12. Gary A. Hengstler, *Psychic's Case to Be Retried,* 72 ABA Journal 23 (1986); Fredric N. Tulsky, *Did Jury's Award Consider Psychic's Loss of Powers?* National Law Journal, April 14, 1986, at 9.

13. Ralph Nader and Wesley J. Smith, *No Contest: Corporate Lawyers and the Perversion of Justice in America* 275 (Random House, 1996).

14. W. Kip Viscusi, *Reforming Products Liability* 1 (Harvard University Press, 1991).

15. Joseph A. Page, *Deforming Tort Law,* 78 Georgetown Law Journal 649, 676–77 n. 139 (1990).

16. Irvin Molotksy, *Reagan Reiterates Support for Liability Suit Limits,* New York Times, May 31, 1986, at A28.

17. *Bigbee v. Pacific Telephone and Telegraph Co.,* 131 Calif. App. 3d 999 (1982), rev'd at 665 P. 2d 947 (Calif. 1983).

18. 665 P. 2d at 952.

19. For the coffee case, I rely on: Charles Allen, *The McDonald's Coffee Spill Case,* Washington Post, April 4, 1995, at A22; Andrea Gerlin, *How Jury Gave $2.9 Million for Coffee Spill,* Pittsburgh Post-Gazette, Sept. 4, 1994, at B2; Mort Hochstein, *Don't Get Burned,* Nation's Restaurant Review, April 15, 1996, at 33; Theresa Howard, *MCD Settles Coffee Suit in Out-of-Court Settlement,* Nation's Restaurant Review, Dec. 12, 1994, at 1; *Judge Cuts $2.9 Million Hot Coffee Award,* Phoenix Gazette, Sept. 15, 1994, at A2; Alan J. Wax, *Coffee-Burn Lawsuit Has Chains Thinking Cool,* Philadelphia Inquirer, Sept. 24, 1994, at D1.

20. Timothy Castle and Carl Peel, *A Hot Issue,* Tea & Coffee Trade Journal, Sept. 1995, at 17.

21. My research assistant, Christopher Lordan of the Roger Williams University School of Law class of 1999, visited two units each from the four chains in September 1998. All of the restaurants were located in Rhode Island and Massachusetts. Except for Wendy's, which was not offering hot chocolate, he ordered both coffee and hot chocolate at each of the eight restaurants.

NOTES TO CHAPTER 2

1. See, e.g., James J. Kilpatrick, *Getting Back to Tort Reform,* San Diego Union-Tribune, June 8, 1986, at C3.

2. *1991's Largest Verdicts,* National Law Journal, Jan. 20, 1992, at S2.

3. Members of Congress follow such hectic schedules that they often do not even have the time to read a daily newspaper. See Fred R. Barnes, *The Unbearable Lightness of Being a Congressman,* New Republic, Feb. 15, 1988, at 18.

4. From American Tort Reform Association's (ATRA's) "Horror Stories!" at www.atra.org/ath.htm (Oct. 25, 1998).

5. *Vandevender v. Sheetz, Inc.,* 490 S.E. 2d 768 (W. Va. 1997).

6. West Virginia's workers' compensation law covers all personal injuries occurring "in the course of and resulting from" employment (W. Va. Code § 23-4-1). The "resulting from" employment requirement is interpreted broadly and includes activities that have only an incidental connection with work.

7. See, e.g., *Jordan v. State Workmen's Comp. Comm'r,* 191 S.E. 2d 497 (W. Va. 1972).

8. Letter to author from Richard E. Anthony, executive director of the Business Roundtable (a PLCC member), dated May 4, 1992.

9. For occupations of state legislators, see National Conference of State Legislatures, *State Legislators' Occupations: A Decade of Change* 2 (1987), reporting that lawyers comprise between 11 and 36 percent of state legislators). See also Alan Rosenthal, *The Decline of Representative Democracy* 31 (Congressional Quarterly Books, 1997), reporting that the proportion of lawyer members of all state legislatures has declined from about 25 percent in the 1960s and 1970s to about 17 percent in 1993.

10. See Kevin Sack, *G.O.P. Moderates Meet to Frown before an Unflattering Mirror,* New York Times, Feb. 15, 1999, at A1.

11. For this section, I rely on: *Republican Filibuster in the Senate Kills Crime Bill,* New York Times, March 20, 1992; Michael Wines, *House Adopts Crime Legislation To Build Jails and Hire Officers,* New York Times, April 22, 1994, at A1, reporting that in the House of Representatives, 87 percent of Democrats voted for and 62 percent of Republicans voted against an anti-crime package sponsored by Democratic congressman Charles E. Schumer of New York.

12. Of the 898 sitting federal judges in 1997–98, 532 were appointed by Presidents Bush (134), Reagan (284), Ford (42), Nixon (101), and Eisenhower (13). See *The American Bench: Judges of the Nation* (9th ed., Reginald Bishop Forster, 1997–98).

13. For this section, I rely on: Jan Hoffman, *Court Balks at Freedom for Convicted Murderer,* New York Times, Dec. 30, 1997, at A13; Anthony Lewis, *Menacing the Judges,* New York Times, Nov. 3, 1997, at A27; Katharine Q. Seelye, *House G.O.P. Begins Listing a Few Judges to Impeach,* New York Times, March 14, 1997, at A24.

14. See Linda Greenhouse, *Judges Seek Aid in Effort to Remain Independent,* New York Times, Dec. 10, 1998, at A16.

15. Louis D. Brandeis, *Other People's Money and How the Bankers Use It* 62 (A. Stokes Co., 1933).

16. For this section, I rely on: James Fallows, *Breaking the News* 203 (Vintage Books, 1996); Thomas E. Mann, *Is the Era of Big Government Over?* Public Perspective, February 1998, at 27; Joseph S. Nye Jr., *In Government We Don't Trust,* Foreign Policy, Sept. 22, 1997, at 99.

17. Patterson analyzed all evaluative references to the major parties' presidential nominees in 4,263 issues of *Time* and *Newsweek* magazines for elections from 1960 through 1992. He discovered that in 1960, 75 percent of the references to John F. Kennedy and Richard Nixon were favorable and 25 percent were unfavorable. He found a nearly steady shift in these ratios over time, and by 1992, only 40 percent of the references to Bill Clinton and George Bush were favorable, and 60 percent were unfavorable. Patterson then compared these data to results of major polls conducted at the end of the presidential campaigns, asking whether voters had an overall positive or negative opinion of the candidates. These data show that from 1936, when Gallup started collecting this information, through the 1960s, voters gave an overall positive rating to all major party presidential candidates but one (Barry Goldwater). From 1980 to 1992, however, voters have had negative opinions of at least one and, more recently, generally both of the candidates. Patterson's comparison of press references and voters' opinions reveals a nearly exact correlation between the two, that is, voters' negative opinions of candidates have risen in tandem with negative press references. Thomas E. Patterson, *Out of Order* 19–23 (Vintage Books, 1993).

18. According to Harris polls, from 1976 to 1998 the percentage of Americans expressing "a great deal of confidence" in the Supreme Court has varied between 22 and 37 percent and, with only a few exceptions, has fluctuated within a range of 27 to 32 percent. See American Political Network, *The Hotline,* Feb. 11, 1998, at 46. Confidence in the Supreme Court may have risen in the last two years. The Harris poll in 1998, cited in *The Hotline* found the highest number (37 percent) expressing great confidence in the Supreme Court.

And a survey conducted for the American Bar Association in 1998 found 50 percent of Americans expressing strong confidence in the Court. It also found that, since 1978, confidence in all levels of the judicial system had risen while public confidence in all other institutions—including Congress, the news media, schools, doctors, and organized religion—had declined. See Linda Greenhouse, *47% in Poll View Legal System as Unfair to Poor and Minorities,* New York Times, Feb. 24, 1999, at A12.

19. *The Federalist* No. 78 (Hamilton).

20. For this section, I rely on: Jack Greenberg, *Crusaders in the Courts* 213–17, 268 (Basic Books, 1994); A. Leon Higginbotham Jr., *Shades of Freedom: Racial Politics and Presumptions of the American Legal Process* 152–68 (Oxford University Press, 1996); Richard Kluger, *Simple Justice* 746 (1976).

21. Lawrence M. Friedman, *A History of American Law* 668 (2d ed., Simon & Schuster, 1985).

22. See *Bad Justice,* New York Times, Feb. 21, 1995, at A18.

23. But see *Product Liability Legislation Defeated as Senate Fails to Curtail Filibuster,* BNA Daily Report for Executives, July 29, 1994, at A123, suggesting that then House Judiciary chairman Jack Brooks may have been an obstacle to House passage of the Products Liability Fairness Act in the House.

24. For this section, I rely on: *Clinton Threatened Veto; Senate Block Bill Limiting Lawsuits,* Washington Post, May 5, 1995, at 8A; *Friends & Foes Rally as Senate Nears Vote on Product Liability,* Liability Week, June 20, 1994, at 11; Neil A. Lewis, *President Vetoes Limit on Liability,* New York Times, May 3, 1996, at A1; *Product Liability Legislation Defeated as Senate Fails to Curtail Filibuster,* BNA Daily Report for Executives, July 29, 1994, at A123, reporting vote to invoke cloture on the Product Liability Fairness Act, S687, failed by a vote of fifty-four to forty-four.

25. See *Product Liability Reform Act of 1998,* S. 2236, 105th Cong., 2d Sess. (1998); Neil A. Lewis, *Bill to Cap Damage Awards May Finally Survive Senate,* New York Times, June 12, 1998, sec. 1 at 18.

26. See *Senate Vote Kills Product Liability Proposal for This Year,* CongressDaily, July 9, 1998 (available on Westlaw at 1998 WL 13130737).

27. See Neil A. Lewis, *Senate Dims Hope for Liability Bill,* New York Times, July 10, 1998, at A1; Neil A. Lewis, *Lott Amendment Benefits Miss. Company; He Told Others Not to Burden Measure,* New Orleans Times-Picayune, July 9, 1998, at A1, an expanded version of a front-page article run the preceding day by the *New York Times.*

28. See W. John Moore, *Lobbying & Law: All Aboard the Gravy Train,* National Law Journal, Oct. 17, 1998.

29. The cap did not apply when defendant engaged in a "pattern or practice of intentional wrongful conduct," in conduct involving "actual malice other than fraud or bad faith," and in libel actions. Alabama Code 1975, § 6-11-21 (1987).

30. Thomas A. Eaton and Susette M. Talarico, *Testing Two Assumptions about Federalism and Tort Reform* 41 Yale Law & Policy Review 371, 399 (1996).

31. Alabama Constitution 1901, art. I, § 11. The cap was invalidated in *Henderson v. Alabama Power Co.*, 627 So. 2d 878 (Ala. 1993).

32. *Henderson v. Alabama Power Co.*, at 887.

33. *Id.* at 893.

34. At least nine states, including California and Missouri, have upheld statutory damage caps.

At least half a dozen states, including Alabama, Ohio, and Texas, have held statutory damage caps to be unconstitutional.

At least two other states, Florida and New Hampshire, have invalidated the amount of damage caps set by statute.

See *Best v. Taylor Machine Works,* 689 N.E. 2d 1057, 1069–78 (Ill. 1997), holding that a statutory cap on compensatory damages for noneconomic injuries was unconstitutional because (1) it imposed the entire burden of anticipated cost savings on one class of injured plaintiffs and was therefore arbitrary and not rationally related a governmental interest, and (2) it violated the principle of separation of powers by invading judicial authority to limit excessive awards; and see cases cited therein at 1077–78.

35. The only states that have a pure appointment system of selecting justices for their highest court are Connecticut, Delaware, Hawaii, Maine, Massachusetts, New Jersey, New York, and Rhode Island.

Ten states have a purely partisan election system. They are Alabama, Arkansas, Illinois, Mississippi, New Mexico, North Carolina, Pennsylvania, Tennessee, Texas, and West Virginia.

The rest have either a supposedly nonpartisan election system or some hybrid combining merit selection and election. See John B. Wefing, *State Supreme Court Justices: Who Are They?* 32 New England Law Review 47 (1997–98).

36. For this section, I rely on: Steve Bates, *Attorneys' Rising Political Clout*, Nation's Business, Feb. 1, 1998, at 19; *The Buying of the Bench* and *Dicey Justice*, The Nation, Jan. 26, 1998, at 11; William Glaberson, *Fierce Campaigns Signal a New Era for State Courts,* New York Times, June 5, 2000, at A1; William Glaberson, *Chief Justices to Meet on Abuses in Judicial Races,* New York Times, Sept. 8, 2000, at A12; W. John Moore, *Lobbying & Law: All Aboard the Gravy Train*, National Law Journal, Oct. 17, 1998; Steven Rosenfeld, *Judges and Campaign Contributions,* Morning Edition, National Public Radio, Nov. 25, 1998; *Tort Reformers Focus on State Supreme Court Elections,* Liability Week, Oct. 26, 1998;

37. For this section, I rely on: *Alabama Supreme Court*, Montgomery Advertiser, Jan. 18, 1999, at 14D; Linda Greenhouse, *Judges Aid in Effort to Re-*

main Independent, New York Times, Dec. 10, 1998, at A16; Roger Parloff, *Is This Any Way to Run a Court?* American Lawyer, May 1997, at 50.

38. See *Key Policy Issues, Alabama,* Metropolitan Corporate Counsel, January 1999, at 24.

39. *Oliver v. Towns,* 1999 WL 14675 *7n.7 (Ala. 1999).

40. See Parloff, *Is This Any Way to Run a Court?* 50.

41. Alexis de Tocqueville, 1 *Democracy in America* 269 (1840; trans. Henry Reeve, Arlington House, 1966).

42. The medical estimate was made by Dr. Irving J. Selikoff of Mount Sinai School of Medicine, the acknowledged expert in the field, in the early 1980s. See Paul Brodeur, *Outrageous Misconduct: The Asbestos Industry on Trial* 6 (1985). The Environmental Protection Agency attempted to ban asbestos until 1990; its ban was overturned by a federal court in *Corrosion Proof Fittings,* 947 F. 2d 1201 (5th Cir. 1991).

NOTES TO CHAPTER 3

1. Regarding Roger Williams and founding of Rhode Island, I rely on: Patrick T. Conley, *Democracy in Decline: Rhode Island's Constitutional Development 1776–1841* at 7–14 (Rhode Island Historical Society, 1977); Paul Johnson, *A History of the American People* 46–50 (Harper Perennial, 1998); William G. McLoughlin, *Rhode Island: A History* 3–4 (W. W. Norton, 1968); and Edward J. Eberle, *Roger Williams' Gift: Religious Freedom in America,* 4 Roger Williams University Law Review 425 (1999).

2. This is perhaps an oversimplification. Williams was neither the first white settler in what is now Rhode Island, nor within a few years, was Williams's settlement of Providence the largest settlement. Nevertheless, Williams is rightfully considered the founder of Rhode Island because the Indians granted him the land for Providence and at Williams's request granted Aquidneck Island, on which larger the settlement of Newport was situated, to the settlers there. See McLoughlin, *Rhode Island.*

3. McLoughlin, *Rhode Island,* 12.

4. *Id.* at 10.

5. *Id.* at 33–34.

6. Roger Williams, *The Bloody Tenet of Persecution* (1644), in 1 *Great American Political Thinkers,* ed. Bernard E. Brown 38, 47–48 (Avon Books, 1983).

7. Daniel J. Boorstin, *The Americans: The Colonial Experience* 8 (Vintage Books, 1958).

8. The seminal statement of separation of church and state is generally considered to be John Locke's *A Letter Concerning Toleration,* published in England in 1689, about forty-five years after Roger Williams's major works

appeared in England. In that document Locke asks, What is a church? then continues:

> I say it a free and voluntary society. . . . No man by nature is bound unto any particular church or sect, but everyone joins himself voluntarily to that society in which he believes he has found that profession and worship which is truly acceptable to God. . . . [S]ince the joining together of several members into this church-society . . . is absolutely free and spontaneous, it necessarily follows that the right of making laws can belong to none but the society itself; or, at least (which is the same thing), to those whom the society by common consent has authorised thereunto.

John Locke, *A Letter Concerning Toleration* 4, in *33 Great Books of Western World,* ed. Mortimer J. Adler (1990).

9. Lawrence M. Friedman, *A History of American Law* 39–40 (2d ed., Simon & Schuster, 1985).

10. Friedman notes that the county courts "were not the absolute base of the system" but heard appeals from magistrates and ad hoc courts that had jurisdiction over small claims, public drunkenness, marriages, and the whipping of Quakers. The description of the county courts as "general instruments of government" is Friedman's. *Id.*

11. See Gordon S. Wood, *The Radicalism of the American Revolution* 80–82 (1991); and Gordon S. Wood, *Creation of the American Republic* 154 (Vintage Books, 1991). See also Conley, *Democracy in Decline* 40–43, regarding the Rhode Island.

12. Friedman, *History of American Law* 41.

13. See Jack C. Rakove, *Politics and Ideas in the Making of the Constitution* 246 (Alfred A. Knopf, 1996).

14. For a concise history of the Glorious Revolution, see Carl T. Bogus, *The Hidden History of the Second Amendment,* 31 University of California Davis Law Review 309, 379–86 (1998).

15. See Rakove, *Politics and Ideas* 245.

16. William Blackstone, 1 *Commentaries* 145, 156.

17. Edward Jenks, *A Short History of English Law: From the Earliest Times to the End of the Year 1911* at 185 (Little, Brown, 1912).

18. See Goldwin Smith, *A Constitutional and Legal History of England* 364 (Scribner's, 1990).

19. See Ronald Walker and Richard Ward, *Walker & Walker's English Legal System* 182 (Michie Butterworth, 1994).

20. See, e.g., Rakove, *Politics and Ideas* 248; Wood, *Creation of the American Republic* 152.

21. Montesquieu, *The Spirit of the Laws,* trans. and ed. Anne M. Cohler et al., 156–57 (Cambridge University Press, 1989).

22. *Id.* at 157.

23. See Pauline Maier, *American Scripture: Making the Declaration of Independence* 110 (Alfred A. Knopf, 1997). See also Rakove, *Politics and Ideas* 246–47; and Wood, *Creation of the American Republic* 160–61.

24. See Wood, *Creation of the American Republic* 150.

25. See *id.* at 33–34; Wood, *Radicalism of the American Revolution* 174–75. See also Thornton Anderson, *Creating the Constitution: The Convention of 1787 and the First Congress* 36–37 (Pennsylvania State University Press, 1993), arguing that there were religious connotations to the corruption theme.

26. See generally M. J. C. Vile, *Constitutionalism and the Separation of Powers* 23–82, 107–30 (2d ed., Liberty Fund, 1998).

27. Anderson, *Creating the Constitution* 168. See also Wood, *Creation of the American Republic* 406–7; Rakove, *Politics and Ideas* 290.

28. See Anderson, *Creating the Constitution* 50–51, describing how at the beginning of the convention Edmund Randolph proposed the three-branch system.

29. The founders worried that a system that attempted to balance power between only two branches was inherently unstable. When executive authority was limited, legislative power swelled, "drawing all power into its impetuous vortex," as Madison famously put it. *The Federalist* No. 48 (Madison). A third branch, the judiciary, was necessary to preserve balance by, among other things, confining the other branches, especially the legislature, "within the limits assigned to their authority." *The Federalist* No. 78 (Hamilton). This theme, though perhaps not fully developed, separated the American system from its British antecedents.

30. See Anderson, *Creating the Constitution* 149–52; Rakove, *Politics and Ideas* 81–82, 186–87; Wood, *Creation of the American Republic* 453–63.

31. Wood, *Creation of the American Republic* 454, quoting Dickinson.

32. For example, the anti-Federalist writer "Brutus," whom some believe to have been Robert Yates, a judge who served as one of New York's three delegates to the Constitutional Convention in Philadelphia, wrote:

> The judicial power will operate to effect, in the most certain but silent and imperceptible manner, what is evidently the tendency of the constitution—I mean, an entire subversion of the legislative, executive and judicial powers of the individual states. Every adjudication of the supreme court, on any question that may arise upon the nature and extent of the general government, will affect the limits of the state jurisdiction. In proportion as the former enlarge the exercise of their powers, will that of the latter ve restricted.

Brutus XI, in *The Anti-Federalist Papers and the Constitutional Convention Debates,* ed. Ralph Ketcham, 293, at 296 (Mentor, 1986).

Two opponents of judicial review among the delegates to the Constitutional Convention were John Francis Mercer of Maryland and Pierce Butler of South Carolina. See M. E. Bradford, *Founding Fathers* 123, 199 (2d ed., University Press of Kansas, 1994).

33. See Rakove, *Politics and Ideas* 175–76. It is not technically correct to talk about acts of the Rhode Island General Assembly being "unconstitutional" during this period, since Rhode Island was still operating under a charter and did not adopt a Constitution until 1843.

34. 2 *The Records of the Federal Convention of 1787,* ed. Max Farrand, 73–80 (Yale University Press, 1937).

35. Shannon C. Stimson, *The American Revolution in the Law,* at 23 (Princeton University Press, 1990).

36. Robert Stevens, *The Independence of the Judiciary: The Case of England,* 72 Southern California Law Review 597 (1999).

37. See, e.g., *Towe v. Martinson,* 1994 WL 486862 *4n. 6 (D. Mont.), noting a federal bankruptcy judge ordered a governmental official with settlement authority to appear at a settlement conference.

38. Oliver Wendell Holmes, *The Common Law* 5 (1881; ed. Mark DeWolfe, Belknap Press, 1963).

39. Alexis de Tocqueville, 1 *Democracy in America* 266–67 (1840; trans. Henry Reeve, Arlington House, 1966).

40. Anthony T. Kronman, *The Lost Lawyer: Failing Ideals of the Legal Profession* 174–273 (Belknap Press, 1993).

41. Thomas Hobbes, *A Dialogue between a Philosopher and a Student of the Common Laws of England* 54 (1681; ed. Joseph Cropsey, University of Chicago Press, 1971).

42. Wood, *Creation of the American Republic* 10. But see Daniel J. Boorstin, *The Americans: The Colonial Experience* 202 (Vintage Books, 1958), arguing that Blackstone "violated the spirit of the common law by confining it in a system."

43. See Mary Ann Glendon et al., *Comparative Legal Traditions* 133 (2d ed., West/Wadsworth, 1994).

44. *Swift v. Tyson,* 41 U.S. 1, 18–19 (1842).

45. *The Virginia Report of 1799–1800* at 211 (Da Capo Press, 1970). See Daniel Sisson, *The American Revolution of 1800* at 333–38 (Alfred A. Knopf, 1974), attributing the *Virginia Report of 1799–1800* to James Madison.

46. *Kuhn v. Fairmont Coal Co.,* 215 U.S. 349, 372 (1910): "The law of a State does not become something outside of the state court and independent of it by being called the common law. Whatever it is called it is the law as declared by the state judges and nothing else" (Holmes, J.).

47. *Black & White Taxicab Co. v. Brown & Yellow Taxicab Co.,* 276 U.S. 518, 532 (1928), Holmes, J., dissenting.

48. 304 U.S. 64 (1938).

49. William James, *Pragmatism's Conception of Truth,* in *Essays in Pragmatism by William James,* ed. Alburey Castell (Hafner Press, 1948).

50. Richard A. Posner, *Economic Analysis of Law* 21–25 (4th ed., Little, Brown, 1992).

51. Tocqueville, 1 *Democracy in America* 269–70.

52. Johnson, *History of the American People* 394.

53. See Carl T. Bogus, *The Death of an Honorable Profession,* 71 Indiana Law Journal 911, 930 (1996).

54. See Boorstin, *The Americans: The Colonial Experiences* 198.

55. See Friedman, *History of American Law* 97.

56. Christopher W. Brooks, *Lawyers, Litigation and English Society since 1450* at 151 (Hambledon Press, 1998).

57. See David Lemmings, *Gentlemen and Barristers: The Inns of Court and the English Bar 1680–1730* at 162–65 (Oxford University Press, 1990).

58. Friedman, *History of American Law* 306.

59. Wood, *Radicalism of the American Revolution* 34.

60. See Friedman, *History of American Law* 607.

61. See Richard L. Abel, *England and Wales: A Comparison of the Profes sional Projects of Barristers and Solicitors,* in *Lawyers in Society: An Overview,* ed. Richard L. Abel and Philip S. C. Lewis, at 39, 40–42 (University of California Press, 1995); and Maimon Schwarzchild, *Class, National Character, and the Bar Reforms in Britain: Will There Always Be an England?* 9 Connecticut Journal of International Law 185, 192–96 (1994).

62. See Stimson, *American Revolution in the Law* 39.

63. Tocqueville, 1 *Democracy in America* 266.

64. See Friedman, *History of American Law* 25, 662 ; Kermit L. Hall, *The Magic Mirror: Law in American History* 11 (Oxford University Press, 1989).

65. See Brooks, *Lawyers, Litigation and English Society* 45–46.

66. Richard L. Marcus et al., *Civil Procedure: A Modern Approach* 115 (2d ed., West Publishing, 1995).

67. Brooks, *Lawyers, Litigation and English Society* 48–49.

68. See Wood, *Radicalism of the American Revolution* 122–23.

69. *Id.*

70. See generally Wood, *Radicalism of the American Revolution.*

71. Friedman, *History of American Law* 146.

72. *Id.* at 146–47.

73. See William E. Nelson, *Americanization of the Common Law: The Impact of Legal Change on Massachusetts Society, 1760–1830* at 68–88 (University of Georgia Press, 1994).

74. See *id.* at 71, 77, stating that the resistance to court reform was one of the causes of Shay's Rebellion. There were other grievances leading to the

rebellion as well. For more about Shay's Rebellion, see Johnson, *History of the American People* 187–88; Howard Zinn, *A People's History of the United States* 90–95 (Harper Perennial, 1980); and Bogus, *Hidden History of the Second Amendment* 309, 391–94.

75. Nelson, *Americanization of the Common Law* 78.

NOTES TO CHAPTER 4

1. For the history of the jury system, I rely on: George Burton Adams, *Constitutional History of England 1851–1925* (reprint, Gaunt, 1996); Goldwin Smith, *A History of England* 54–59 (4th ed. 1974); Edward Jenks, *A Short History of English Law: From the Earliest Times to the End of the Year 1911* (Little, Brown, 1912); Matthew P. Harrington, *The Law-Finding Function of the American Jury*, 1999 Wisconsin Law Review 377 (1999); Stephen Landsman, *The Civil Jury in America: Scenes from an Unappreciated History*, 44 Hastings Law Journal 579 (1993); Douglas Smith, *The Historical and Constitutional Contexts of Jury Reform*, 25 Hofstra Law Review 377 (1996).

2. Jenks, *Short History of English Law* 46. See also R. J. Walker and Richard Ward, *Walker & Walker's English Legal System* 196–203 (Michie Butterworth, 1994).

3. Smith, *History of England* 408–9 (1996).

4. See W. A. Speck, *Reluctant Revolutionaries: Englishmen and the Revolution of 1688* at 67–68, 184–85, 221–24 (Oxford University Press, 1988).

5. *Id.* at 67.

6. Adams, *Constitutional History of England* at 354.

7. For a description of the underlying facts of the Zenger case, I rely on: William Lowell Putnam, *John Peter Zenger and the Fundamental Freedom* (McFarland, 1997); Eben Moglen, *Considering Zenger: Partisan Politics and the Legal Profession in Provincial New York*, 94 Columbia Law Review 1495 (1994).

8. See Paul Johnson, *A History of the American People* 97–98 (Harper Perennial, 1998).

9. Putnam, *John Peter Zenger* 22–23, quoting Raymond W. Postgate, *Murder, Piracy and Treason* 126 (1949).

10. Moglen, *Considering Zenger* at 1513.

11. Putnam, *John Peter Zenger* at 88.

12. *Id.* at 89.

13. *Id.* at 97.

14. *Id.* at 102 (edited without ellipses).

15. *Id.* at 103.

16. *Id.* at 108.

17. *Id.* at 114.

18. *Id.*

19. *Id.* at 116.

20. Daniel J. Boorstin, *The Americans: The Colonial Experience* 333 (Vintage Books, 1958).

21. *Wilkes v. Wood,* 98 Eng. Rep. 489 (K.B. 1763); *Huckle v. Money,* 95 Eng. Rep. 768 (K.B. 1763). See also Arvel B. Erickson and Martin J. Havran, *England: Prehistory to the Present* 293–94, 301–3 (Praeger, 1968); Smith, *History of England* 467–70; R. K. Webb, *Modern England: From the Eighteenth Century to the Present* 76–81 (Dodd, Mead, 1968); Peter D. G. Thomas, *John Wilkes: A Friend to Liberty* 27–56 (1996).

22. Erickson and Havran, *England* 293.

23. Webb, *Modern England* 76.

24. William B. Willcox, *The Age of Aristocracy 1688 to 1830* at 133 (Heath, 1976).

25. Thomas, *John Wilkes* 1.

26. Wilcox, *Age of Aristocracy* 132.

27. Thomas, *John Wilkes* 19.

28. *Id.* at 29.

29. *Huckle v. Money* 769.

30. *Id.*

31. Arkansas, Delaware, Maine, and New Jersey named cities after Lord Camden, as did counties in Georgia, Missouri, and North Carolina.

32. See Edmund S. Morgan, *The Birth of the Republic, 1763–89* at 16 (3d ed., University of Chicago Press, 1992).

33. *Id.* at 48, 59.

34. *The Federalist* No. 83 (Hamilton).

35. For example, the Massachusetts Convention, which ratified the Constitution in February 1788, recommended the following constitutional amendment: "In civil actions between Citizens of different States every issue of fact arising in Actions at common law shall be tried by a Jury if the parties or either of them request it." See *The Anti-Federalist Papers and the Constitutional Convention Debates* 219 (ed. Ralph Ketcham, Mentor, 1986). The Virginia Convention recommended adoption of the following amendment: "That, in controversies respecting property, and in suits between man and man, the ancient trial by jury is one of the greatest securities to the rights of the people, and to remain sacred and inviolable." *Id.* at 220.

36. Ketcham, *Anti-Federalist Papers* 173.

37. Thornton Anderson, *Creating the Constitution: The Convention of 1787 and the First Congress* 152–55 (Pennsylvania State University Press, 1993).

38. See Jack H. Friedenthal et al., *Civil Procedure* 507 (2d ed., West/Wadsworth, 1993).

39. See Harrington, *Law-Finding Function of the American Jury* 388, quoting Jefferson.

40. *The Federalist* No. 83 (Hamilton).

41. When representing a man named Harry Croswell, a Federalist newspaper editor prosecuted for seditious libel under the Alien and Sedition Acts in 1804, Hamilton argued to the Supreme Court of New York that the jury should be the finder of both fact and law in criminal cases as well as in cases involving libel. It is not possible, however, to know whether this represented his personal view or was merely the position he was advocating on behalf of his client. See Clinton Rossiter, *Alexander Hamilton and the Constitution* 102–5 (Harcourt, Brace & World, 1964).

42. See Harrington, *Law-Finding Function of the American Jury.*

43. *Id.* at 436, quoting Pound.

44. See Terence Ingman, *The English Legal Process* 303–19 (6th ed., Financial Training, 1983); Walker and Ward, *Walker & Walker's English Legal System* 198–99.

45. See *Ward v. James,* 1 Q.B. 273, 290 (1966).

46. *Id.* at 301.

47. *Teamsters Local No. 391 v. Terry,* 494 U.S. 558 (1990); *Tull v. U.S.,* 481 U.S. 412 (1987); *Curtis v. Loether,* 415 U.S. 189 (1974); *Ross v. Bernhard,* 396 U.S. 531 (1970); *Dairy Queen, Inc. v. Wood,* 369 U.S. 469 (1962); and *Beacon Theaters, Inc. v. Westover,* 359 U.S. 500 (1959).

48. *Ross v. Bernhard,* 396 U.S. 531, 538 n. 10 (1970).

49. "We hold that the right to jury trial attaches to those issues in derivative actions as to which the corporation, if it had been suing in its own right, would have been entitled to a jury." *Id.* at 532.

50. *Teamsters Local No. 391 v. Terry,* 494 U.S. 558, 592 (1990), Kennedy, J., with O'Connor and Scalia, JJ., dissenting.

51. The Supreme Court has held that the Seventh Amendment "requires trial by jury in actions unheard of at common law, provided that the action involves rights and remedies of the sort traditionally enforced in an action of law, rather than in an action in equity or admiralty." *Pernell v. Southall Realty,* 416 U.S. 363, 375 (1974). Since the common law is a living system that can accommodate new forms of action, this can be interpreted to mean (speaking generally) that the right to a jury trial exists in both traditional and modern common law actions involving claims for money damages.

52. *NLRB v. Jones & Laughlin Steel Corp.,* 301 U.S. 1 (1937); *Atlas Roofing Co. v. Occupational Safety and Health Review Commission (QSHRC),* 430 U.S. 442 (1977).

53. See *Granfinanciera, S.A. v. Nordberg,* 492 U.S. 33 (1989); *Commodity Futures Trading Comm'n v. Schor,* 478 U.S. 833 (1986).

54. *Teamsters Local No. 391 v. Terry,* 494 U.S. 558, 574 (Brennan concurring).

55. *See* Paula L. Hannaford, et al., *How Judges View Civil Juries,* 46 De-

Paul Law Review 247, 253 (1998). *See also* Brian J. Ostrom et al., *A Step Above Anecdote: A Profile of the Civil Jury in the 1990s*, Judicature, March–April 1996, at 233, 234 (reporting that 2.7 percent of tort cases reach a jury trial in the state courts).

56. 28 U.S.C. § 1861.

57. In the 1996 presidential election, only 48.99 percent of the voting age population actually voted. See *The New York Times 1998 Almanac* 109 (1997).

58. 28 U.S.C. § 1866(c).

59. 28 U.S.C. § 1870.

60. See, e.g., Vicki L. Smith, *The Feasibility and Utility of Pretrial Instruction in the Substantive Law*, 14 Law & Human Behavior 235 (1990).

61. See Federal Rule Civil Procedure 49.

62. See *Smith v. Phillips*, 455 U.S. 209, 217 (1982), holding that due process requires "a jury capable and willing to decide a case solely on the evidence before it."

63. *Galloway v. U.S.*, 319 U.S. 372, 407 (1943), Black, J., dissenting.

64. See Fed. R. Civ. P. 56(c).

65. Fed. R. Civ. P. 50.

66. *Garrison v. U.S.*, 62 F. 2d 41, 42 (4th Cir. 1932).

67. *Dimick v. Schiedt*, 293 U.S. 474 (1935).

68. *Johansen v. Combustion Engineering, Inc.*, 170 F. 3d 1320 (11th Cir. 1999); *In re Bd. of County Sup'rs of Prince William County*, 143 F. 3d 835 (4th Cir. 1998). The courts' reasoning is based on *BMW of North America, Inc. v. Gore*, 517 U.S. 559 (1996).

69. Two circuit court cases that appear to disagree are *Continental Resources, Inc. v. OXY USA, Inc.*, 101 F. 3d 634 (10th Cir. 1966); and *Lee v. Edwards*, 101 F. 3d 805 (2d Cir. 1996).

70. *Dimick v. Schiedt*, 293 U.S. 474, 485 (1935).

71. See, e.g., *Hattaway v. McMillian*, 903 F. 2d 1440 (11th Cir. 1990).

72. The original researchers reported their results in Harry Kalven and Hans Zeisel, *The American Jury* (Little, Brown, 1964); and Harry Kalven, *The Dignity of the Civil Jury*, 50 Virginia Law Review 1055 (1964), describing studies conducted by Kalven and Zeisel for the University of Chicago Jury Project. Summary descriptions of this and other studies described may be found in Paula L. Hannaford et al., *How Judges View Civil Juries*, 48 DePaul Law Review 247 (1998); and Neil Vidmar, *The Performance of the American Civil Jury: An Empirical Perspective*, 40 Arizona Law Review 849, 853 (1998).

73. R. Perry Sentell Jr., *The Georgia Jury and Negligence: The View from the Bench*, 26 Georgia Law Review 85 (1991); and R. Perry Sentell Jr., *The Georgia Jury and Negligence: The View from the (Federal) Bench*, 27 Georgia Law Review 85 (1991).

74. *The View from the Bench,* National Law Journal, Aug. 10, 1987, at 1 (poll taken by the *National Law Journal*).

75. See Hannaford et al., *How Judges View Civil Service* 249.

76. *Judges' Opinions on Procedural Issues: A Survey of State and Federal Trial Judges Who Spend at Least Half Their Time on General Civil Cases,* 69 Boston University Law Review 731, 746–50 (1989).

77. See Vidmar, *Performance of the American Civil Jury* 858–59.

78. Ostrom et al., *A Step Above Anecdote* 235.

79. See also W. Kip Viscusi, *Reforming Products Liability* 51 (1991), reporting a 37 percent plaintiff win rate in products liability.

80. Another study found that plaintiff win rates were 60 percent against individuals and 63 percent against corporations, while a third study found rates of 50 percent and 61 percent, respectively. See Valerie P. Hans, *Realities of Jurors' Treatment of Corporate Defendants,* 48 DePaul Law Review 327, 338, 341 (1998). Despite the variations, all three studies point in one direction: any pro-plaintiff bias is more than compensated for by the fact that plaintiffs may face more difficult legal battles when suing corporations.

81. See Vidmar, *Performance of the American Civil Jury* 868–69, discussing studies by three different groups of researchers.

82. For example, one study found that the plaintiff win rate varied from 33 percent in Massachusetts to 75 percent in North Dakota. See Viscusi, *Reforming Products Liability* 239 n. 16, reporting the results of a 1989 study by the U.S. General Accounting Office.

83. Vidmar, *Performance of the American Civil Jury* 853.

84. Viscusi, *Reforming Products Liability* 88. Viscusi suggests the awards are irrational when he speaks about ways to "rationalize procedures for determining damages." The adjective *explosive* comes from the title of his chapter "The Explosive Mathematics of Damages."

85. *Id.* at 101.

86. Vidmar, *Performance of the American Civil Jury* 885; Neil Vidmar, *Pap and Circumstance: What Jury Verdict Statistics Can Tell Us about Jury Behavior and the Tort System,* 28 Suffolk University Law Review 1205, 1234 (1994).

87. Ostrom et al., *A Step Above Anecdote* 237–38.

88. See Jeffrey Ball and Milo Geyelin, *GM Ordered by Jury to Pay $4.9 Billion,"* Wall Street Journal, July 12, 1999, at A3; Andrew Pollack, *Paper Trail Haunts G.M. after It Loses Injury Suit,* New York Times, July 12, 1999, at A12.

89. See *World Almanac and Book of Facts 1999* at 122 (Press Publishing, 1998), reporting that General Motors' 1997 revenues totaled $177.2 billion, the largest of any American corporation; *Burn Victim Plans Large Donation,* Boston Globe, July 13, 1999, at F3, reporting GM's profit was $6.3 billion in 1997 and $3.1 billion in 1998.

90. See Ball and Geyelin, *GM Ordered by Jury* A3, reporting that GM's stock closed at $66.125, down $1.625, on Friday, July 9, 1999; and Wall Street Journal, July 13, 1999, at C8, reporting GM's stock closed at 68 ¹¹/₁₆, up 2⁹/₁₆, on Monday, July 13, 1999.

91. See Vidmar, *Performance of the American Civil Jury* 893.

92. Viscusi, *Reforming Products Liability* 87.

93. *Ealy v. Richardson-Merrell, Inc.*, 897 F. 2d 1159 (D.C. Cir. 1990), *cert. denied* 498 U.S. 950 (1990).

94. See id. at 870–71; Valerie P. Hans, *The Contested Role of the Civil Jury in Business Litigation*, Judicature, March–April 1996, at 242, 246–47.

95. See Hans, *Contested Role of the Civil Jury* 244–46.

96. See *id*; Alan Wolfe, *One Nation, After All* 219, 267 (Penguin, 1998).

97. See Theodore Eisenberg and James A. Henderson Jr., *Inside the Quiet Revolution in Products Liability*, 39 UCLA Law Review 731, 741 (1992).

98. *Id.* at 776.

99. *Judges' Opinions on Procedural Issues* 731, 746, reporting polling data of one thousand judges by Louis Harris and Associates, Inc.

100. *Wilks v. American Tobacco Company*, 680 So. 2d 839 (Miss. 1996). See also Mark Hansen, *To Lawyer's Surprise, Cancer Suit Lost*, 79 ABA Journal 40 (1993); *Miss. Jurors Clear 2 Cigarette Firms in Smoker's Death*, Commercial Appeal (Memphis), June 18, 1993, at A1, *Death Cause Not Certain, Jury Is Told*, Commercial Appeal (Memphis), June 12, 1993, at A15.

101. E.g., Rule 292 of the Texas Rules of Civil Procedure, allowing verdicts with a concurrence of ten members of a twelve-member jury or five members of a six-member jury. See also Friedenthal et al., *Civil Procedure* 530.

102. Telephone interview with Don Barrett, Esquire (July 26, 1999).

103. Clay S. Conrad, *Jury Nullification: The Evolution of a Doctrine* xix (Carolina Academic Press, 1998).

104. *Judges' Opinions on Procedural Issues* 746.

105. Richard L. Rosenzweig has suggested that the requirement that the plaintiff show the defendant's conduct was a substantial factor in the injury presents plaintiffs with unintended obstacles because jurors are confused by the word *substantial*. Instead of understanding it to mean "[n]ot negligible, or not so insignificant that no ordinary mind would think such conduct a cause," as the term is defined in *Restatement of Torts* (§ 431 cmt.), jurors tend to think it is meant to place an extremely heavy burden on the plaintiff, tantamount to raising the plaintiff's burden of proof on causation from a preponderance of the evidence to beyond all reasonable doubt. Rosenzweig writes that this formulation "often provides juries with a basis for civil jury nullification where the jury does not wish to award damages for reasons of bias or prejudice either toward the plaintiff or litigation." Richard L. Rosenzweig, *"Substantial Factor"—Plaintiff's Everest*, Pittsburgh Law Journal, May 1998, at 35.

106. This vignette is based on personal experience. I was counsel for the plaintiff and spoke with jurors after they had been dismissed. The case was tried in the U.S. District Court for the Eastern District of Philadelphia in the 1980s.

107. Lon L. Fuller, *The Forms and Limits of Adjudication*, 92 Harvard Law Review 353, 366 (1978). Richard A. Posner holds much the same view. He believes that "common law concepts must be justified by demonstrating their provenance in sound public policy," while legislation is "not motivated by the public interest as such" but serves the interest of powerful groups. Richard A. Posner, *The Problems of Jurisprudence* 249, 354 (Harvard University Press, 1990).

NOTES TO CHAPTER 5

1. *Proctor v. Davis*, 628 N.E. 2d 1203, 1217 (Ill. 1997).

2. *Fortune 500 Largest U.S. Corporations*, Fortune, May 15, 1995, at 226, F-59.

3. *Aetna Casualty & Surety Co. v. Yeats*, 122 F. 2d 350, 352–53 (4th Cir. 1960). In Illinois, a trial judge may order a new trial when she finds the verdict is "against the manifest weight of the evidence." *Gillespie v. Chrysler Motors Corp.*, 553 N.E. 2d 291, 301 (Ill. 1990).

4. *Proctor v. Davis*, 682 N.E. 2d at 1216.

5. See *In re Estate of Wernick*, 535 N.E. 2d 876, 885 (Ill. 1989).

6. *Proctor v. Davis*, 682 N.E. 2d at 1216.

7. *Id.* at 1216, 1217.

8. Matt Kelley, *Jury Awards $127 Million to Man Who Lost Eye*, Associated Press, October 19, 1991 (available on Westlaw at 1991 WL 6205750).

9. Although the judge's decision was formally entered on the court docket later, it was publicly announced on Friday, October 18, 1991. Again, it is not clear whether news reports were carried before the market close; a wire service report is dated the following day.

10. The two largest pharmaceuticals, Merck and Johnson & Johnson, gained ground while number three, Bristol Myers Squibb lost 3.3 percent of value from the close on October 17 to the close on October 22, 1991.

11. Donna Rosato, *Money: Dow Down*, USA Today, Oct. 22, 1991, at 1B.

12. *Judge Slashes Damage Award in Upjohn Case*, United Press International, Aug. 15, 1992 (available on LEXIS/NEXIS). See also *Judge Cuts Upjohn's Punitive Damages*, Chicago Tribune, Aug. 15, 1992, at 5. But see John Flynn Rooney, *Judge Slashes $124-Million Punitive Damages Jury Award to $35 Million*, Chicago Daily Law Bulletin, Aug. 14, 1992, at 1.

13. Upjohn stock fell from 30⅛ on June 27, 1994 (the day before the decision) to 29¾ on June 29, 1994 (the day after the decision).

14. See Geoffrey Cowley, et al., *Sweet Dreams or Nightmare*, Newsweek, Aug. 19, 1991, at 44; Bruce H. Dobkin, M.D., *Body and Mind: Sleeping Pills*, New York Times, Feb. 5, 1989, at Sec. 6, page 39.

15. Jamie Talan, *Millions Reach for Halcion*, Newsday, Oct. 29, 1991, at 65.

16. See Andrew Blum, *High Stakes: Wonder Drugs Are Focus of Criminal, Civil Actions*, National Law Journal, Oct. 22, 1990, at 1.

17. Cowley et al., *Sweet Dreams or Nightmare* 44.

18. See Cowley, *id.* (for *Newsweek* quote); Jeremy Webb, *Sleeping Pill Ban Puzzles Doctors*, New Scientist, Oct. 12, 1991, at 13 (for Grundberg allegation).

19. See *Upjohn Co. Fined $600,000 for Keeping Sloppy Records of Samples Given to Physicians*, Drug & Cosmetic Industry, September 1991, at 84.

20. See Webb, *Sleeping Pill Ban*; and *Banning a Pill*, Maclean's, Oct. 14, 1991, at 31.

21. *Time to Go Public on Clinical Trials*, New Scientist, Oct. 12, 1991, at 11.

22. See Jonathan Gabe and Michael Bury, *Halcion Nights: A Sociological Account of a Medical Controversy*, Journal of the British Sociological Association, August 1996, at 30.

23. Michael L. Millenson, *Upjohn Hit by Debate on Halcion*, Chicago Tribune, March 9, 1992, at C1.

24. E.g., John Carey and Joseph Weber, *How the FDA Let Halcion Slip Through*, Business Week, June 17, 1996; *Jury Finds Upjohn Partly at Fault in Murder Case Linked to Halcion*, Wall Street Journal, Nov. 13, 1992, at B10; *Upjohn Co.: FDA Concludes Its Inquiry over Halcion Sleeping Pills*, Wall Street Journal, Nov. 25, 1992; Jacqueline Mitchell, *Racing the Clock: Upjohn Takes a Hit, and It Isn't the Only One the Drug Maker Faces*, Wall Street Journal, Oct. 2, 1991, at A1.

25. Clare Dyer, *Both Sides Win in Upjohn Libel Case*, British Medical Journal, June 4, 1994, at 1455; Clare Dyer, *Memo Suggests Upjohn Concealed Halcion Side Effects*, British Medical Journal, March 12, 1994, at 677; Clare Dyer, *Upjohn Libel Case over "Wild" Claims Open in Court: Criticism of the Sleeping Pill Halcion*, British Medical Journal, Jan. 22, 1994, at 221.

26. Gabe and Bury, *Halcion Nights*.

27. E.g., Bob Gibbins, *Secrecy versus Safety*, ABA Journal, December 1991, at 74; Mark Hasen, *Does Halcion Spur Aggression? Evidence Kept Secret in Upjohn's Defense of Sleeping-Pill Suits*, ABA Journal, November 1991, at 24; Andrew Blum, *Upjohn Asks High Court to Protect Halcion Info*, National Law Journal, July 22, 1996, at A7; Andrew Blum, *Halcion Updates*, National Law Journal, June 1, 1992, at 6; Andrew Blum, *High Stakes: Wonder Drugs Are Focus of Criminal, Civil Actions*, National Law Journal, Oct. 22, 1990.

28. *Halcion and Prozac*, Consumer Reports, January 1993, at 22.

29. William Styron, *Prozac Days, Halcion Nights*, The Nation, Jan. 4, 1993, at 1.

30. John Schwartz and Bob Cohn, *The Drug Did It: A Tough Sell in Court,* Newsweek, April 1, 1991; Cowley et al., *Sweet Dreams or Nightmares;* Geoffrey Cowley, *Hard Times for Halcion,* Newsweek, Oct. 14, 1991, at 61; Geoffrey Cowley, *Halcion Takes Another Hit,* Newsweek, Feb. 17, 1992, at 58; Geoffrey Cowley, *Fueling the Fire over Halcion,* Newsweek, May 25, 1992, at 84; Geoffrey Cowley, *More Halcion Headaches,* Newsweek, March 7, 1994, at 50; Geoffrey Cowley et al., *Halcion: A Damaging Report,* Newsweek, May 2, 1994, at 6; Carla Koehl et al., *Pill Report,* Newsweek, May 27, 1996, at 6.

31. A search of the LEXIS/NEXUS database in the current and archived news files, conducted on July 23, 1998, found a total of 892 stories containing the words *Halcion, Upjohn,* and *FDA,* compared to only 26 with the words *Depo-Medrol, Upjohn,* and *FDA.* A search in the LEXIS/NEXUS newspaper and magazine database found fourteen stories in general-circulation periodicals (i.e., not legal trade publications) about *Proctor v. Davis v. Upjohn,* compared to ninety-two about *Grundberg v. Upjohn.*

32. The Upjohn Company, *Annual Report 1991,* at 35. *Proctor* was, in fact, the only individual case identified, although Upjohn was, in its own words, a defendant in "a substantial number of products liability suits." The only other sum mentioned with respect to potential litigation liability was an estimate that Upjohn's share of environmental remediation (i.e., clean-up) costs at a total of forty EPA "Super Fund" sites was $20 million. Upjohn noted it was pursuing post-trial remedies in the *Proctor* case, and predicted that its "ultimate liability [in all products liability and environmental cases] should not have a material adverse effect" on the company's financial position.

33. See Michael Rustad, *In Defense of Punitive Damages in Products Liability: Testing Tort Anecdotes with Empirical Data,* 78 Iowa Law Review 1, 56 (1992).

34. 980 F. 2d 171 (3rd Cir. 1992). The trial judge issued a judgment notwithstanding the verdict to set aside the entire verdict because of a lack of evidence of wrongful conduct. The U.S. Court of Appeals for the Third Circuit affirmed that judgment in part but ordered a new trial on one plaintiff's tort claim. 980 F. 2d 171 (3rd Cir. 1992), cert. denied 507 U.S. 921 (1993). In the second trial, the jury found that the defendant had acted wrongfully but also found that plaintiff had suffered no damages, and accordingly the trial court entered a final judgment awarding plaintiff nothing. See *Defense Verdicts: A Roundup of Major 1994 Cases,* National Law Journal, April 24, 1995, at A24. The Third Circuit affirmed that judgment. *Industry Network System, Inc. v. Armstrong World Industries, Inc.,* 118 F. 3d 1575 (1997).

35. 886 F. 2d 1109 (9th Cir 1989), earlier decision reversing summary judgment by district court. See also National Law Journal, Jan. 20, 1992.

36. *Underwriters at Lloyd's London v. The Narrows,* 846 P. 2d 118 (Alaska 1993). The case was settled before a new trial. See James A. McGuire and

Kristin Dodge McMahon, *Bad Faith, Excess Liability and Extracontractual Damages,* 72 University of Detroit Mercy Law Review 49 (1994). Although a new trial may have resulted in a judgment in plaintiff's favor, and presumably plaintiff obtained something in settlement (queries to attorneys handling the case went answered, probably because the settlement is subject to a confidentiality agreement), I have listed zero as the final award since the original award was vacated in its entirety.

37. No. 89CZ696 (Douglas Dist. Ct., Colo.). Following reductions in the jury award by the trial judge, in an unpublished opinion the Colorado Court of Appeals reduced the compensatory award to $5,360,000 and remanded the case to the trial court to reconsider the punitive award in light of its opinion. Colorado law limits punitive damages to the amount of compensatory damages, so under this ruling the total award—compensatory plus punitive—could not have exceeded $10,760,000. I list $10.8 million in the table, although the case was settled before the case proceeded further. This information was from Alvin M. Cohen, Esq., counsel for Crown Point, via e-mail on Nov. 29, 2000. See also J. Stratton Shartel, *Lower Awards, Post-Verdict Reversals or Reductions Characterize Top 1991 Verdicts,* Inside Litigation, March 1992, at 1.

38. 36 Cal. App. 4th 936 (1994).

39. No. 312743 (San Mateo, Calif., Superior Ct.). See Scott Graham, *First District Spikes $57 Million Punitive Award,* The Recorder (American Lawyer Media), May 19, 1995, at 1.

40. 986 F. 2d. 1463 (5th Cir. 1993).

41. No. 7420/85 (Rockland Co., N.Y., Superior Ct.). The $25.9 million figure represented the present value of a structured verdict consisting of a $9.6 million payment and an annuity secured by a bond posted by the defendant. See *Some Awards Are Just Uncollectable,* National Law Journal, Jan. 20, 1992, at S13.

42. *Bseirani v. Mahshie,* 881 F. Supp. 778 (N.D.N.Y. 1995).

43. See Marc Galanter, *Real World Torts: An Antidote to Anecdote,* 55 Maryland Law Review 1093, 1115 (1996).

44. Rooney, *Judge Slashes $124-Million Punitive Damages Jury Award* 1, quoting Cook County Circuit Judge Leonard L. Levin.

45. See Jacqueline Mitchell, *Upjohn's Parfet, Vice Chairman, Is Leaving Firm,* Wall Street Journal, Sept. 20, 1993, at B10. Upjohn was, more than most, a family owned and controlled company. Members of the Upjohn family had served as CEOs of the company from its founding until 1987. In 1991, Upjohn family members sat on the company's six-member executive committee and held the positions of president and executive vice president for administration. See also The Upjohn Company, *Annual Report 1991,* at 45.

46. Brief of Appellant The Upjohn Company in the Appellate Court of Illinois, at 18.

47. See H. Denman Scott et al., *Physician Reporting of Adverse Drug Reactions: Results of the Rhode Island Adverse Drug Reaction Reporting Project,* 263 Journal of the American Medical Association 1785 (1990).

48. See Michael D. Green, *Bendectin and Birth Defects: The Challenges of Mass Toxic Substances Litigation* 63–83 (University of Pennsylvania Press, 1996).

49. Appellate Brief of Plaintiffs, at 2.

50. Harlan F. Stone, *The Common Law in the United States,* 50 Harvard Law Review 4, 5 (1936).

51. Jay M. Feinman, *Implied Warranty, Products Liability, and the Boundary Between Contract and Tort,* 75 Washington University Law Quarterly 469, 477 (1997).

52. See, e.g., Tom W. Bell, *Public Choice in Law and Cyberspace,* 97 Michigan Law Review 1746, 1752 (1999); Michael C. Dorf and Charles F. Sabel, *A Constitution of Democratic Experimentalism,* 98 Columbia Law Review 267, 455 (1998); Fran Ansley, *Poverty Law and Policy,* 81 Georgetown Law Journal 1757, 1812 (1993); Cass R. Sunstein, *Administrative Substance,* Duke Law Journal 607, 611 (1991), all suggesting that the common law consists of torts, contracts, and property.

53. Richard A. Posner, *The Problems of Jurisprudence* 247 (Harvard University Press, 1990).

54. Frank H. Easterbrook, *Statutes' Domains,* 50 University of Chicago Law Review 533, 544 (1983).

55. Stone, *Common Law in the United States* 4.

56. *Barker v. State of Vermont,* 744 A. 2d 864 (1999). In dissent, one justice argued that the court should craft a remedy without waiting for the legislature, not because family law is a common law subject but because it is the duty of the courts to protect and define rights.

57. *State* ex rel. *Ohio Academy of Trial Lawyers v. Sheward,* 715 N.E. 2d 1062 (Ohio 1999).

58. The reenacted legislation contained provisions purporting to overrule the Ohio Supreme Court's prior decisions that had held the measures to be unconstitutional. The court invoked the doctrine of separation of powers with respect to the legislature's attempt to determine the constitutionality of its own legislation.

59. Leaving aside, of course, that the Constitution may be amended.

60. See S. F. C. Milsom, *Historical Foundations of the Common Law* 353–74 (Butterworths, 1969).

61. See Lawrence M. Friedman, *A History of American Law* 284–91 (2d ed., Simon & Schuster, 1985).

62. *U.S. v. Hudson and Goodwin,* 11 U.S. (7 Cranch) 32 (1812).

63. See Lawrence M. Friedman, *Crime and Punishment in American His-*

tory 64–65 (1993); Wayne R. LaFave and Austin W. Scott Jr., 1 *Substantive Criminal Law* 88–103 (1986).

64. *Rex v. Manley,* 1 K.B. 529 (1932). See discussion in LaFave and Scott, 1 *Substantive Criminal Law* 91.

65. LaFave and Scott, 1 *Substantive Criminal Law* 91.

66. Florida Statutes Annotated § 775.01 (West 1992).

67. *State v. Egan,* 287 So. 2d 1 (Fla. 1973). This decision continues to be cited and relied on by Florida courts. See, e.g., *Clayton v. Willis,* 489 So. 2d 813, 817 (Fla. App. 1986).

68. Official Comment to Uniform Commercial Code § 1–102.

69. Gordon S. Wood, *The Radicalism of the American Revolution* 324–25 (Random House, 1991).

70. Friedman, *History of American Law* 348.

71. See Patrick T. Conley, *Democracy in Decline: Rhode Island's Constitutional Development 1776–1841* at 127 (Rhode Island Historical Society, 1977), quoting a letter by Madison dated April 2, 1787. See also William G. McLoughlin, *Rhode Island: A History* 101–4 (W. W. Norton, 1986); Garry Wills, *A Necessary Evil. A History of Distrust of Government* 95–96 (Simon & Schuster, 1999).

72. Wood, *Radicalism of the American Revolution* 264–65; Gordon S. Wood, *Creation of the American Republic, 1776–1787* 609 (W. W. Norton, 1986).

73. See *The Federalist* No. 10 (Madison), in which Madison fretted over how government would deal with the unequal distribution of property.

74. Friedman, *History of American Law* 230.

75. See *id.* at 275–79.

76. U.S. Constitution art. 1, § 10 (contract clause); amend. 14 (due process clause).

77. *Lochner v. N.Y.,* 198 U.S. 45 (1905).

78. In this respect, the Ohio Supreme Court's decision declaring tort reform measures to be unconstitutional has a similar ring. "Majoritarian preferences are transitory," wrote the court as it defended tort law against legislative intrusion. *State* ex rel. *Ohio Academy of Trial Lawyers v. Sheward* at 1103.

79. There are, however, small signs that courts may be on the verge of giving the contract clause of the Constitution increased attention. See, e.g., *Wisconsin Central Limited v. Public Service Comm.,* 95 F. 3d 1359, 1370–71 (7th Cir. 1996).

80. See, e.g., Friedman, *History of American Law* 358–61.

81. Laurence H. Tribe, 1 *American Constitutional Law* 1343 (3d ed., Foundation Press, 2000).

82. Labor law came into being as a recognizable field sometime between the Supreme Court's decision in *Loewe v. Lawlor,* 208 U.S. 274 (1908), which

analyzed secondary boycotts in terms of antitrust law, and the enactment of the first federal labor law, the Wagner Act, in 1935.

Fixing a birthdate for corporate law is more difficult. America was colonized by chartered overseas trading companies, which were, in effect, corporations; and most of the American states enacted general incorporation statutes during the eighteenth century. It was not until the beginning of the twentieth century, however, when the first large American corporation was organized (United States Steel Corp. in 1901), that the field took on real significance. The National Conference of Commissioners on Uniform State Laws proposed the Uniform Business Act in 1928. According to a standard treatise, "After the onset of the Great Depression in 1932, corporate litigation increased with the bringing and consequent regulation of shareholder derivative actions and judicial recognition of greater duties owed by management." Harry G. Henn and John R. Alexander, *Laws of Corporations* 27 (West, 1983).

83. *United States Trust Co. v. N.J.*, 431 U.S. 1, 22–23 (1976).

84. Friedman, *History of American Law* 276.

85. Friedman identifies contract law as the most similar field of law in both England and America. *Id.* at 278.

86. *Id.* at 467.

87. G. Edward White, *Tort Law in America: An Intellectual History* 3 (Oxford University Press, 1980).

88. Regarding the transcontinental railroad, I rely primarily on Walter Licht, *Working for the Railroad: The Organization of Work in the Nineteenth Century* 164–212 (Princeton University Press, 1983). See also Daniel J. Boorstin, *The Americans: The Democratic Experience* 118–21 (Vintage Books, 1973); Friedman, *History of American Law* 479; Paul Johnson, *A History of the American People* 531–37 (Harper Perennial, 1997); Howard Zinn, *A People's History of the United States* 246 (Harper Perennial, 1980).

89. See Licht, *Working for the Railroad* 190–91.

90. See Michael B. Katz, *In the Shadow of the Poorhouse: A Social History of Welfare in America* 191 (Basic Books, 1986).

91. See Licht, *Working for the Railroad* 177, quoting letter from John Douglas to William Osborn.

92. Daniel J. Boorstin, *The Americans: The National Experience* 39 (Vintage Books, 1965).

93. *Farwell v. Boston & Worcester R.R. Corp.*, 45 Mass. 49 (1842).

94. *Id.* at 59.

95. Useful discussions of the case can be found in Leonard W. Levy, *The Law of the Commonwealth and Chief Justice Shaw* 166–82 (Harvard University Press, 1957); Friedman, *History of American Law* 301–2; and Posner, *Problems of Jurisprudence* 252–54.

96. "[T]he common law consists of a few broad and comprehensive princi-

ples, founded on reason, natural justice, and enlightened public policy, modified and adapted to the circumstances of all the particular cases which fall within it. These general principles of equity and policy are rendered precise, specific, and adapted to practical use, by usage, which is the proof of their general fitness and common convenience," wrote Shaw in another case. See Boorstin, *The Americans: The National Experience* 41–42, quoting this language from Shaw's opinion in *Norway Plains Co. v. Boston & Maine Railroad,* and expressing the view that this represented American pragmatism.

97. See John Fabian Witt, Note, *The Transformation of Work and the Law of Workplace Accidents, 1842–1910,* 107 Yale Law Journal 1467, 1478 (1998). It should be noted that railroad accidents also injured large numbers of passengers. For obvious reasons, railroads were more concerned about passenger than about worker safety, and thus some significant incentive for self-regulation existed. The courts never insulated railroads from lawsuits from passengers, however, perhaps because the courts believed passenger confidence was critical to the railroad development and was supported by giving passengers the right to recover for injuries. In any event, these cases came into the tort system and created additional safety pressures, benefiting passengers and workers alike. See Licht, *Working for the Railroad* 181, discussing frequent boiler explosions and derailments that injured workers and passengers.

98. Levy, *Law of the Commonwealth* 178–82.

99. John Hoyt Williams, *A Great & Shining Road: The Epic Story of the Transcontinental Railroad* 16–17 (Times Books, 1988).

100. Johnson, *History of the American People* 533–34.

101. See Friedman, *History of American Law* 182.

102. *Chicago, Milwaukee & St. Paul Railway Co. v. Ross,* 112 U.S. 377 (1884).

103. *Id.* at 391–92, quoting F. Wharton, *A Treatise on the Law of Negligence* § 232a (2d ed., 1878).

104. See White, *Tort Law in America* 54. See also generally White's discussion about the fellow-servant and vice-principal doctrines at pages 51–56.

105. *Baltimore & Ohio Railroad Co. v. Baugh,* 149 U.S. 368, 384 (1893).

106. See W. Page Keeton, ed. *Prosser and Keeton on the Law of Torts* 572 (5th ed., West, 1984), listing examples of such cases at notes 37–41.

107. Eugene Wambaugh, *Workmen's Compensation Acts: Their Theory and Their Constitutionality,* 25 Harvard Law Review 129, 130 (1911).

108. See Keeton, ed., *Prosser and Keeton on the Law of Torts* 573.

109. See Katz, *In the Shadow of the Poorhouse* 192.

110. I rely for this section primarily on James Weinstein, *Big Business and the Origins of Workmen's Compensation,* 8 Labor History 156 (1967). See also Michael Kazin, *The Populist Persuasion: An American History* 49–65 (Basic Books, 1995); Katz, *In the Shadow of the Poorhouse* 191–95.

111. See Weinstein, *Big Business* 168.
112. Katz, *In the Shadow of the Poorhouse* 194.
113. *Food Lion, Inc. v. Capital Cities/ABC, Inc.,* 194 F. 3d 505 (4th Cir. 1999).

NOTES TO CHAPTER 6

1. *Webster's New Universal Unabridged Dictionary* 1444 (1989).
2. *Carroll v. Otis Elevator Co.,* 896 F. 2d 210 (7th Cir. 1990).
3. *Id.* at 215 (Easterbrook, concurring).
4. *Statistical Abstract of the United States 1999,* at table 1074.
5. For information regarding the national maximum speed limit, I rely on: New Jersey Department of Transportation, *18 Month Study Report on the 65 MPH Speed Limit in New Jersey* (2000); National Highway Traffic Safety Administration (NHTSA), *Report to Congress: The Effect of Increased Speed Limits in the Post–NMSL Era,* February 1998; Henry Payne, *Double-Nickel Falls, So Do Fatalities,* Pittsburgh Post-Gazette, June 13, 1999, at A16; *Data Link Highway Speeds to Rise in Fatalities,* Star-Ledger (Newark, N.J.), Jan. 15, 1999, at 2.
6. For information regarding the war against drunk driving, I rely on: *Statistical Abstract of the United States 1999,* table 1048 (119th ed.); Lawrence M. Friedman, *Crime and Punishment in American History* 280–82 (Basic Books, 1993); Bruce L. Benson et al., *Can Police Deter Drunk Driving?* 32 Applied Economics 357 (2000); Joseph R. Gusfield, *Risky Roads,* Society, March/April 1991, at 10; Mike A. Males, *The Minimum Purchase Age for Alcohol and Young-Driver Fatal Crashes: A Long-Term View,* 15 Journal of Legal Studies 181 (1986); Joey Kennedy, *Drunk Driving Makes a Comeback*, Redbook, May 1997, at 89; B. Drummond Ayres Jr., *Big Gains Are Seen in Battle to Stem Drunken Driving,* New York Times, May 22, 1994, at 1.
7. See Ellen MacKenzie, *Review of Evidence Regarding Trauma System Effectiveness Resulting from Panel Studies,* 47 Journal of Trauma: Injury, Infection and Critical Care S34 (1999); N. Clay Mann et al., *Systematic Review of Published Evidence Regarding Trauma Effectiveness,* 47 Journal Trauma: Injury, Infection and Critical Care S25 (1999). See also Sheryl Weinstein, *Flaws Persist in Trauma Network,* New York Times, June 26, 1994, sec. 13NJ at 1.
8. For information regarding NHTSA and crashworthiness, I rely on: telephone interviews with Sally Greenberg (July 25, 2000) and David Pittle (July 18, 2000), both of Consumers Union; Jerry L. Mashaw and David L. Harfst, *The Struggle for Auto Safety* (Harvard University Press, 1990); John D. Graham, *Product Liability and Motor Vehicle Safety,* in *The Liability Maze,* ed. Peter W. Huber and Robert E. Litan (Brookings Institution, 1991); Ralph Nader and Joseph A. Page, *Automobile-Design Liability and Compliance with*

Federal Standards, 64 George Washington Law Review 415 (1996); Joan Claybrook and David Bollier, *The Hidden Benefits of Regulation: Disclosing the Auto Safety Payoff,* 3 Yale Journal on Regulation 87 (1985); *Cars Are Getting Safer,* Consumer Reports, April 1994, at 250; Matthew L. Wald, *Revised Rules for Air Bags Will Reduce Their Power,* New York Times, May 5, 2000.

For discussions of administrative agencies and capture, public choice, and ossification theories, I rely on: James Q. Wilson, *Bureaucracy* (Basic Books, 1989); Thomas W. Merrill, *Capture Theory and the Courts: 1967–1983,* 72 Chicago-Kent Law Review 1039 (1997); Richard J. Pierce Jr., *Seven Ways to Deossify Agency Rulemaking,* 47 Admin. Law Journal 59 (1995); Myron Levin, *Who's Watching Out for Safety? Does an Agency Revolving Door Sacrifice Auto Standards?,* Los Angeles Times, Jan. 5, 2000, at G1.

9. The quote is from committee chair Senator Abraham Ribicoff (D–Conn.) during the public hearings.

10. Mashaw and Harfst, *Struggle for Auto Safety* 69.

11. *Id.* at 167.

12. Merrill, *Capture Theory and the Courts* 1067.

13. *Id.* at 1070.

14. Murry Richtel, *The Simpson Trial: A Timid Judge and a Lawless Verdict,* 67 University of Colorado Law Review 977, 978 (1996), coining the term *judicial-centricism.* Judge Richtel defines *judicial-centricism* only as "black robes disease" and does not define the latter term at all. My definition comes from my hearing and using the term within the trial bar in Philadelphia, where I practiced law from 1973 to 1991.

15. NHTSA, *FY2000 Budget in Brief* 19.

16. *Chrysler Corp. v. Dep't of Transp.,* 472 F. 2d 659, 671 (6th Cir. 1972).

17. *Id.* at 676.

18. The EPA's asbestos ban was overturned in *Corrosion Proof Fittings v. EPA,* 947 F. 2d 1201 (5th Cir. 1991). See also Paul Brodeur, *Outrageous Misconduct: The Asbestos Industry on Trial* (Pantheon, 1985); Dennis Cauchon, *Nobody Can Plead Ignorance: At Least 1 Million Likely to Die over 30 Years in Poor Nations,* USA Today, Feb. 8, 1999, at 1A; *Model for Asbestos Settlements,* ABA Journal, April 1993, at 22.

19. Thomas O. McGarity, *The Courts and the Ossification of Rulemaking: A Response to Professor Seidenfeld,* 75 Texas Law Review 525, 541 (1997).

20. For information about judicial appointees, I rely on: Neil A. Lewis, *President Criticizes G.O.P. for Delaying Judicial Votes,* New York Times, July 31, 2000, at A10; Kamen, *Trial and Error,* Washington Post, May 19, 2000, at A29; Kamen, *Clinton Nominates Hatch Friend to Bench,* Washington Post, July 28, 1999, at A8; David Byrd, *Clinton's Untilting Federal Bench,* National Law Journal, Feb. 19, 2000, at 555; Robert S. Greenberger, *GOP Fights to Limit Scope of Clinton's Judicial Legacy,* Wall Street Journal, May 24, 1999, at

A32; Stephen Pomper, *The Gipper's Constitution: Legacy of Reagan's Judicial Appointments,* Washington Monthly, Dec. 1, 1999, at 25; Garland W. Allison, *Delay in Senate Confirmation of Federal Judicial Nominees,* 80 Judicature 8, 10 (1996); and Sheldon Goldman and Elliot Slotnick, *Clinton's First Term Judiciary: Many Bridges to Cross,* 80 Judicature 254, 261, 269 (1997).

21. Pierce, *Seven Ways* 61.

22. Mashaw and Harfst, *Struggle for Auto Safety* 121, quoting Hartke.

23. *Motor Vehicle Manufacturers Assn. V. State Farm Mutual Automobile Ins. Co.,* 463 U.S. 29, 34 (1983).

24. *U.S. v. General Motors Corp.,* 841 F. 2d 400 (D.C. Cir. 1988).

25. During his 2000 presidential primary campaign, Senator John McCain (R–Ariz.) released five hundred letters he had written during a two-year period to regulatory agencies on behalf of major contributors, constituents, and others. In these letters, McCain urged regulators to act expeditiously or asked questions about specific matters. According to former senator Warren Rudman (R–N.H.), who chaired the Senate Ethics Committee, this is appropriate as long as the member of Congress does not "advocate for a [particular] result." Elaine S. Povich, *Power of Senator McCain's Pen,* Newsday, Jan. 14, 2000, at A22, quoting Rudman. See also Adam Zagorin and John F. Dickerson, *When Does Money Matter?* Time, Jan. 17, 2000, at 52. One suspects there is an art of writing these letters to convey subtly to agency staff just how interested the member is in the matter. When the author sits on the congressional committee that oversees the agency or sets its budget, the agency may take genuine interest quite seriously.

26. See Jerry Heaster, *Congress, Not the IRS, Is the Problem,* Kansas City Star, April 25, 1999, at N1, discussing how Senator William Roth (R–Del.) made personal political mileage out of bashing the IRS, including writing a book titled *The Power to Destroy: How IRS Became America's Most Powerful Agency; How Congress Is Taking Control;* Editorial, *Auditing the IRS; Fix the Agency, Don't Just Bash It,* Star Tribune (Minneapolis), Sept. 29, 1997, at 12A, discussing how Roth held Senate Finance Committee hearings to bash the IRS but failed to schedule hearings to confirm a new IRS commissioner or to consider thoughtful reform bills because "beating up on the IRS is good theater and good politics," thereby contributing to a "siege mentality" within IRS; and Matthew Rees, *Congress and the IRS,* Weekly Standard, Oct. 13, 1997, at 12, describing how Roth's staff sifted through one thousand discontented taxpayers to find four witnesses with "the most compelling and credible stories" of IRS abuse for Roth's hearings.

27. *A Weakened I.R.S.,* New York Times, April 16, 2000, at WK-14. See also David Cay Johnson, *Investigations Uncover Little Harassment by I.R.S.,* New York Times, Aug. 15, 2000, at A-1; David Cay Johnson, *I.R.S. More Likely to Audit Poor and Not the Rich,* New York Times, April 16, 2000, at A-1.

28. Wilson, *Bureaucracy* 88.

29. For the NCAP program, I rely on: telephone interview with David Pittle; and Harry Stoffer, *Budget Pinch Cuts NHTSA Crash Tests,* Automotive News, Nov. 8, 1999, at 56.

30. For information regarding NHTSA's budget, I rely on: NHTSA *Budget in Brief* for the 2001, 2000, 1999, and 1998 fiscal years. See also Joan Claybrook, *Congress's Part in the Firestone Crisis,* New York Times, Sept. 4, 2000, at A19; Diana T. Kurylko, *Curry Wows Consumer Advocates,* Automotive News, April 2, 1990, at 39; Harry Stoffer, *NHTSA Banking on Proposed Budget Hike,* Automotive News, Feb. 14, 2000, at 20.

31. NHTSA had 666 employees in 1991 and 600 in 1999. See Joseph M. Callahan, *NHTSA Shifts Gears,* Automotive Industries, August 1991, at 45; Myron Levin, *Agency Oversees U.S. Fuel Rules,* Los Angeles Times, Dec. 5, 1999, at 43.

32. For information regarding the Firestone tire problem, I rely on: Keith Bradsher, *Documents Show Firestone Knew of Rising Warranty Costs,* New York Times, Sept. 8, 2000, at C1; Keith Bradsher, *Explorer Tires Had to Carry a Heavy Load,* New York Times, Aug. 23, 2000, at C1; Keith Bradsher and Matthew L. Wald, *More Indications Hazards of Tires Were Long Known,* New York Times, Sept. 7, 2000, at A1; Keith Bradsher and Matthew L. Wald, *Link between Tires and Crashes Went Undetected in Federal Data,* New York Times, Aug. 8, 2000, at A1; *Safety Groups Applaud Firestone Action but Say Decision to Recall Tires Was Late,* BNA Product Safety & Liability Report, Aug. 14, 2000, at 735.

33. Donald Reed, *NHTSA Reauthorization,* Automotive Engineering, October 1989, at 96, quoting Gordon.

34. See Charles Lewis and the Center for Public Integrity, *The Buying of the President 2000* (Avon Books, 2000); and Don Van Natta Jr., *Companies Ended Soft Donations but Still Play the Influence Game,* New York Times, Aug. 4, 2000, at A1.

35. For information regarding the Ford Bronco II, I rely on: telephone interview with Edgar F. Heiskell III, Esq. (Aug. 2, 2000), together with documents furnished by Mr. Heiskell from his litigation files; *Clay v. Ford Motor Co.,* 215 F. 3d 663 (6th Cir. 2000); *Ford Motor Co. v. Ammerman,* 705 N.E. 2d 539 (Ind. Ct. App. 1999); *Gamblin v. Ford Motor Co.,* 513 S.E. 2d 467 (W. Va. 1998); *Moya v. Ford Motor Co.,* 1197 U.S. Dist. LEXIS 23568 (E.D. Calif. 1997); David Goetz, *Long-Discontinued Bronco II Remains a Thorn in Ford's Side,* Courier-Journal (Louisville, Ky.), March 16, 2000, at 14B; Tom Incantalupo, *Ford's Berated Bronco II Goes the Way of the Edsel,* Newsday, Jan. 5, 1990, at 51; Benjamin Pimentel, *Ford Crash Verdict Stays at $26 Million,* San Francisco Chronicle, June 9, 2000, at A22; Christopher Jensen, *Agency Blames Self for Allowing Ford to Withhold Tests,* Plain Dealer (Cleveland), Dec. 5,

1999; Levin, *Who's Watching Out for Safety?*; Barry Meier, *Bronco II Accidents Pose New Questions for Ford Safety,* New York Times, June 15, 1992 at A1; Mark Rollenhagen, *Ford to Fight $14 Million Award in Bronco II Crash,* Plain Dealer (Cleveland), May 21, 1998.

36. *Traxler v. Ford Motor Co.,* 576 N.W. 2d 398, 402 (Mich. App. 1998).

37. For information regarding SUVs, I rely on: Keith Bradsher, *Was Freud a Minivan or S.U.V. Kind of Guy,* New York Times, July 17, 2000, at A1; Keith Bradsher, *Ford Is Conceding S.U.V. Drawbacks,* New York Times, May 12, 2000, at A1; Keith Bradsher, *Automakers Modifying S.U.V.'s to Reduce Risk to Other Drivers,* New York Times, March 21, 2000, at A1; Keith Bradsher, *Tests Find Light Trucks Pose Hazards to Drivers of Cars,* New York Times, June 3, 2000, at A12; Keith Bradsher, *Further Problems of Safety Found for Light Trucks,* New York Times, Dec. 12, 1997, at A1; Keith Bradsher, *Big Insurers to Increase Rates on Large Vehicles,* New York Times, Oct. 17, 1997, at A1; Keith Bradsher, *A Deadly Highway Mismatch Ignored,* New York Times, Sept. 24, 1997, at A1; James L. Gilbert et al., *The Trouble with Sport Utility Vehicles,* Trial, November 1996, at 40; Marianne Lavelle, *New Rules for Those Fun Trucks,* U.S. News & World Report, Feb. 15, 1999, at 26; Robert M. N. Palmer and William Petrus, *LTVs: "Safer" at What Cost?,* Trial, January 2000, at 44; Paul Rauber, *Arms Race on the Highway,* Sierra, November/December 1999, at 20; *Ford Lands on Its Feet,* Los Angeles Times, April 22, 1989, sec. 4 at 1.

38. Lee Iacocca, *Iacocca: An Autobiography* 297 (Bantam Books, 1984).

39. For more about the growing importance of advocacy organizations in American democracy, see Jeffrey M. Berry, *The New Liberalism: The Rising Power of Citizens Groups* (Brookings Institute, 1999).

40. *Brown v. Sears, Roebuck & Co.,* 514 So. 2d 439 (La. 1987), *reh. denied,* 516 So. 2d 1154 (1988).

41. David B. Harrison, *Liability for Injury on, or in Connection with, Escalators,* 1 A.L.R. 4th 144 (1980).

42. I know of no data reflecting what portion of filed cases result in published court opinions. Data suggest, however, that between 2 and 8 percent of tort injuries result in litigation and about 4 percent of products liability cases reach trial. See Michael J. Sacks, *Do We Really Know Anything about the Behavior of the Tort Litigation System—And Why Not?,* 140 University of Pennsylvania Law Review 1147, 1184–85, 1227–29 (1992). I arrived at my one in five hundred estimate by multiplying 5 percent (as a rough estimate of the percentage of injuries resulting in litigation) by 4 percent, which yields 0.2 percent, i.e., one in five hundred. This is admittedly a crude estimate. Some cases that never reach trial are the subject of published court opinions granting the defendant's motion to dismiss. I assume, however (based on gut instinct alone),

that at least as many cases that are tried never become the subject of published opinions.

43. *Hunt v. City Stores, Inc.,* 387 So. 2d 585 (1980).

44. Graham, *Product Liability and Motor Vehicle Safety* 127.

NOTES TO CHAPTER 7

1. For the facts relating to MacPherson's accident, Brackett and Corbin, and trial testimony, I rely on David W. Peck, *Decisions at Law* 38–69 (Dodd, Mead, 1961). For information about cars generally and the early-twentieth-century automobile industry, I rely on Christopher Finch, *Highways to Heaven: The Auto Biography of America* (HarperCollins, 1992); James J. Flink, *America Adopts the Automobile 1895–1910* (MIT Press, 1970); and especially on Paul C. Wilson, *Chrome Dream: Automobile Styling since 1893* (Chilton, 1976).

2. Wilson, *Chrome Dream* 26.

3. *Id.* at 105, referring to the spoke/disk issue. With respect to the brou-haha about whether hydraulic tests showed wire was stronger than wood or vice versa, Wilson writes: "All of this had negligible effect on public preference. Their widespread adoption on passenger cars depended on their aesthetic appeal." *Id.* at 71.

4. Peck, *Decisions at Law* 44.

5. 152 Eng. Rep. 402 (Ex. 1842).

6. *Id.* at 405.

7. E.g., *Huset v. J.I. Case Threshing Machine Co.,* 120 F. 2d 865, 871 (8th Cir. 1903).

8. *MacPherson v. Buick Motor Co.,* 111 N.E. 1050 (N.Y. 1916).

9. *Ultramares Corp. v. Touche,* 174 N.E. 441, 445 (N.Y. 1931).

10. *Stamp v. Eighty-Sixth Street Amusement Co.,* 159 N.Y. Supp. 683 (Sup. Ct. 1916). For simplicity's sake, I refer to the injured woman as the plaintiff, although in accordance with the custom of the time, her husband sued on her behalf.

11. L.R. 3 H.L. 330 (1868). For simplicity's sake, I ignore the fact that the defendants were tenants rather than the landowner.

12. *Brown v. Kendall,* 60 Mass. 292 (1850).

13. *Restatement of the Law of Torts* § 519 (1938).

14. I leave aside the fact that the doctrinal basis was implied warranty rather than tort, for the two are functionally similar if not identical. The court held "that under modern marketing conditions, when a manufacturer puts a new automobile in the stream of trade and promotes its purchase by the public, an implied warranty that it is reasonably suitable for use as such accompanies it into the hands of the ultimate purchaser." *Hennigsen v. Bloomfield Motors, Inc.,* 161 A. 2d 69, 84 (N.J. 1960).

15. *Restatement (Second) of Torts* § 402A (1964).

16. *Restatement (Second) of Torts* § 402A (Preliminary Draft No. 6, 1958).

17. *Restatement (Second) of Torts* (Council Draft No. 8, 1960).

18. 38 ALI Proceedings 87 (1961).

19. *Id.* at 87–88.

20. *Restatement (Second) of Torts* § 402A cmt. g.

21. See James A. Henderson Jr. and Aaron D. Twerski, *Will a New Restatement Help Settle Troubled Waters: Reflections*, 42 American University Law Review 1257, 1260 n. 17 (1993).

22. *Hennigsen v. Bloomfield Motors, Inc.*, 161 A. 2d 69 (N.J. 1960. *Greenman v. Yuba Power Products, Inc.*, 377 P. 2d 897 (Calif. 1963).

23. See *Heaton v. Ford Motor Co.*, 435 P. 2d 806 (Ore. 1967).

24. For my description of the Pinto, I rely on: *Grimshaw v. Ford Motor Co.*, 174 Cal. Rptr. 348 (1981); Russell Mokhiber, *Corporate Crime and Violence* 371–82 (Sierra Club Books, 1988); Francis T. Cullen et al., *Corporate Crime under Attack: The Ford Pinto Case and Beyond* 145–308 (Anderson, 1987); Robert Lacey, *Ford: The Men and the Machine* 579–86 (Little, Brown, 1986); Lee Iacocca, *Iacocca: An Autobiography* 161–62 (Bantam Books, 1984); Dennis A. Gioia, *Why I Didn't Recognize Pinto Fire Hazards,* in *Corporate and Governmental Deviance,* ed. M. David Ermann and Richard J. Lundman (Oxford University Press, 1996); Gary T. Schwartz, *The Myth of the Ford Pinto Case*, 43 Rutgers Law Review 1013 (1991); Reginald Stuart, *Ford Auto Company Cleared in 3 Deaths,* New York Times, March 14, 1980, at A1; *Three Cheers in Dearborn,* Time, March 4, 1980, at 24.

25. The *Grimshaw* case represents something of an exception. The Pinto was struck from behind after it stalled on a superhighway, perhaps as a result of some other defect.

26. *Evans v. General Motors Corp.*, 359 F. 2d 822, 824 (7th Cir. 1966).

27. *Id.* at 825.

28. *Huff v. White Motor Corp.*, 565 F. 2d 104 (7th Cir. 1977). Both *Huff* and *Evans* were decided under Indiana law.

29. *Id.* at 108.

30. *Id.*

31. See *Tafoya v. Sears Roebuck & Co.*, 884 F. 2d. 1330, 1337 n. 14 (10th Cir. 1989).

32. 719 F. Supp. 385 (W.D. Pa. 1989), *aff'd* 898 F. 2d 139 (3d Cir. 1990).

33. The same approach may be found in cases involving a host of other products. See Carl T. Bogus, *The Third Revolution in Products Liability,* 72 Chicago-Kent Law Review 3, 13–15 (1996); and Carl T. Bogus, *War on the Common Law: The Struggle at the Center of Products Liability,* 60 Missouri Law Review 1, 37 (1995).

NOTES TO CHAPTER 8

1. Craig R. McCoy and Clea Benson, *City Considers Novel Suit against Gun Makers,* Philadelphia Inquirer, Jan. 8, 1998, at A1.

2. After Rendell left office, Philadelphia filed an action against fourteen gun manufacturers. See Fox Butterfield, *Philadelphia Sues Gun Makers over Availability of Weapons,* New York Times, April 12, 200, at A14.

3. This was my own inference from news accounts. See, e.g., Clea Benson, *Lawyer Who Drafted Gun Lawsuit Quits,* Philadelphia Inquirer, Jan. 21, 1998, at B1; and Mark Cohen, *Half-Cocked,* Philadelphia Magazine, June 1998, at 29. Though I know a number of players in the drama—including Edward Rendell, who was one of my partners in a Philadelphia law firm before he became mayor and I became an academic lawyer—none has ever told me anything about the internal discussions within the Rendell administration or communications with the media during this period.

4. See, e.g., James Dao and Don Van Natta Jr., *N.R.A. Is Using Adversity to Its Advantage,* New York Times, June 12, 1999, at A10, reporting that Senator Rick Santorum (R–Pa.) received $19,700 in NRA campaign contributions, making him the biggest beneficiary of NRA financial support in the nation; Michael Rezendez, *Clinton, NRA Find Battle Offers Mutual Benefits,* Boston Globe, Oct. 15, 1995, at 1, reporting that former Senator Harris Wofford (D–Pa.) believed gun control was "a decisive factor" in his loss to Santorum in 1994; David L. Michelmore, *Santorum Finances Brighten,* Pittsburgh Post-Gazette, Oct. 22, 1994, at A5, reporting the NRA contributed $8,800 to Santorum's 1994 campaign and spent an additional $44,617 urging its 230,000 Pennsylvania members to support Santorum; and Greg Gattuso, *Finance Controversies Open Election Year,* Fund Raising Management, March 1994, at 11, reporting the NRA contributed $9,900 to Senator Arlen Specter (R–Pa.) and spent an additional $166,000 urging its members to support Specter, who, notes the article, "has never voted against the NRA position."

5. See David Fireston, *Gun Lobby Begins a Concerted Attack on Cities' Lawsuits,* New York Times, Feb. 9, 1999, at A1.

6. See John Gibeaut, *Gunning for Change,* ABA Journal, March 2000, at 48, 49.

7. Fox Butterfield, *Major Gun Makers Talk with Cities on Settling Suits,* New York Times, Oct. 22, 1999, at A1.

8. See Eric Rosenberg, *U.S. Readies Suit against Gun Manufacturers,* San Francisco Examiner, Dec. 15, 1999, at A-12.

9. See Tom Schoenberg, *Washington D.C.'s Gun Suit a Long Shot,* Connecticut Law Tribune, Nov. 29, 1999, at 5.

10. See *FBI Uniform Crime Reports 1998,* table 2.10 at 18 (1999), regarding

percentage of firearm murders committed with handguns. Determining the ratio of handguns to long guns in the United States is more complicated, but data suggest handguns comprise roughly half of all guns. See Gallup Poll Monthly, August 1996, at 38, reporting that 50 percent of Americans owning one gun own a handgun and 46 percent owning two or more guns own a handgun; Violence Policy Center, *Firearms Production in America* 147 (1995), providing data showing that the wholesale value of handguns compared to all firearms manufactured in the United States increased from 43.2 percent in 1983 to 49.9 percent in 1994. For a risk-utility analysis of handguns, see Carl T. Bogus, *Pistols, Politics and Products Liability,* 59 University of Cincinnati Law Review 1103 (1991).

11. I have addressed issues relating to gun control policy in Carl T. Bogus, *The Strong Case for Gun Control,* American Prospect, Summer 1992, at 19.

12. W. Page Keeton, ed., *Prosser and Keeton on the Law of Torts* 616 (5th ed., 1984).

13. "A public nuisance . . . is a substantial and unreasonable interference with a right held in common by the general public, in the use of public facilities, in health, safety, and convenience. . . . A public nuisance may be abated or enjoined by public authorities, even if it is not specifically declared to be a nuisance or a crime by statute." Dan B. Dobbs, *The Law of Torts* 1334 (West Group, 2000).

14. See Richard Willing, *"Damages Here Could Be Eye-Popping": even if Big Tobacco Prevails Later, Verdict Could Be Big Loss,* USA Today, July 8, 1999, at 3A.

15. See Peter Pringle, *Cornered: Big Tobacco at the Bar of Justice* 265 (Henry Holt, 1998).

16. See *id.* at 55.

17. See *id.*

18. The tobacco companies reached individual settlements with Mississippi, Florida, Texas, and Minnesota and a global settlement with forty-six states for $206 billion. See *U.S. Sues Tobacco Industry,* Star Tribune (Minneapolis), Sept. 23, 1999, at 1A.

19. See *id.*

20. See, e.g., Mark Hansen, *Crack in Tobacco Armor,* ABA Journal, May 1996, at 22; Barry Meier, *Tobacco Industry Loses First Phase of Broad Lawsuit,* New York Times, July 8, 1999, at A1; *Philip Morris to Challenge $81 Million Award,* 27 BNA Product Safety & Liability Report 331, April 2, 1999.

21. Seymour Martin Lipset, *American Exceptionalism: A Double-Edged Sword* 31 (W. W. Norton, 1996).

22. *Id.* at 19.

23. Alan Wolfe, *One Nation, After All* 219 (1998), interpreting and agreeing with Lipset's work.

24. *Id.* at 267.

25. For the history of the medical community's and the public's awareness of an association between smoking and illness, I rely on Richard Kluger, *Ashes to Ashes: America's Hundred-Year Cigarette War, the Public Health, and the Unabashed Triumph of Philip Morris* 66–73, 129–62 (Alfred A. Knopf, 1996); Pringle, *Cornered* 114–33. Polling data on the public attitude toward addictiveness are from a national telephone survey, sponsored by *NBC News* and the *Wall Street Journal,* conducted during April 18–20, 1998, and obtained from the Roper Center at the University of Connecticut.

26. The question of whether and to what extent health ramifications are suffered by nonsmokers exposed to secondhand smoke remains open, if not medically at least in the perceptions of juries. See, e.g., *No Liability Is Found in Secondhand-Smoke Case,* New York Times, June 3, 1999, at A16.

27. This often-repeated example may have originated in Robert D. Cooter and Thomas S. Ulen, *Law and Economics* 45 (Scott, Foresman, 1988).

28. Some scholars believe it is appropriate for courts, without a legislative mandate, to treat a particular product differently from other products. The term *enterprise liability* is sometimes used to stand for this proposition, that is, for imposing strict liability on a product with unique characteristics even though liability would not be imposed under generally applicable rules. I am not an advocate of this kind of enterprise liability and do not believe that imposing strict liability on tobacco and handguns does so. On the contrary, I believe that strict liability is properly imposed on these products under existing doctrine, and that failing to do so grants these industries a form of specialized immunity from products liability law. See Carl T. Bogus, *The Third Revolution in Products Liability,* 72 Chicago-Kent Law Review 3 (1996); Carl T. Bogus, *War on the Common Law: The Struggle at the Center of Products Liability,* 60 Missouri Law Review 1 (1995); Carl T. Bogus, *Pistols, Politics, and Products Liability,* 59 University of Cincinnati Law Review 1103 (1991).

29. Particularly influential was a three-part series describing internal documents of the Brown & Williamson Tobacco Corporation obtained by the *New York Times*: Philip J. Hilts, *Cigarette Makers Debated the Risks They Denied,* New York Times, June 16, 1994, at A1; Philip J. Hilts, *Tobacco Maker Studied Risk but Did Little about Results,* New York Times, June 17, 1994, at A1; Philip J. Hilts, *Grim Finds Scuttled Hope for "Safer" Cigarette,* New York Times, June 18, 1994, at A1. The series was quickly followed by further revelations. See, e.g., Warren E. Leary, *Cigarette Company Developed a Potent Gene-Altered Tobacco,* New York Times, June 27, 1994, at A1, reporting testimony by FDA commissioner David A. Kessler that Brown & Williamson secretly developed tobacco that would deliver twice the amount of nicotine.

30. See, e.g., Sheryl Stolberg, *FTC Reveals It Has New Evidence in Joe Camel Case,* Los Angeles Times, March 27, 1997, at D1; Pringle, *Cornered* 166–70.

31. See, e.g., Philip J. Hilts, *Philip Morris Blocked '83 Paper Showing Tobacco Is Addictive, Panel Finds*, New York Times, April 1, 1994, at A21, reporting that in 1983 the Philip Morris Companies learned from their own research that nicotine was addictive and actively suppressed this information. Reports also surfaced regarding Brown & Williamson's effort to stop CBS from broadcasting an interview with the company's former head of research, Jeffrey Wigand, who testified that Brown & Williamson deliberately manipulated nicotine delivery in its cigarettes. E.g., Barnaby J. Feder, *Former Tobacco Executive to Begin Telling Secrets to Grand Jury*, New York Times, Dec. 13, 1995, at A21.

32. See Pringle, *Cornered* 68–71, 77–81, including, within a center insert of photographs, the picture of the CEOs being sworn in at the congressional hearing; Philip J. Hilts, *Tobacco Company Chief Denies Nicotine Scheme in Testimony*, New York Times, June 24, 1994, at A1.

33. See Pringle, *Cornered* 177–93. The story of Jeffrey Wigand, former vice president of research of Brown & Williamson, whose interview for the CBS show *60 Minutes* was not broadcast because of threatened legal action by Brown & Williamson, was dramatized by the film *The Insider* (Buena Vista, 1999).

34. *See* Linda Saad, *A Half-Century of Polling on Tobacco*, Public Perspective, August 1998, at 1.

35. Americans opposed the bill by a slight margin. See *id*. For a description of the bill and its demise, see David E. Rosenbaum, *Cigarette Makers Quit Negotiations on Tobacco Bill*, New York Times, April 9, 1998, at A1.

36. Also consistent with a belief in individual responsibility is Americans' overwhelming support for "the right of non-smokers to a smoke-free environment" over "the right of smokers to smoke everywhere." See Saad, *Half-century of Polling*, reporting both polls.

37. See Saad, *Half-century of Polling*.

38. See *id*.

39. David W. Moore, *Most Americans Feel Tobacco Companies Not Liable for Smoking-Related Deaths*, Gallup Poll Monthly, April 1997, at 18.

40. Thirteen percent said smokers and the companies were equally to blame, and 2 percent had no opinion. Poll conducted by the Gallup Organization, Sept. 23–26, 1999 (accession number 0341027; question number 020), available in the LEXIS "News" file.

41. Poll conducted by *ABC News* on April 17, 1997 (accession number 0288568; question number 004), available in LEXIS "News" file.

42. Poll conducted by Gallup Organization, Sept. 23–26, 1999 (accession number 0341028; question number 021), available in LEXIS "News" file.

43. For an estimate of the costs of treating smoking-related diseases, see Philip J. Hilts, *Sharp Rise in Smokers' Health Care Costs*, New York Times, July 8,

1994, at A12, reporting a study by the Centers for Disease Control and Prevention placing the health care costs of smoking-related illnesses at $50 billion.

44. For a comprehensive analysis of the externalization of cigarette costs, see Jon D. Hanson and Kyle D. Logue, *The Costs of Cigarettes: The Economic Case for Ex Post Incentive-Based Regulation*, 107 Yale Law Journal 1167 (1998).

45. See *FBI Uniform Crime Reports*, table 2.10 at 18.

46. See *id.* at 27–29, reporting that firearms were used in 38.2 percent of 446,625 robberies in 1998.

47. Based on a U.S. population of about 270 million and a nonfatal firearm-injury rate of 38.6 per 100,000. See Joseph L. Annest et al., *National Estimates of Nonfatal Firearm-Related Injuries*, JAMA, June 14, 1995, at 1749, developing the rate of nonfatal firearm-related injuries treated in hospital emergency rooms.

48. Since 1959, at least fifteen Gallup polls have asked the question "Do you have a gun in your home?" The most recent poll of which I am aware (November 1996) reported 44 percent answering "Yes." That number has ranged from a low of 43 percent (1972) to a high of 51 percent (1993); the variance probably has more to do with sample size and representativeness than with actual fluctuations in gun ownership. For example, two polls conducted six months apart in 1993 reported gun ownership at 48 percent and 51 percent, and two polls conducted four months apart in 1996 yielded 38 percent and 44 percent. I use 46 percent because it is the median number of all fifteen polls, and the median of the six polls conducted since 1990 falls between 46 percent and 47 percent. See Gallup Poll Monthly, November 1996, at 39.

49. The rate of smoking and handgun ownership are about the same. Roughly one-quarter of the adults smoke and roughly one-quarter of homes contain a handgun. See Leslie McAneny, *Despite Growing Concerns, Most Non-Smokers Oppose Stringent Bans*, Gallup Poll Monthly, March 1994, at 21, reporting 27 percent of Americans smoke; Gallup Poll Monthly, November 1996, at 37–38, reporting handgun ownership.

50. See, generally, Dobbs, *Law of Torts* §§ 334–35 at 876–83. This has been an area of such activity that one annotation cataloging cases exceeds three hundred pages in length. Tracy A. Bateman and Susan Thomas, *Landlord's Liability for Failure to Protect Tenant from Criminal Acts of Third Persons*, 43 A.L.R. 5th 207 (1996).

51. See pages 000–000 (chapter 4).

52. *Ira S. Bushey & Sons, Inc. v. U.S.*, 398 F. 2d 167, 171 (2d Cir. 1968).

53. *Indiana Harbor Belt Railroad v. American Cyanamid Co.*, 916 F. 2d 1174, 1177 (7th Cir. 1990), citations omitted.

54. See, e.g., David Hemenway and Douglas Weil, *Phasers on Stun: The Case for Less Lethal Weapons*, 9 Journal of Policy Analysis & Management 94 (1990).

55. See Stephen Labaton and Lowell Bergman, *Documents Indicate Ford Knew of Engine Defect but Was Silent,* New York Times, Sept. 12, 2000, at A1.

56. See M. David Ermann and Richard J. Lundman, eds., *Corporate and Governmental Deviance* at 39 (Oxford University Press, 1996), describing the work of Marshall B. Clinard.

57. *Id.* at 38

58. Kermit Vandivier, *Why Should My Conscience Bother Me?* in *Corporate and Governmental Deviance,* ed. Ermann and Lundman, at 118.

59. For the story of the Rely tampon, I rely on: Alecia Swasy, *Rely Tampons and Toxic Shock Syndrome,* in *Corporate and Governmental Deviance,* ed. Ermann and Lundman, at 278; *Annotation: Products Liability: Toxic Shock Syndrome,* 59 A.L.R. 4th 50 (2000); *Company Found Negligent in Toxic Shock Disease Suit,* New York Times, March 20, 1982, at 8; Sandy Rovner, *Toxic Shock: Fighting over Tampon Labels,* Washington Post, Aug. 1, 1989, at Z-7; Richard Severo, *Mystery of Toxic Shock Cases Is Unfolding at Disease Center,* New York Times, Oct. 9, 1980, at A1; *Tampons Are Linked to Rare Disease,* New York Times, June 28, 1980, at 17; *Tampons: Not Relied On,* The Economist, Sept. 27, 1980, at 100; *Tampon Rule in Effect as Shock Cases Decline,* New York Times, Dec. 20, 1982, at A16; *Toxic Shock Case Weighed by Court,* New York Times, Nov. 4, 1982.

60. Swasy, *Rely Tampons and Toxic Shock Syndrome* 287–88. Swasy's account also appears in her book *Soap Opera: The Inside Story of Proctor & Gamble* (Times Books, 1993).

61. John D. Graham, *Product Liability and Motor Vehicle Safety,* in *The Liability Maze: The Impact of Liability Law on Safety and Innovation,* ed. Peter W. Huber and Robert E. Litan, at 126 (Brookings Institution, 1991). See also Robert S. Peck et al., *Tort Reform 1999: A Building without a Foundation,* Florida State Law Review 397, 420–33 (2000), critiquing industry estimates of the tort tax.

Index

Abinger, Lord, 175–76, 183–84
Abou Khadra v. Bseironi, 109
Adams, John, 60
Additur, 88
Administrative Agencies: and capture,
   162; and cylcing, 148, 153; generally,
   166–67; and ossification, 153. *See also
   individual agencies*
Adverse Drug Reaction (ADR) Reports,
   113
Alabama Tort Reform Act, 37
Alabama Trial Lawyers Association, 39
Alexander, Lamar, 10
American Automobile Manufacturing As-
   sociation, 10
American Bar Association (ABA), 31, 38
American Chemical Council, 10
American Creed, 200–201
American Federation of Labor (AFL), 134
American Judicature Society, 38
American Law Institute (ALI), 9. *See also*
   Restatements of the Law of Torts; Re-
   statement (Second) of Torts
American National Standards Institute
   (ANSI), 139–40, 169–70, 172
American Petroleum Institute, 10
American Tobacco Company. See *Wilks v.
   American Tobacco Co.*
American Tort Reform Association (ATRA),
   23, 27, 29, 34–38; membership of, 35
Anderson, Thornton, 49
Anderson v. General Motors Corp., 92–93
Anti-federalists, 50, 78
Apple Computer Litigation, In re, 109
Aristotle, 53
Articles of Confederation, 47–48
Asbestos, 150–51
Assumption of Risk, 96–100

Automobile Industry: early years of,
   173–74; and research and development
   for auto safety, 145. *See also particular
   manufacturers and models*

Balachey, Michael E., 213
*Baltimore & Ohio Railroad Co. v.
   Blaugh,* 132–33, 245n. 105
Barrett, John, W. (Don), 97–98
Baxter Healthcare Corporation, 36
B. F. Goodrich Company, 213–15
*Bighee v. Pacific Telephone & Telegraph
   Co.,* 18–19
Big Business: and George W. Bush, 10; and
   increasing political influence of, 211–12;
   and industrial revolution, 135; and tort
   reform, 9, 30, 34–40; and worker's com-
   pensation, 133–34. *See also particular
   companies and trade associations*
Black Robes Disease. *See* Judicial
   centricism
Blackstone, William, 41, 46, 54, 129
Boehly, William, 162
Boggs, Lillburn W., 131
Boorstin, Daniel, 45, 73
Brackett, Edgar T., 175–78
Bradford, William, 68
Brandeis, Louis D., 3, 32, 88
Brennan William, 82
Brown v. Board of Education, 33, 40
Brown v. Sears, Roebuck & Co., 169–71,
   250n. 40
Burger King, 20
Bushell's case, 66–67, 76, 78
Bush, George H. W., 31; and selection of
   judges, 151–52
Bush, George W., 4, 7, 10
Business Roundtable, 29

Calabresi, Guido, 8
Camden, Lord. See Pratt, Charles
Cardozo, Benjamin N., 88, 178–84
Carr, Bob, 155
Carroll v. Otis Elevator Co., 139–40,
    171–72, 249n. 2
Carver, Hartwell, 131
Cat Burglar case, 18
Center for Auto Safety, 166
Centers for Disease Control (CDC), 216,
    217
Cervantes, 201
Chamber of Commerce, 10, 29, 38
Chevrolet Malibu, 92
Chicago, Milwaukee & St. Paul Railway
    Co. v. Ross, 131–32, 245n. 102
Civil Justice Reform. See Tort Reform
Civil Law Tradition, 52–53
Claybrook, Joan, 146
Clinton, William J., 7, 30, 35; and selec-
    tion of judges, 152–53
Committee for Family Values, 39
Common Law: and criminal law, 119–22;
    English origins of, 62– 65; four legs of,
    115–37; generally, 8–9; and private law,
    127; and societal values, 98–101
Common Sense Legal Reforms Act, 7
Compensatory damages, 16
Concise Oil & Gas Partnership v.
    Louisiana, 109
Constitutional law, 118–19
Consumer Product Safety Commission
    (CPSC), 5, 146
Consumers Union, 166
Contingent Fee System, 8
Contract Clause, 124
Contract With America, 6
Corbin, Harold H., 175
Corrosion Proof Fittings v. EPA, 151,
    247n. 18
Cosby, William, 68–69
Cost externalization: defined, 203–4;
    and guns, 207–8, 210–11; and tobacco,
    207
Courts, public confidence in, 32–34
Crashworthiness doctrine, 145–50,
    153–55, 192–93, 209
Crown Point Center Ltd. v. Mellon Bank
    Corp., 109
Curry, Jerry R., 162

Danforth, John C., 6–8, 16–17, 22–23,
    102
DeLancy, James, 69, 72
DeLay, Tom, 31
Democratic Party, 31
Depo-Medrol, 12–16, 112–14
Des Moines Register, 29
Dickerson, F. Reed, 187–88
Dickinson, John, 49
Dodd, Christopher J., 6
Dole, Elizabeth, 9
Dole, Robert, 31, 35
Dowie, Mark, 166
Dram shop litigation, 144, 209
Drug Enforcement Administration (DEA),
    107
Drunk Driving, 143–45
Dunkin' Donuts, 20

Easterbrook, Frank H., 117
Ecclesiastes, 201
Ecclesiastical courts, 44, 116
Ecks v. Nizen, 109
England's civil war, 46
Enterprise liability, 255n. 28
Environmental Protection Agency (EPA),
    138, 146
Erie Railroad Co. v. Tomkins, 57
Escalators, 139–40, 169–72
Evans v. General Motors. Corp., 192,
    252n. 26

Family law, 116–17
Farwell v. Boston & Worcester Railroad
    Corp., 129, 176, 244n. 93
Federal Aviation Administration (FAA), 5,
    138
Federal Bureau of Investigation (FBI), 7
Federal Trade Commission (FTC), 160
Federalists, 77–78
Fellow Servant Rule, 129–34
Fineman v. Armstrong, 109
Firestone tires, 157–58, 212
Food and Drug Administration (FDA), 4,
    12; and Halcion, 106–8. 138; and Rely
    tampon, 217
Food Lion, Inc. v. Capital Cities/ABC,
    Inc., 136, 246n. 113
Food Marketing Institute, 10
Ford Bronco II, 159–69, 212

Ford Explorer, 157–58, 162
Ford Motor Company, 165, 173. *See also*
  particular models
Ford Pinto, 168–69, 190–92, 212
Friedman, Lawrence M., 34, 46, 127
Friendly, Henry J., 210
Fuller, Lon L., 101

General Motors Corporation, 145, 149;
  and X-cars, 155
Generic liability, 195–96, 209
Gingrich, Newt, 6
Glorious Revolution, 46, 71
Gompers, Samuel, 134
Gorham, Nathaniel, 50
Gorton, Slade, 158
Graham, John D., 172
Greenberg, Jack, 33
Greenman v. Yuba Power Products, Inc.,
  189, 252n. 22
Grimshaw v. Ford Motor Co., 191–92,
  252n. 24
Grundberg, Ilo, 106–8

Haimes v. Temple University Hospital,
  17–18
Halcion, 84, 106–8
Hamilton, Alexander, 33, 49, 60, 64; and
  jury system, 77–79, 123
Hamilton, Andrew, 70–73
Hans, Valerie P., 236n. 80
Harfst, David L., 146
Harr, Jonathan, 85
Harrington, Matthew P., 79
Hartke, Vance, 153
Harvard Law School, 54, 61
Hatch, Orrin G., 152
Heaton v. Ford Motor Co., 189,
  252n. 23
Heiskell, Edgar F., 159–63
Helms, Jesse, 6
Hennigsen v. Bloomfield Motors, Inc.,
  189, 252n. 22
Hobbes, Thomas, 54
Holmes, Oliver Wendell, 53, 57
Huckle v. Money, 75, 233n. 21
Huff v. White Motor Corp., 193,
  252n. 28
Hughes, Charles E., 88
Hughes, Evans, 33

Iacocca, Lee, 165, 190, 212
Individual responsibility, 201–11
Inns of Court, 60–61
Insurance Institute of Highway Safety
  (IIHS), 143, 163–64
Internal Revenue Service (IRS), 156

James, William, 57
Jeep CJ series, 159–60, 163, 165
Jefferson, Thomas, 60, 78
John Birch Society, 33
Johnson, Paul, 131
Joyce, Sherman, 23
Judges: life tenure of, 49, 51; selection of,
  151–53
Judicial centricism, 148–51
Judicial review, 49–51
Jury system: contemporary, England,
  79–80; discipline devices, 82–88; empir-
  ical data, 88–96; judge-jury agreement,
  88–90; jury attitudes and biases, 94–96;
  jury nullification, 98; jury verdicts v.
  final judgments, 93–94; origins of,
  66–79, 82
Jury verdicts, largest in 1991, 109–10

Kam, Alan J., 213
Kennedy, Anthony M., 31, 81
King George III, 47–48
Kronman, Anthony T., 53–55, 57

Langdell, Christopher Columbus, 54
Law-and-economics, 54, 54–59; and fel-
  low servant rule, 129
Lieberman, Joseph I., 4
Lipset, Seymour Martin, 200–201
Litchfield Law School, 61
Lochner era, 125–26
Locke, John, 46, 227n. 8
Lott, Trent, 36
LTV Aerospace Corporation, 214

MacPherson v. Buick Motor Co., 173–84,
  191, 251n. 8
Madison, James, 49–50, 56–57, 124
Malpractice, 136–37
Marshall, John, 60
Mashaw, Jerry L., 146
Mason, George, 50, 78
Massachusetts Bay Colony, 42, 45

McCain, John, 9, 11, 248n. 25
McDonald's, 4, 19–20
McLoughlin, William, 43
Mead, William, 66, 78
Merrill, Thomas W., 148
Mitchell, George, 35
Montesquieu, 47, 49
Mothers Against Drunk Driving (MADD), 143, 166
Motor Vehicle Manufacturers Assn. v. State Farm Mutual Automobile Ins. Co., 154, 248n. 23

Nader, Ralph, 145–46, 166–67
Narrows v. Underwriters, 109
National Association of Manufacturers, 29
National Commission on Product Safety, 146
National Highway Traffic Safety Administration (NHTSA), 4; established, 146; FARS program, 158, 167; and Ford Pinto, 190–91; NCAP program, 156–57; recall program, 155–56, 167–68; rulemaking, 146–55; Standard 208, 146–55; and TFI, 213. *See also* Administrative Agencies; *and particular vehicles*
National Insurance Consumer Organization, 219
National Labor Relations Board (NLRB), 81
National Rifle Association (NRA), 197
Nelson, William E., 64
Nuisance doctrine, 198–99

Occupational Safety and Health Administration (OSHA), 5, 81, 138
O'Connor, Sandra Day, 81
Ohio Supreme Court, 118
O'Neal, Robert, 97
Otis Elevator Company, 170

Patterson, Thomas E., 32, 224n. 17
Penn, William, 66, 78
Performance-based regulation, 149
Pharmaceutical Manufacturers Association, 23
Philadelphia, PA, 197
Pierce, Richard J., 153

Pitt, William (The Younger), 48
Plaintiff's success rate, 95
Posner, Richard A., 54, 57–58, 117, 210
Pound, Roscoe, 79
Pragmatism, 56–59
Pratt, Charles, 74
Premises liability, 209
Press, 135–36
Privity rule, 175–79, 183–85
Proctor & Gamble, 216–18
Proctor v. Davis: award reduced, 37; Danforth's description of, 7, 22–24; effect on Upjohn stock, 105–11; facts of, 11–17, 29; rationality of verdict, 102–5; and search for truth, 112–15
Product category liability, *See* generic liability.
Product Liability Coordinating Committee (PLCC), 29, 36
Products Liability, *See* specific topics.
Products Liability Fairness Act, 6, 23, 35–36
Prosser, William L., 186–88, 199
Psychic powers case. See *Haimes v. Temple University Hospital*
Public Citizen, 154
Punitive Damages, 16; 26–27, 37; first cases awarding, 75; Illinois law of, 104–5; in *Proctor v. Davis,* 103–6; and products liability actions, 109; and Rely tampons, 218
Puritans, 42

Quakers, 43, 66
Quayle, J. Danforth, 4, 17–18, 22

Railroads, transcontinental, 127–33
Reagan, Ronald, 4, 18, 22; and auto regulation, 155; and selection of judges, 151–52
Rehnquist, William, 152
Rely tampons, 216–18
Remittur, 87–88
Rendell, Edward G. 197
Reno, Janet, 7
Republican Party, 6, 30–31, 158
Restatement of the Law of Torts, 184–85
Restatement (Second) of Torts, 145, 185–89

Rhode Island, 43, *See also* Williams, Roger
Rockefeller, Jay, 36
Rosenzweig, Richard L., 237n. 105
Roth, William, 248n. 26
Rowland, John G., 30
Rylands v. Fletcher, 181–82, 251n. 11

Santesson v. Travelair Ins. Co., 109
Scalia, Antonin, 81
See, Harold F., Jr., 38
Separation of powers, 42, 229 nn. 29, 32
Seven Bishops, Case of, 62, 72, 76
Seventh Amendment, 78, 80–82, 87
Shaw, Lemuel, 129–31, 133, 176, 181
Shay's Rebellion, 64
Shelby, Richard, 155
Shetterly v. Crown Control Corp., 194–96, 252n. 32
Smart gun, 210
Smith, Anderson. See *Wilks v. American Tobacco Co.*
Smith, Jerry E., 151
Sports utility vehicles (SUVs), 4, 163–66, 185
Starr, Kenneth W., 156
Stimson, Shannon C., 51
Stone, Harlan F., 88, 115, 117
Story, Joseph, 56–57
Sutherland, George, 88
Suzuki Samurai, 163, 165
Swasy, Alecia, 218, 258n. 60
Swift v. Tyson, 56
Syracuse University, 156

Texans for Lawsuit Reform, 10
Texas Civil Justice League, 10
Thalidomide, 113–14
Thick Film Ignition (TFI), 212–13
Thurmond, Strom, 33
Tocqueville, Alexis de, 39, 53, 60–62
Tort reform: in Alabama, 38–40; agenda, 34–40; effect on public attitudes, 95; in Ohio, 38, 118; in Texas, 10. *See also* American Tort Reform Association
Tort tax, 218–19

Toxic Shock Syndrome (TSS), 216–18
Trial lawyers, 8, 39, 168–69
Tribe, Laurence H., 125

Uniform Commercial Code (UCC), 122
United States v. *see name of defendant*
Upjohn, 12–16, 104. *See also* Depo-Medrol; Halcion; *Proctor v. Davis*
U.S. Department of Agriculture (USDA), 138
U.S. Trust Co. v. New Jersey, 126, 244n. 43
U.S. v. Hudson and Goodwin, 119, 242n. 62

Vandevender v. Sheetz, Inc., 24–29, 37
Vandivier, Kermit, 213–15
Van Dyke, William, 177–78
Vermont Supreme Court, 117
Vidmar, Neil, 91
Viscusi, W. Kip, 18, 91, 93

Waller v. Truck Ins. Exchange, 109
Warren, Earl, 33–34
Webster, Daniel, 60
Wendy's, 20
White, Byron R., 81
Wilkes, John, 73–76
Wilkes v. Wood, 75, 233n. 21
Wilks v. American Tobacco Co., 96–100, 209
Williams, Roger, 42–45
William the Conqueror, 66
Wilson, James, 50
Wilson, James Q., 156–57
Wilson, Paul C., 173–74
Winsten, Jay, 143
Winterbottom v. Wright, 175–76, 178, 251n. 5
Wolfe, Alan, 201
Wood, Gordon S., 54, 123
Worker's compensation system, 133–35

Xanax, 107

Zenger, John Peter, 68–73, 76, 78

About the Author

Carl T. Bogus is an associate professor at the Roger Williams University School of Law in Bristol, Rhode Island, where he teaches Torts, Product Liability, Evidence, and Administrative Law. His writings about products liability and other topics have appeared in law reviews, professional journals, college and law school textbooks, and the *American Prospect, The Nation,* and *Tikkun* magazines. He is a winner of the prestigious Ross Essay Award from the American Bar Association.

Professor Bogus received his A.B. and J.D. degrees from Syracuse University and was an editor of the *Syracuse Law Review.* He practiced law for eighteen years in Philadelphia, concentrating in complex commercial litigation. After leaving practice, he taught for four years at Rutgers University School of Law in Camden, New Jersey. He has been teaching at Roger Williams since 1996.

Judging by the frequency with which it makes an appearance in television news shows and late-night stand-up routines, the frivolous lawsuit has become an integral part of our national culture. A woman sues McDonald's because she was scalded when she spilled her coffee. Thousands file lawsuits claiming they were injured by Agent Orange, silicone breast implants, or Bendectin, although scientists report these substances do not cause the diseases in question. The United States, conventional wisdom has it, is a hyperlitigious society, propelled by avaricious lawyers, harebrained judges, and runaway juries. Lawsuits waste money and time and, moreover, many are simply groundless.

Carl T. Bogus is not so sure. In *Why Lawsuits Are Good for America,* Bogus argues that common law works far better than commonly understood. Indeed, Bogus contends that while the system can and occasionally does produce "wrong" results, it is very difficult for it to make flatly irrational decisions. Blending history, theory, empirical data, and colorful case studies, Bogus explains why common law, rather than being outdated, may be more necessary than ever.

As Bogus sees it, the common law is an essential adjunct to governmental regulation—essential, in part, because it is not as easily manipulated by big business.

Bogus makes a compelling case for the necessity of safeguarding the system from